# fun with the family
# Upstate New York

hundreds of ideas for day trips with the kids

First Edition

**Mary Lynn Blanks**

**gpp**®

travel

Guilford, Connecticut

All the information in this guidebook is subject to change. We recommend that you call ahead to obtain current information before traveling.

To buy books in quantity for corporate use or incentives, call **(800) 962-0973** or e-mail **premiums@GlobePequot.com.**

Editor: Amy Lyons
Project Editor: Lynn Zelem
Layout: Joanna Beyer
Text Design: Nancy Freeborn and Linda R. Loiewski
Maps: Rusty Nelson © Morris Book Publishing, LLC
Spot photography throughout © Photodisc and © RubberBall Productions

Library of Congress Cataloging-in-Publication Data is available on file.

ISBN 978-0-7627-5408-3

Printed in the United States of America
10 9 8 7 6 5 4 3 2 1

# Contents

# About the Author

An avid explorer and experienced world traveler, Mary Lynn Blanks toured and trekked across almost every continent during her childhood. After attending Florida State University on a theater scholarship, she moved to New York City and joined the casts of ABC's *All My Children* as Tara and later CBS's *As the World Turns* as Annie. Fulfilling a lifelong dream, she then ran away with the circus . . . writing and coproducing original television and radio programs and commercials for Ringling Bros. and Barnum & Bailey Circus. Unofficially known as the "Vanna White of Concacaf," she is also an FAA-licensed pilot, a PADI-certified scuba diver, and the proud mom of sons Christopher and Nicholas. She is also the author of *Fun with Family Metro New York*.

# Acknowledgments

Researching the riches of New York would not have been possible without the assistance of the wonderful people at the tourist offices, parks, and attractions listed. You'd be hard pressed to find a more helpful and enthusiastic group, and I urge you to contact them for more information.

A special thanks to my editor Amy Lyons, who guided me through this edition with wit, wisdom, and infinite patience.

To all my friends and family who supported and sustained me through this journey, I am deeply indebted. Their faith in my talent allowed me to believe in myself and find my voice. A very special thanks to Chuck Blazer, Elaine Kaufman, Dr. Ruth Westheimer, Donna de Varona, Robin Eisenmann, Callan White, Cece Verardi, Shelley Tahlor-Levine, Nina Chertoff, Nicole Orth-Pallavicini, Kathy Schultz, Beverly Monsky, Leo Bookman, Bobby Supino, my soccer, and FIFA family of fabulous females, Marci, Stuart, Jason, Samantha, Dylan, Drew, Logan, Cameron, and my wonderful sons Chris and Nick.

And finally, to my mom and dad, Lola and John Blanks, and my sister, Lisa, all presently touring another dimension, I owe perhaps the most. From London to Leningrad, Istanbul to Indonesia, my parents journeyed with us to just about every Pan American port of call, encouraging our exploration of new experiences and different cultures. It was their gift of the world when I was young that sparked the fire of adventure and discovery within me and nurtured my sense of wonder. My hope is to pass this gift on to my children and perhaps to yours. Enjoy the trip!

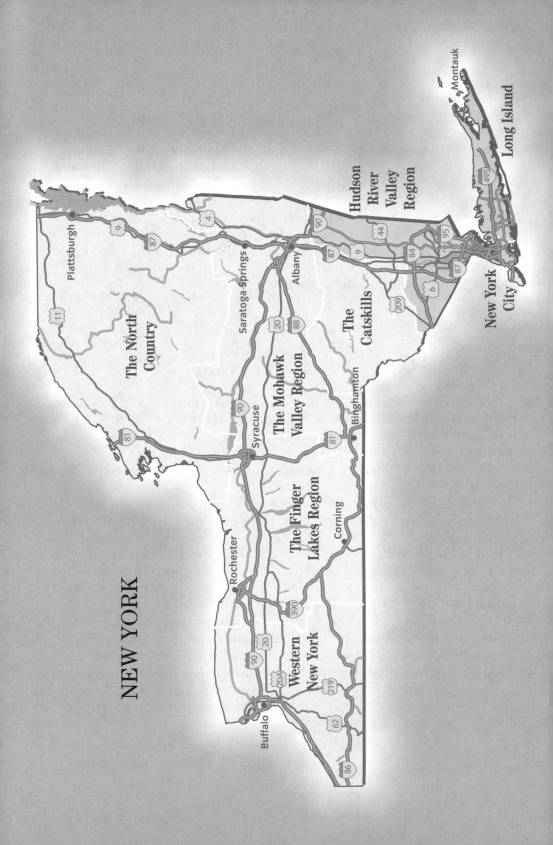

# Introduction

Like a magician's scarf, the glaciers of the last ice age grazed across the face of New York, transforming the land into a myriad of geological shapes and spectacular beauty. Over half the state is blanketed in thick, verdant forests, bejeweled with thousands of sapphire lakes, laced with ribbons of trout-laden streams, and edged in sugar sand beaches. For this edition, the journey begins in the Catskills, home to hemlock cathedrals and legendary folk tales. Travel through the Leatherstocking Country of the Mohawk Valley, the Finger Lakes, and the ancient Adirondacks, homeland of the Haudenosaunee. Further west is the grandeur of Niagara Falls, a spectacle that's lured visitors from all over the world for generations. Each chapter features facets of that region's scenic wonders, rich heritage, and cultural diversity that will appeal to folks of all ages.

Unlike solo travels, where there's a footloose freedom, family travel requires more planning and flexibility. Everyone should be included in the process. As New York is perennially renewing and re-creating itself, things change. Contact the places listed, either by phone or Web site, to get up-to-the-minute information about special events and vacation packages; to confirm hours of operation, admissions, reservations; and to ask about accommodations for special needs your family may have.

At the beginning of each chapter is a quick reference map, and each region is explored is a circular loop, but to open your options and customize your route, you'll want to get a detailed road map. The age recommendations are pretty subjective, but you know your children best. It's a plus if you can tour historical sites relevant to their school studies, especially when festivals and special events are scheduled. Revolutionary War encampments, pioneer days, and powwows can transform a dry history lesson into a virtual-reality time travel trip worthy of Jules Verne and H. G. Wells.

Each chapter has a short list of suggested children's books relevant to that region. While many are fictionalized accounts of the area's history, they add depth and richness to the tapestry of traveling that a mere guidebook cannot. It's tough to top reading "Rip

## More Family Fun in the Metro New York City Area

If you will be spending time in the Metro New York area—including the five boroughs, the Hudson River Valley region, and Long Island—be sure to pick up a copy of our sister book *Fun with the Family Metro New York* (GPP Travel).

Van Winkle" by a Catskill campfire, or *Last of the Mohicans* from a path in an ancient forest.

As you travel through upstate New York, think of yourselves not as tourists, but rather as explorers. As Henry David Thoreau wrote, "The question is not what you look at, but what you see." By sharing the adventure of discovery with your family, you will discover much about each other as well. These are fleeting years, so get out there, have fun with your family, and collect a treasury of memories.

### Rates for Attractions

| $ | up to $5 |
| $$ | $6 to $10 |
| $$$ | $11 to $20 |
| $$$$ | more than $20 |

### Rates for Restaurants

| $ | most entrees under $10 |
| $$ | most $10 to $15 |
| $$$ | most $16 to $20 |
| $$$$ | most over $20 |

### Rates for Accommodations

| $ | up to $100 |
| $$ | from $100 to $150 |
| $$$ | from $151 to $200 |
| $$$$ | more than $200 |

# Attractions Key

The following is a key to the icons found throughout the text.

| | | | |
|---|---|---|---|
| **SWIMMING** | | **FOOD** | |
| **BOATING / BOAT TOUR** | | **LODGING** | |
| **HISTORIC SITE** | | **CAMPING** | |
| **HIKING / WALKING** | | **MUSEUM** | |
| **FISHING** | | **PERFORMING ARTS** | |
| **BIKING** | | **SPORTS/ATHLETICS** | |
| **AMUSEMENT PARK** | | **PICNICKING** | |
| **HORSEBACK RIDING** | | **PLAYGROUND** | |
| **SKIING/WINTER SPORTS** | | **SHOPPING** | |
| **PARK** | | **PLANTS/GARDENS/NATURE TRAILS** | |
| **ANIMAL VIEWING** | | **FARM** | |

# The Catskills

Older than the Adirondacks, the Catskills are a delightful dichotomy. Romantically primeval and mysterious, this ancient plateau was once the hunting grounds of the Lenape, who believed the area to be the abode of the Great Spirit. Since the mid-1800s, the paintings of Thomas Cole and Frederick Church, along with the literature of Washington Irving and John Burroughs, have attracted tourists to the region, and resorts sprang up in response. Along with the wilderness and wildlife, there's a wild life of a different nature that exists today. From flume zooming at water parks to fly-fishing on the Willowemoc, there are train trips, petting zoos, putt-putt palaces, and more, all planned to please everyone in the family.

## DRIVING TIPS

From the west bank of the Hudson River in Kingston, NY 28 cuts through Ulster County and the Catskill Forest Preserve and Park, a 700,000-acre reserve of public and private land. Continue through the rolling hills of Delaware County or head north near Arkville on NY 30 to intersect with NY 23A. Follow NY 23A through the heart of Greene County and the higher peaks region, all the way to the west bank of the Hudson River in Catskill. NY 30 also follows the east branch of the Delaware River south and connects with NY 17 through the center of Sullivan County and to the scenic NY 98, which winds along the Delaware River. The region is reachable from I-87 on the eastern border and by I-88 on the far western edge.

# Kingston

On US 9W, on the eastern edge of the Catskills, along the Hudson River.

This quiet town was originally named "Wiltwyck" (Wild Place) by the Dutch, who founded a settlement here in 1652, making it the third-oldest city in the state. Later controlled by the British and renamed Kingston, the village was briefly the colonists' state capital during

# THE CATSKILLS

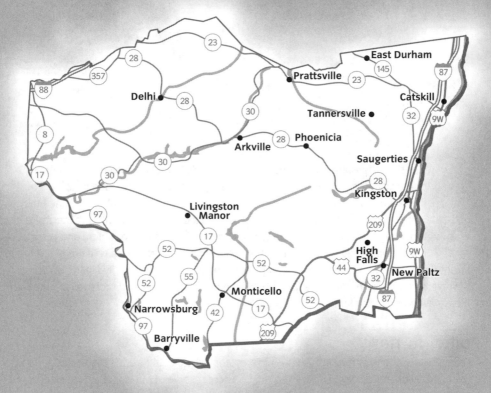

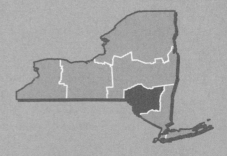

the Revolutionary War. Stop by the Kingston Urban Cultural Park Visitor Center at 308 Clinton Ave. in the historic Stockade District (845-339-0720) for a guided or self-guided walking tour of the area. Of special interest are the Old Dutch Church, the Senate House, and the Ulster County Courthouse (where Sojourner Truth won a lawsuit that rescued her son from slavery). Afterward, head down to the **Rondout Visitor Center** at 20 Broadway for a stroll around the revitalized river port. On summer Saturdays, the Catskill Mountain Railroad operates a new 2-mile round-trip train tour, the Kingston Shuttle, occasionally offering special "Teddy Bear Rides," complete with milk and cookies (BYOB . . . Bring Your Own Bear). Seasonal events throughout the town include an art fair, the Tall Tales Festivals, holiday lighting celebrations, band concerts on the riverfront, and the ever-popular "Reenactment of the Burning of Kingston." For more information contact (800) 331-1518, (845) 331-0080, or (845) 338-7534; www.kingston-ny.gov or www.nps.gov.

### Hudson River Maritime Museum (all ages)

50 Rondout Landing; (845) 338-0071; www.hrmm.org. Open daily May through Oct, 11 a.m. to 5 p.m., by chance or appointment. Museum and Lighthouse Tour, adults $, children 6 to 12 $, under 6 **free.**

This small museum is dedicated to preserving the maritime heritage of the Hudson River and has changing indoor exhibits, as well as several vintage vessels docked outside. Watch craftspeople restoring and rigging wooden ships next door, then hop aboard a boat to tour the biggest beacon on the Hudson, the nearby Rondout Lighthouse.

### Rondout Lighthouse Tours (all ages)

50 Rondout Landing; (800) 378-8145 or (845) 336-8145; www.ulster.net. Public tours operate every Sat, Sun, and holiday Mondays, from Memorial Day weekend to Labor Day, at 12:15 and 2 p.m. $$$; discount if you present your ticket from the Hudson River Maritime Museum. New tours are being added to the smaller Rondout II lighthouse.

Exhibitions and period furnishings illustrate the history of the lighthouse and lives of its keepers. Enjoy the view of the area from the tower.

### Trolley Museum and Tour (all ages)

89 East Strand, Rondout Landing; (845) 331-3399; www.tmny.org. Open weekends and holidays Memorial Day to Columbus Day, noon to 5 p.m. $.

Check out subway and rapid transit cars past and present, then ride the trolley 1.5 miles along the riverfront on original tracks to Kingston Point for a picnic.

### Forsyth Nature Center (all ages)

467 Broadway; (845) 331-1682 ext. 117; www.forsythnaturecenter.org. Open year-round. Memorial Day weekend through Labor Day, Mon through Fri 7 a.m. to 7 p.m., Sat and Sun 9 a.m. to 5 p.m.; Oct through May, Mon through Fri 7 a.m. to 5 p.m., Sat and Sun 9 a.m. to 1 p.m. **Free.** Some programs have fees.

The Forsyth Zoo and educational facility combined to create this new center, which has fifteen animal exhibits and five themed gardens, including demonstration pens showing honey making, composting, maple syruping, and more. Kids will enjoy the Kingston Kinderland playground, and there are picnic areas and tennis courts. Special interactive and educational programs are offered throughout the year.

### Volunteer Fireman's Hall and Museum  (ages 4 and up)

**265 Fair St.; (845) 331-0866; www.kingston-ny.gov; Open Apr through Oct, Fri 11 a.m. to 3 p.m. and Sat 10 a.m. to 4 p.m.; June through Aug, Wed through Fri 11 a.m. to 3 p.m. and Sat 10 a.m. to 4 p.m. Free.**

Housed in an 1857 fire station, this small museum has several ornate antique fire engines, artifacts, and other interesting firefighting memorabilia.

### Slabsides  (all ages)

**Burroughs Drive, West Park; (845) 473-4208; www.amnh.org. House open two days a year, so call for dates. Sanctuary is open year-round dawn to dusk. Free.**

Located within the 170-acre John Burroughs Sanctuary, this was one of three homes belonging to the legendary literary naturalist, and the one where he spent his last years. A rough-sided rustic cabin, hence the name, is furnished just as he left it, and it's open to visitors only twice a year. Still, you can take a peek inside the windows and pretend Mr. Burroughs will be right back, or take a hike on the very trails that inspired the Grand Old Man of Nature.

## Where to Eat

**Deising's Bakery and Coffee Shop.** 111 N. Front St.; (845) 338-1327; www.deisings .com. Fresh-baked goods, soups, sandwiches, and a children's menu. $

**Hoffman House.** 94 N. Front St.; (845) 338-2626; www.hoffmanhousetavern.com. Housed in a 1711 National Historic Landmark with fireplaces and a lovely patio, this restaurant offers a menus including steaks, seafood, homemade pasta, apple cobbler, and cheesecake. $$$

**Jane's Homemade Ice Cream and Restaurant.** 305 Wall St.; (845) 338-8315; www .janesicecream.com. Fresh homemade ice cream (more than sixty flavors!), soups, sandwiches, and daily specials. $

## Where to Stay

**Courtyard by Marriott, Kingston.** 500 Frank Sottile Blvd.; (845) 382-2300; www.mar riott.com. Babysitting, barbecue, picnic area, indoor pool. $$

# Hudson River Rides (all ages)

**North River Cruises,** West Strand Park, Broadway, Kingston; (845) 679-8205; www.northrivercruises.com. $$$

**Hudson River Cruises,** Rondout Landing; (845) 340-4700 or (800) 843-7472; www.hudsonrivercruises.com. $$$

**Hampton Inn Kingston.** 1307 Ulster Ave.; (845) 382-2600; www.kingston.hamptoninn .com. Eighty-one rooms, complimentary hot breakfast, refrigerator and microwave in every room, Internet, indoor pool, fitness center, guest laundry, flat-screen TV ($). $$$$

**Holiday Inn.** 503 Washington Ave.; (845) 338-0400. Two hundred and twelve rooms, indoor pool, recreation center, and restaurant. $$$$

# Woodstock, Bethel, and Phoenicia

West on NY 28.

Situated on the banks of Esopus Creek, Phoenicia is the tubing capital of the Catskills, if you are twelve or older. For those under the age limit recommended by the tube-rental shops, the rails are the way to ride. Woodstock is known for its famous 1969 music festival (although the actual concert took place in Bethel, about 70 miles away on Max Yasgur's dairy farm) and its legendary Byrdcliffe Arts and Crafts Colony.

## Catskill Mountain Railroad  (all ages)

P.O. Box 46, NY 28, Shokan, about 28 miles west of the New York State Thruway exit 19; (845) 688-7400; www.catskillmtrailroad.com. Two different stations for boarding. Weekends and holidays, late May through late Sept; fall foliage trips in Oct. $$$ adults, $$ children, under 4 free.

Travel by train 12 miles round-trip between the Empire State Railway Museum in Phoenicia and Mount Pleasant, a route that takes you along the scenic banks of Esopus Creek. Special events are scheduled, and the fall foliage rides are spectacular.

## Empire State Railway Museum  (all ages)

NY 28, off High Street, Phoenicia Station 12464; (845) 688-7501; www.esrm.com. Open Sat, Sun, and holidays, Memorial Day through Columbus Day 11 a.m. to 4 p.m. Donation.

Several vintage steam locomotives, a 1913 Pullman dining car, and other exhibits highlighting the history of railroading in the region are displayed in and around the restored 1899 Delaware & Ulster Railroad station. In Dec, Santa trades his sleigh for a train and rides into town with the RR String Band.

## Emerson Kaleidoscope  (ages 4 and up)

Emerson Place, 5340 NY 28, Mount Tremper; (877) 688-2828; www.emersonresort.com/ theshow. Open daily 10 a.m. to 5:30 p.m. Adults $, children under 12 free.

At 60 feet tall, this is the world's largest kaleidoscope. Step into the viewing chamber (actually the silo of an 1841 barn) and experience a magical multimedia seasonal sound and light show the 'scopes of your childhood could only dream about.

### Woodstock Farm Animal Sanctuary (all ages)

35 Van Wagner Rd., Willow (8 miles past Woodstock); (845) 679-5955; www.woodstockfas .org. Visiting days are weekends Apr through Oct, 11 a.m. to 4 p.m. Adults $$, children 12 and under $, free 3 and under.

The WFAS is a shelter providing care for neglected and abused animals. It promotes farm-animal welfare and educates the public about how animals are treated.

### Bethel Woods Center for the Arts (all ages)

200 Hurd Rd., Bethel; (866)781-2922 information; (845) 583-2079 museum; (845) 295-2448 Harvest Festival; www.bethelwoodscenter.org. Adults $$$, children $$, under 2 free.

Reclaim the spirit of the '60s at this vast 100-million-dollar outdoor performing arts center and museum, located on 2,000 pastoral acres that once were the site of the original Woodstock Festival. The museum explores the experience of the festival, and the legacies of that era, with multimedia exhibits, programs, and educational events. Concerts are offered June through Sept at three venues: the Pavilion Stage that accommodates 15,000 folks, the 1000-seat outdoor Terrace Stage, and the original Woodstock site, with a 30,000-people permit. On Sunday, from the end of Aug through Columbus Day weekend, the annual Harvest Festival occurs, with corn and hay mazes, pony rides, a craft village, a farmers market, arts and crafts workshops, live music, festival food, a children's area, and a "Gathering of the Scarecrows."

### Lake Superior State Park (all ages)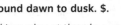

342 Dr. Dugan Rd., Bethel; (845) 583-7908; http://nysparks.state.ny.us/parks/87/details.aspx. Beach open Memorial Day through Labor Day; park is open year-round dawn to dusk. $.

Swim at the beach, rent a rowboat or paddleboat, go fishing or hiking, play at the playground, or have a picnic at the pavilion or a snack at the concession stand.

### Belleayre Mountain (all ages)

181 Galli Curci Rd., off NY 28, Highmount; (845) 254-5600 or (800) 942-6904; www.belle ayre.com. Ski resort open the day after Thanksgiving through Mar; lifts run 9 a.m. to 4 p.m. Beach open Memorial Day through mid-June, weekends only, 10 a.m. to 6 p.m.; mid-June to Sept, Mon through Fri 10 a.m. to 6 p.m.; Sat, Sun, and holidays 10 a.m. to 7:30 p.m. $$$$.

# Tube **Rentals**

**Town Tinker Tube.** 10 Bridge St., Route 28, Phoenicia; (845) 688-5553; www .towntinker.com.

**FS Tube and Raft.** 4 Church St., Phoenicia; (845) 688-7633 or (866) 4FS-TUBE; www.fstuberental.com.

# Panther Mountain Meteor Impact Site

About 400 million years ago, a huge meteor crashed into what is now the Catskill Mountains. At the time, the area was covered by a shallow sea, and the 6-mile crater was gradually filled in with sediment. Over eons, the layers of rock were pushed upwards, forming Panther Mountain, and the Esopus and Woodland Creeks encircled the site. To explore this scenic geologic formation, head south on CR 47, about 7 miles past Oliverea, to the NYSDEC Giant Ledge trailhead. For more information, check out the Panther Mountain Web site at www.catskillcenter.org/panther.

In winter this resort offers forty-seven trails, glades, and parks, plus eight lifts, a vertical drop of 1,400 feet, ski lessons, and Kids Camp. Child care is available for children ages one to six. In summer, swim at the Belleayre Beach on Pine Lake Hill; rent a rowboat, kayak, or pedal boat; plan a picnic; or go fishing. Eco-Adventures are offered to families on weekends, a Junior Naturalist Program is just for kids, and breathtaking views from the Belleayre Sky Ride are a blast. Concerts are scheduled July to Sept at the Belleayre Music Festival, so check the Web site for current shows.

## Where to Eat

**The Bear Cafe.** 295 Tinker St., Woodstock; (845) 679-5555; www.bearcafe.com. New American cuisine from steaks and salmon to half-pound cheeseburgers served streamside or fireside, with seasonal cobbler and homemade ice cream. $$$–$$$$

**Garden Cafe.** 6 Old Forge Rd., Woodstock; (845) 679-3600; Eclectic vegetarian cuisine serving organic, fresh, local whole foods. Everything is homemade and nothing is microwaved, and they have a children's menu. $$–$$$

**Peekamoose Restaurant and Tap Room.** 8373 NY 28, Big Indian; (845) 254-6500; www.peekamooserestaurant.com. Gourmet New American cuisine, using seasonal local produce, with casual fare served in the tavern, a creative kids' menu, and an extensive beer and wine list. $$.

**Sweet Sue's.** 49 Main St., Phoenicia; (845) 688-7852. A pancake paradise with great sandwiches. $

# Also in the Area

**Tibetan Buddhist Monastery.** Karma Triyana Dharmachakra, 352 Meads Mountain Rd., Woodstock; (845) 679-5906; www.kagyu.org.

## Where to Stay

**Emerson Resort & Spa.** 5340 NY 28, Mount Tremper; (877) 688-2828; www.emersonresort.com.; Families stay at the log Lodge, with twenty-seven rooms and suites, including free Wi-Fi, flat-screen TVs, access to the spa, Country Store, conference center, and Phoenix Restaurant. $$$$

**Full Moon Resort.** Valley View Road (CR 47), Oliverea; (845) 254-5117; www.fullmoon resort.com. Located on one hundred beautiful acres, Full Moon offers rooms at the Valley View House with private bath or shared hall bath, plus seven other guesthouses and four smaller cottages, most with kitchen, living room, and bath. Full Moon is dedicated to the celebration of music, art, and nature, and has frequent concerts and festivals, as well as a spring-fed swimming pool and a rustic cafe serving breakfast, barbecue, and chocolate-dipped strawberries. $$$

**Woodland Valley Campground.** 1319 Woodland Valley Rd., off NY 28, Phoenicia; (845) 688-7647. Open mid-May to Columbus Day. Seventy-two tent and trailer sites, picnic area, hot showers, fishing, and hiking trails to the Panther Mountain Meteor Impact Site. $

# Arkville, Delhi, East Meredith, and Roxbury

Continue west on NY 28.

Native Americans called this area Pakatakan, and at the turn of the twentieth century the town supported a successful artists' colony. Stop by the unusual Round Barn (NY 30, in nearby Halcottsville) to stock the larder at the Pakatakan Farmers Market every Saturday, May through October, from 9 a.m. to 3 p.m. The largest town in Delaware County, Delhi is centered around historic Courthouse Square, where on Wednesday, June through September, from 9 a.m. to 2 p.m., you can purchase produce from local farms and orchards. Nearby Walton is the home of the Delaware County Fair, as well as the site of the annual Memorial Day Civil War reenactment of the Battle of Honey Hill. Roxbury also offers time-travel trips on four days each summer, with horse-drawn coach rides and games played by the nineteenth-century baseball team, the Roxbury Nine.

### Delaware & Ulster Railroad  (all ages)

**43510 NY 28, D&U Depot, Arkville; (845) 586-3877 or (800) 225-4132; www.durr.org. Open weekends and holidays Memorial Day through Oct; Wed through Sun, July through Labor Day. Departure times vary by date (board fifteen minutes before). Adults $$, children 3 to 12 $, under 3 free. Rip Van Winkle Flyer $$$$.**

Ride the DURR, nicknamed the "Up and Down" because of the hilly terrain, from Arkville to Roxbury and back again, aboard old "Doodlebug," a vintage steam train. Special rides are scheduled throughout the season, ranging from mock railroad robberies to Twilight on the Rails, a little night music in the mountains. To experience the Golden Age of

Railroading, hop aboard the Rip Van Winkle Flyer, a newly refurbished streamliner, for a two-hour-and-fifteen-minute lunch trip through the Catskills.

### Bear Spring Mountain State Park (all ages)

512 E. Trout Brook Rd., Downsville; (607) 865-6989; www.nysparks.com. $.

Created in 1885 to protect the region's water resources, this rustic park has forty-one tent and trailer sites, a sandy beach, a picnic pavilion, showers and restrooms, horse stalls, and 24 miles of multiuse trails to explore.

### Delaware County Historical Association Museum (ages 8 and up)

46549 NY 10, Delhi; (607) 746-3849; www.dcha-ny.org. Open Memorial Day through Oct 15, Tues through Sun 11 a.m. to 4 p.m.; Oct 16 through late May, Mon through Fri 10 a.m. to 3 p.m. $.

This museum has a complex of restored historical buildings and a gallery with changing regional exhibits. On-site is the Frisbee house (no, not that Frisbee) with rooms decorated in different period styles and a children's room with antique toys. Outside explore the Husted Hollow Schoolhouse, a tollhouse, a blacksmith shop, a gun shop, and an easy nature trail.

### Hanford Mills (all ages) ·

Corner of NY 10 and CR 12, East Meredith; (607) 278-5744 or (800) 295-4992; www.hanford mills.org. Open Tues through Sun, mid-May through mid-Oct, and on Memorial Day, Labor Day, and Columbus Day, 10 a.m. to 5 p.m. Adults $$, children 12 and younger free.

Experience the past at this fully restored water-powered rural industrial complex. This was nineteenth-century one-stop shopping at its best, for farmers had grain ground, builders had lumber cut, creameries had containers made, and homemakers could buy flour here. Sixteen historic structures are spread out on seventy acres, but the heart of the complex is the huge whirring and creaking waterwheel. Seasonal events such as the Independence Day celebration include sampling freshly made ice cream and competing in a fishing derby, tug-of-war, sack races, and frog-jumping contests (BYOF).

### Stone & Thistle Farm (all ages)

1211 Kelso Rd., East Meredith; (607) 278-5800; www.stoneandthistlefarm .com. Farm store open year-round 9 a.m. to 6 p.m.; farm tours Sun at 11 a.m., Memorial Day to Columbus Day, $, under 3 free; tour with brunch $$.

Tour a working sustainable organic farm and creamery, with naturally raised goat, pigs, rabbits, Scottish Highland cattle, chickens and turkeys. Watch border collies at work, or be a "Farmer for a Day" by milking goats, herding sheep, collecting eggs, or harvesting and preparing food from the kitchen gardens. Feast at their fabulous Fable Restaurant housed in an 1860 Greek Revival farmhouse.

### Woodchuck Lodge and Burroughs Memorial Field (all ages)
**Hardscrabble Road, Roxbury; (607) 326-7641 or (607) 326-3722; www.roxburyny.com.**
**Free.**

This was the naturalist John Burroughs's boyhood home. It was sold out of the family, then later bought back by Henry Ford and returned to Burroughs as a gift. He was buried on his eighty-fourth birthday at the foot of his favorite "Boyhood Rock," on which he played as a child. Programs for families include farming, gardening, and nature experiences that teach folks how to "listen to the land."

### Plattekill Mountain (all ages)
**NY 30 South (Plattekill Mountain Road), Roxbury; information (607) 326-3500; snow conditions (800) NEED-2-SKI; www.plattekill.com. $$.**

Family-friendly, all-season resort, with skiing, snowboarding, and snow tubing in winter. Thirty-five trails, with three lifts, and a vertical drop of 1,100 feet. Child care is available for kids six months and up. Kids under seventeen ski **free** with paying adult. In summer, mountain bike and hike along more than 60 miles of trails, or get a panoramic view from the Plattekill Skyride, available on weekends.

## Where to Eat

**The Cheese Barrel.** 798 Main St., Margaretville; (845) 586-4666. Homemade soups and sandwiches, plus gourmet coffee and cheeses. $

**Delhi Diner.** 95 Main St., Delhi; (607) 746-2207. Delicious Delhi deli. $

**Miller's Bar-B-Q.** 29735 NY 10, Walton; (607) 865-4721. Great barbecued chicken. $$

## Where to Stay

**Andes Hotel.** 110 Main St., Andes; (845) 676-4408; www.andeshotel.com. Ten rooms in a historic 1850 inn, cable TV, Wi-Fi, restaurant, tavern with six TVs, live music, and barbecues. $–$$

**Buena Vista Motel.** 18718 NY 28, Andes Road, Delhi; (607) 746-2135; www.buenavista motel.com. Thirty-three rooms and studio apartments, Wi-Fi, cable TV, free breakfast, picnic area. $

## Catskills **Farm Fun**

**Widmark Honey Farms.** US 44/NY 55, Gardiner; (845) 255-6400.

**Arrowhead Maple Syrup Farm Tour.** 5941 US 209, Kerhonkson; (845) 626-7293. Open Feb through Mar.

**Lyonsville Sugarhouse and Farm.** 591 CR 2, Kripplebush-Krumville Road, Accord; (845) 687-2518.

**Armstrong's Elk Farm.** 936 Hervey Sunside Rd., Cornwallville; (518) 622-8452.

## Delaware County Agritainment

**Maple Shade Farm.** 2066 CR 18, Delhi; (607) 746-8866; www.mapleshadefarm ny.com. Open late Sept to Nov. $.

**Sunflower Farm.** 834 Crescent Valley Rd., Bovina; (607) 832-4418; Open Labor Day through Halloween. $.

**Harmony Hill Retreat.** 694 McKee Hill Rd., East Meredith; (877) 278-6609; www.harmony hillretreat.com. Sleep in a tree house, yurt, or mountain chalet on seventy acres of woods and meadows, take a Wild Plant Walk and learn about edible and medicinal plants, then spiral around a fieldstone labyrinth at this peaceful spiritual retreat. $$$$. Child care is available for kids six months and up. Kids under seventeen ski free with paying adult. $$$$

**The Roxbury Motel.** 2258 CR 41, Roxbury; (607) 326-7200; www.roxburymotel.com. This is a very cool place. There will be no doilies here, thank you! Decorated with wild colors and bold patterns, the themed rooms and suites are inspired by Fred Flintstone, George Jetson, Austin Powers, *Bewitched, I Dream of Jeannie,* and *The Partridge Family.* Kitchenettes and studios, equally dramatically decorated, are also available. All rooms have TVs with DVD and MP3 players, access to a DVD library of over 400 movies, Internet, refrigerators, microwaves, coffee machines, plus a coed mini-spa with a sauna, fireplace, and hot tub. Ask about special offers and packages that combine area activities with room stays. $–$$$$

# Hunter and Tannersville

Originally named Greenland Mountain, Hunter today offers a wealth of activities, including skiing, cycling, picnicking, hiking, and mountain biking, along with seasonal festivals ranging from Celtic celebrations to a raucous Oktoberfest.

During the mid-1800s, the bark from the once abundant hemlock forests of the Catskills provided the necessary tannin for tanning leather, the industry that gave Tannersville its name.

### St. John the Baptist Ukrainian Church and Grazhda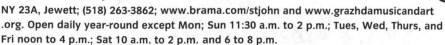

**NY 23A, Jewett; (518) 263-3862; www.brama.com/stjohn and www.grazhdamusicandart .org. Open daily year-round except Mon; Sun 11:30 a.m. to 2 p.m.; Tues, Wed, Thurs, and Fri noon to 4 p.m.; Sat 10 a.m. to 2 p.m. and 6 to 8 p.m.**

In the early '60s, as a tangible expression of their skill and heritage, Ukrainian folk artists and local residents conceived and constructed this incredible complex without any nails, and adorned the inside with intricate icons and folk symbols carved from sugar pine. Buffet lunch is offered on Sun, and concerts at Grazhda are scheduled on Sat.

### Hunter Mountain (all ages)

NY 23A, Hunter, 2 miles west of Tannersville; (800) HUNTERMTN; (800) FOR-SNOW (snow conditions); www.huntermtn.com and www.ridehunter.com; fly-fishing (800) 486-8376. Ski season runs daily from the end of Nov through Apr, 8:30 a.m. to 4 p.m.; summer sky ride weekends July through Oct, 11 a.m. to 4:40 p.m. Ask about family package rates and free ski times for kids. $$$$.

Renowned as the Snowmaking Capital of the World (they can make forty tons of snow a minute), Hunter offers fifty-eight trails and twelve lifts covering three mountains, with a vertical drop of 1,600 feet. The Snowtubing Park has nine chutes and two tube tows. Programs for children include Playcare (ages six months to six years), Explorers (skiers ages four to six), Mountaineers (ages seven to twelve), snow tubing for folks over 42 inches tall, and weekend intensive workshops for kids ages four through seventeen, with lessons and equipment rentals available. In summer, Skyride to the summit of Hunter Mountain in a four-passenger chairlift, or hike and bike numerous trails lacing the area, including the difficult Devil's Path. For fish fans, half- and full-day fly-fishing excursions are offered, with lessons and rod and reel included.

### Dancing Bear Theater (all ages)

Main Street, Hunter; (518) 263-4233. $–$$.

Musicals, revues, comedies, dramas, and children's theater workshops throughout the year.

### North-South Lakes (all ages)

CR 18, Haines Falls (a few miles east of Tannersville); (518) 589-5058 or (518) 357-2289; campground reservations (800) 456-CAMP or www.reserveamerica.com; www.dec.ny.gov/outdoor/24487.html. $$. Open May through late Oct, daily 9 a.m. to dusk. Beaches open when lifeguard available, Memorial Day through Labor Day. Free.

Early Native Americans believed the two lakes were the eyes of a fallen giant, and the nearby escarpment was a sacred ground known as "The Great Wall of Manitou." On a clear day you can see five states from that sacred space. Today this popular area has 219 tent and trailer campsites with hot showers; two lakes; two beaches; picnic pavilions and areas; a playground; canoe, kayak, paddleboat, and rowboat rentals; fishing (bass, bullhead, and pickerel); and some spectacular hiking trails. Organized recreational activities are offered daily from the end of June to Labor Day, and may include nature hikes, crafts, games, and live entertainment. For an easy and safe hike, head 1 mile east of Haines Falls on NY 23. Leave your car at the parking area and walk carefully along the road to the

## Also in **the Area**

**Dolan's Lake.** 7955 Main St., Hunter; (518) 263-4020.

**Five State Lookout.** Mohican Trail, Route 23.

# Captivating Catskill **Children's Hikes**

These are easy hikes for little tykes, and fun for grown-ups, too.

**Huckleberry Point.** CR 16, Platte Clove; (845) 256-3026. Hike 3½ miles round-trip, with very nice vistas of the Hudson River Valley and Hunter Mountain.

**Boulder Rock.** CR 18 to North and South Lake State Campground, Haines Falls; (518) 357-2289. This easy 1½-mile trail visits the site of the magnificent Catskill Mountain House, long since gone, but the breathtaking view remains.

**Colgate Lake.** CR 78, East Jewett; (inside Catskill Park Forest Preserve); (518) 357-2441. This 4-mile round-trip is a moderate hike that takes you past wilderness ponds and streams, filled with wildlife from frogs and fish to deer and salamanders.

**Diamond Notch Falls.** CR 6, Spruceton; (inside Catskill Forest Preserve); (518) 402-8013. An easy 3-mile round trip hike to a waterfall and a brook and back.

**Dry Brook.** CR 49A at Stuart's Turn, Mapledale; (518) 473-9518. There's nothing dry about this 4-mile round-trip trail, as it follows a riverbank where otter, raccoon, mink, coyote, and bobcat roam.

**Long Pond.** CR 84 to Flugertown Road, Willowemoc; (518) 473-9518. Trek this easy 2-mile round-trip trail to a pond teeming with tadpoles, water striders and whirligig beetles.

**Alder Lake.** CR 54, Turnwood; (845) 256-3082. A level, 2-mile loop around the lake.

**Little Spring Brook.** NY 206 to Little Spring Brook Road, Roscoe. This easy 3-mile hike takes you past a frog pond and a babbling brook.

trailhead on the other side. From there it is a short, easy walk to the base of Kaaterskill Falls, which, at 260 feet, are higher than Niagara Falls.

## The Mountain Top Arboretum (all ages)

CR 23C, Maude Adams Road, Tannersville; (518) 589-3903; www.mtarbor.org. $.

Open year-round, this public preserve and garden is located in the high peaks region of the Catskills and functions as both a living museum and an ongoing research project. All flora is labeled, allowing you to self-guide yourself through wildflowers and fifty species of conifers. Seasonal programs are offered and include lessons on pine tree pruning and growing local ginseng.

## Where to Eat

**Bear Creek Restaurant.** Corner of NY 214 and NY 23A, Hunter; (518) 263-3839; www .bearcreekrestaurant.com. Fun family restaurant serving pasta, ribs, steaks, and a peanut butter and white-chocolate mousse, plus an arcade. Outside, there's a mini-golf course and a driving range, as well as horse and pony rides. $$

**Last Chance Antiques and Cheese Café.** 602 Main St., Tannersville; (518) 589-6424; www.lastchanceonline.com. Gourmet cafe and takeout featuring soups, sandwiches, salads, steaks, burgers, pastas, homemade pastries, chocolate fondue, 100 imported cheeses, 300 imported beers, a children's menu, and campfire s'mores toasted at your table. $$

## Where to Stay

**Catskill Mountain Lodge.** 334 NY 32A, Palenville; (518) 678-3101 or (800) MTN–LODGE; www.catskillmtlodge.com. Deluxe rooms with balconies and fireplaces, double and single rooms, cabins and rustic cottages, free wireless Internet, playground, outdoor heated pool, kiddie pool, game room, gym, and the Kindred Spirits Steakhouse & Pub on the premises. $$$

**Kaatskill Mountain Club.** 62 Liftside Dr., Hunter; from Ethel Court Road, follow signs to the club; (800) 486-8376; www.kaatskillmtn club.com. Rooms, suites, and condos (one has six bedrooms), year-round outdoor heated pool, two outdoor hot tubs, spa, health club, steam and sauna, video-game room, high-speed Internet, in-room movies, and food offerings from Van Winkles (a full-service restaurant), Sabatini's Pizza, Jerry's Deli, a weekend sushi bar, and the Plaza Cafe on-site. $$$

# Prattsville

Take NY 10 to NY 23.

Zadock Pratt wanted to build the largest tannery in the world in Schoharie Kill. Having accomplished that, he set out to rebuild the entire town. Creating one of the first planned communities in the state (renamed in his honor), Pratt's people planted hundreds of trees along widened streets trimmed with slate sidewalks and constructed dozens of beautiful Greek Revival homes. Textile factories, gristmills, churches, hotels, and schools were built, along with a bank that dispensed currency with Pratt's picture on it.

## Zadock Pratt Museum (all ages)

**West end of Main Street (NY 23); (518) 299-3395; www.prattmuseum.com. Open weekends Memorial Day through Columbus Day, 1 to 5 p.m., or by appointment. $.**

For all of his civic-minded projects, Zadock Pratt was quite a character. He had a penchant for practical jokes, staged elaborate battle reenactments, and challenged folks to games of skill and strength. His remarkable life is documented inside his former home, in pictures and artifacts, and outside in the symbolic bas-relief cliffside carvings known as Pratt Rock.

# Windham

Continue on NY 23 into Windham.

Nicknamed the "Gem of the Catskills," this region was settled by New England colonists in the late eighteenth century.

### Windom Mountain Resort (all ages)

**33 Clarence D. Lane Rd.; (518) 734-4300; (800) 754-9463 for lodging information; (518) 734-6974 skating area; www.windhammountain.com. Open in season Mon through Fri 9 a.m. to 4 p.m., weekends and holidays 8 a.m. to 4 p.m. $$$$. Skating area open Fri 4 to 9 p.m., Sat and holidays 10 a.m. to 9 p.m., Sun 10 a.m. to 5 p.m. $.**

More intimate than Hunter, Windham ski resort offers forty-six trails for all levels, ten lifts, and snowboard and ski lessons for ages 4 and up. The Children's Learning Center offers organized activities for nonskiers ages two to seven, private lessons for three-year-olds, group Mini-Mogul lessons (age four to seven) and Mountain Master Skier & Rider lessons (ages eight to twelve). For totally skill-less shrieking fun, however, try snow tubing at Windham's Adventure Park, as you slide flat on your back down a 650-foot snow-covered slope. Even three-year-olds can do it! There are three restaurants, a sushi bar, and a Starbucks on-site. A new addition is the 120-foot-by-60-foot ice-skating area, located at the Windham Mountain Adventure Park on South Street, where in summer you can play paintball, climb a wall, skate or bike the Skateboard Park, or bounce on a bungee trampoline.

## Where to Eat

**Bistro Brie & Bordeaux.** 5386 NY 23 (Main Street); (518)738-4911; www.bistro andbordeaux.com. Housed in the former nineteenth-century home of the *Windham Journal* newspaper, this charming classic French bistro in the Catskills serves steak frites, scallops, shrimp, snails, salmon, bouillabaisse, crème brûlée, and a "les enfants" menu. $$–$$$

**Chalet Fondue.** 55 NY 296; (518) 734-4650; www.chaletfondue.com. German Alpine cuisine, with fireplaces, fondue, and hot apple strudel. $$

## Where to Stay

**Point Lookout Mountain Inn.** 7604 NY 23, (518) 734-3381; www.pointlookoutinn .com. Rooms with mountain and valley views, 150 movies (many Disney classics), free Wi-Fi, game room, bocci ball, live entertainment, and in-house dining at the Victorian Rose Restaurant or outside in season at the Cliffside, both with kids' menus and on a clear day the vista of five states. $$

**The Winwood Inn.** NY 23, in center of Windham; (518) 734-3000; www.winwoodinn .com. Rooms, suites, and one- and two-bedroom condos next to Windham Mountain, with a movie theater, tennis court, outdoor pool, recreation center, fitness center, nature trail, and dining at the Trail's End Tavern & Grill. Children under seventeen free anytime, with adult in same room. $$$–$$$$

# East Durham

Take NY 23 east to NY 145 north.

Dubbed the Irish Alps, the town of East Durham has been attracting immigrants from the Emerald Isle since the 1880s. Wear green and be seen here Memorial Day weekend for the East Durham Irish Festival, complete with bagpipes, fresh-baked soda bread, and river dancing in the streets.

### Zoom Flume  (all ages)
**91 Shady Glen Rd., East Durham; (518) 239-4559 or (800) 888-3586; www.zoomflume.com. Open June through Labor Day, weekdays 10 a.m. to 6 p.m., weekends to 7 p.m. $$$–$$$$.**

The largest water park in the Catskills, Zoom Flume offers a full day of family fun in the sun. Slip-slide down a 600-foot water chute as you raft the rapids on the "Wild River Ride," plunge in total darkness down into the "Black Vortex," float around the Lazy River, or wrestle the "Mighty Anaconda." The Lagoon Activity Pool offers pint-size thrills, and there are easy nature trails and a playground to explore.

### Durham Center Museum  (all ages)
**NY 145, 2 miles west of East Durham; (518) 239-8461. Open mid-May through Columbus Day, Thurs through Sun 1 to 4 p.m. Winter hours by appointment. $.**

This volunteer-run museum in an 1825 schoolhouse began as a collection of unusual, historical, or just downright interesting objects amassed by town resident Vernon Haskins. Fossils and minerals, Native American artifacts, pioneer tools, genealogical records, military relics, sculptures, typewriters, toys, and more can be seen here.

### Irish American Heritage Museum  (all ages)
**2267 NY 145, East Durham; museum (518) 634-7497; www.irishamericanheritagemuseum .org. Open Memorial Day through Labor Day, Wed through Sun noon to 4 p.m. $.**

Special cultural programs and educational exhibits highlighting the history of the Irish in America are offered at this excellent museum.

## Cinema **under the Stars**

Greene County is the home of a memorable but vanishing breed of entertainment: the drive-in movie. Catch a flick at one of the open-air retro movie arenas below for a family-style fifties flashback.

**Hi-Way Drive-In.** US 9W, Coxsackie; (518) 731-8672; www.hiwaydrivein.com.

**Greenville Drive-In.** 10700 NY 32, Greenville; (518) 966-8500; www.greenville drivein.com.

# Horsing around **Greene County**

**K&K Equestrian Center.** CR 67, East Durham; (518) 966-5272.

**Bailiwick Ranch and Catskill Equestrian Center.** 118 Castle Rd., Catskill; (518) 678-5665.

**Tanglewood Ranch.** 438 Cornwallville Rd., Cornwallville; (518) 622-9531.

**Rough Riders Ranch.** CR 23C, East Jewett; (518) 589-9159.

**Lazy S Ranch.** 637 Hervey St., Cornwallville; (518) 239-8995.

**Windham Equestrian Center.** NY 23, Windham; (518) 734-3592.

**Bear Creek Recreational Park.** NY 23A and Route 214, Hunter; (518) 263-3839.

**Bronck Museum** (ages 6 and up)
90 CR 42, off US 9W, Coxsackie; (518) 731-6490; www.gchistory.org. Open Memorial Day through mid-Oct, Wed through Fri noon to 4 p.m.; Sat and Monday holidays 10 a.m. to 4 p.m.; and Sun, Memorial Day, Labor Day, and Columbus Day, 1 to 4 p.m. $, children under 5 and members **free.**

Eight generations of the Bronck family worked this farm, a complex of Dutch Colonial homes and nineteenth-century barns filled with period furniture, antiques, spinning wheels, looms, carriages, and other historical artifacts. Out back is the family and slave cemetery, a visual lesson in disparate lifestyles.

## Where to Eat

**Hollowbrook Inn & Restaurant.** 10616 NY 32, Greenville; (518) 966-4683 or (518) 966-4684; www.hollowbrookinn.com. Steak, seafood, sauerbraten, pasta, salads, sandwiches, plus a children's menu. $–$$

**The Shamrock House.** NY 145, East Durham; (518) 634-2897 or (888) 634-2897; www .shamrockhouse.com. Shepherd's pie, fish-and-chips, steak, and chicken. Half orders available for children. A variety of accommodations are also available. $$

## Where to Stay

**Blackthorn Resort.** 348 Sunside Rd.; (518) 634-2541; www.blackthornresort.com. Dude ranch with rooms and efficiencies, some with terrace and mountain views, campsites and RV hookups, an outdoor pool, fishing, lake, mini-golf, horseback and pony rides, rock climbing, go-karts, mini-golf, batting cages, hayrides, a haunted house, a magic show, games, dining, and babysitting. $$–$$$

**The Country Place Resort.** Shady Glen Road, East Durham; (800) 888-3586; www .thecountryplace.com. Affiliated with the Zoom Flume Water Park, it offers admission and accommodation packages, plus heated pool, tennis, Internet, fishing, paddleboats, outdoor sports, and evening activities. $$–$$$

**Hull-O-Farms.** 10 Cochrane Rd., Durham; (518) 239-6950; www.hull-o.com. Milk a

## Also in **the Area**

**Mahayana Buddhist Temple and Monastery.** Ira Vail Road, off CR 23B, Cairo; (518) 622-3619.

**Round Top Raptor Center.** 733 Bald Hill Rd. North, Round Top; (518) 622-0118; www.roundtopraptorcenter.com.

cow, feed the pigs and goats, go fishing in the ponds, pick a pumpkin, and enjoy a barbecue or a hayride or get lost in a corn maze. Lodging is in private homes on or next to the 300-acre farm and comes with three homegrown and home-cooked meals a day. $$$–$$$$, children five to fourteen $$, under five $.

# Catskill

Take NY 67 east to Coxsackie, then head south on NY 385 to Catskill.

The surrounding hillsides sheltered moonshine stills during Prohibition, but the moonshine of the mountains today is of the celestial variety. Folks say Rip Van Winkle slumbered for twenty years here, but there's so much to do in this area that you won't have time for so much as a cat(skill) nap.

### Cedar Grove  (all ages)
218 Spring St.; (518) 943-7465; www.thomascole.org. **Open May through Oct, Thurs, Fri, Sat, and Sun 10 a.m. to 4 p.m. or by appointment. Tours of the main house, adults $$, seniors and students $.**

The home of Thomas Cole, the founder of the Hudson River School of art welcomes visitors for guided tours. With a view of the Catskills, the home overlooks the Hudson River, the subject of many of Cole's paintings. The grounds are **free** to the public, and include the Hudson River School Art Trail, which maps the famous sites and overlooks that have been rendered since the nineteenth century.

### Bailiwick Ranch & Discovery Zoo  (all ages)
118 Castle Rd.; (518) 678-5665; www.bailiwickranch.com. **Trail rides available every day Apr through Oct, by appointment weekdays Nov through Mar. Zoo open daily early Apr through Sept, 10 a.m. to 6 a.m.; Oct weekends only, 10 a.m. to 4 p.m. $$$$.**

A variety of trail rides are offered, for cowboys and cowgirls over the age of seven, from half-hour to all-day trips, as well as sunset dinner rides and overnight camping adventures. There's also a zoo housing exotic and farm animals, with a petting and feeding area, three reptile shows a day, and a bounce house. Play paintball in a five-acre forest with a picnic area, or pause at the picnic area, playground, or gift shop.

### RamsHorn-Livingston Sanctuary (all ages)

Grandview Avenue, Catskill; (518) 325-5203; www.audubon.org and www.scenichudson .org. Open dawn to dusk. **Free.**

This 480-acre preserve of tidal swamp forests and fallow farm fields is filled with birds, and it's a breeding ground for American shad and bass. There are more than 3½ miles of trails, and there's a 28-foot observation tower for a scenic view.

## Where to Eat

**Creekside Restaurant & Bar.** 160 Main St.; (518) 943-652; Serving traditional American cuisine, located between the Hop-O-Nose Marina and the Catskill Creek, with beautiful water views, outdoor patio seating in season, and live music on weekends. $$

**Hagar's Harbor Restaurant & Marina.** 10 Brick Row Extension, Athens; (518) 945-1854. Dockside dining and indoor dining room with live music every weekend. $$

## Where to Stay

**Carl's Rip Van Winkle Motor Lodge.** 810 CR 23B, Leeds (just west of New York State Thruway exit 21); (518) 943-3303; www .ripvanwinklemotorlodge.com. Rooms and cabins on 160 wooded acres, with a gazebo, outdoor pool, kiddie pool, playground, and cribs on request. $

**Red Ranch Motel.** 4555 NY 32; (518) 678-3380 or (800) 962-4560; www.redranchmotel .com. Rooms with refrigerators, kitchenettes, cable TV, swimming and kiddie pools, play area, game room, and restaurant. $

**The Stewart House.** 2 N. Water St.; (518) 945-1357; www.stewarthouse.com. This Victorian inn has nine lovely rooms, some overlooking the Hudson, a fabulous gourmet restaurant, and a new outdoor cafe, the River Garden. For larger families, there's a large secluded lodge nearby with nine bedrooms on ninety-four private acres. $$$$

**Wolff's Maple Breeze.** 360 Cauterskill Rd.; (518) 943-3648 or (800) 777-9653; www .wolffsresort.com. Rooms and suites, outdoor pool, three lakes, rowboats, fishing, a playground, game room, hayrides, tennis, lawn games, mini-golf and driving range, supervised children's activities, and restaurant. $$$

# Family Fun **Centers**

**Catskill Sportsplex.** 1113 CR 23B, Leeds; (518) 947-0611.

**Hoe Bowl Lanes Family Recreation Center.** 305 W. Bridge St., Catskill; (518) 943-4980; www.hoebowl.com.

**Purling Roller Rink.** Mountain Ave, Cairo; (518) 622-9117; www.purlingroller rink.com.

**Supersonic Speedway & Fun Park.** NY 145, East Durham; (518) 634-7200.

# Saugerties

Take NY 23 east to US 9W south.

### Opus 40 and Quarryman's Museum  (all ages)

50 Fite Rd., Saugerties; (845) 246-3400; www.opus40.org. Open Memorial Day weekend through Columbus Day weekend, Fri through Sun, plus Monday holidays, 11:30 a.m. to 5 p.m. Adults $$, children $, under 6 free but must be supervised.

This is a six-acre environmental sculpture chiseled from an abandoned bluestone quarry by one man, Harvey Fite. Fun to explore and marvel at, *Opus 40* is especially enchanting during the regularly scheduled sunset concerts, so plan for a picnic dinner on the grounds.

### Saugerties Village Beach  (all ages)

43 Partition St.; (845) 246-2919.

Set on the Esopus Creek, this beach has sand, a playground, swimming dock, fishing area, and restrooms. Open for swimming July 1 to Sept 1. Lifeguard on duty from 10 a.m. to 6 p.m.

### Esopus Bend Nature Preserve  (all ages)

Shady Lane, off US 9W, Saugerties; (845)247-0664; www.esopuscreekconservancy.org. Open daily dawn to dusk. Donation.

An abandoned farm for over forty years, this unique 161-acre preserve, located at a dramatic bend in the Esopus Creek, has reverted to its natural form, with forests filled with foxes and fawns, and meadows exploding with wildflowers. There are four trails winding though a variety of habitats, and activities include guided nature, butterfly, and bird walks, canoe and kayak tours, and animal-tracking adventures.

### Saugerties Lighthouse  (all ages)

168 Lighthouse Dr.; www.saugertieslighthouse.com. Donation suggested. $.

Tour this lighthouse (unless it's occupied by overnight guests) Memorial Day through Labor Day, weekends and holidays from noon to 3 p.m. This is the only lighthouse on the Hudson River accessible by land, via a 0.5-mile nature trail open dawn to dusk. Stands of willows and wildflowers will lead you to the middle of the Hudson River, where a small museum inside the lighthouse houses artifacts that document the reconstruction of this historic landmark.

## Where to Eat

**Café Tamayo.** 89 Partition St.; (845) 246-9371; www.cafetamayo.com. Intimate place specializing in local seasonal gourmet cuisine, prix fixe or a la carte available, and special dietary requests accommodated. $$$$

**Krause's Homemade Candy.** 41 S. Partition St.; (845) 246-8377; www.krauses chocolates.com. Three generations of confectioners have created more than fifty flavors of freshly made hand-dipped chocolates,

## New York **Trivia**

The population of New York is over nineteen million, which ranks third after California and Texas.

caramels, butter crunch, peanut brittle, and fudge. $

**Miss Lucy's Kitchen.** 90 Partition St.; (845) 246-9240; www.misslucyskitchen.com. Seasonal market menu that changes daily, serving all-natural meats, poultry, wild-caught fish, locally grown produce, homemade desserts and ice cream, plus a $5 kids' menu. $$$$

**New World Home Cooking.**1411 NY 212; (845) 246-0900; www.ricorlando.com. Global soul food cuisine using local and organic bounty of the county, from barbecue to tofu, including Vietnamese salads, po'boy catfish sandwiches, sides of brown rice and black beans, and cheddar quesadillas on the kids' menu. $$$

## Where to Stay

**Saugerties Lighthouse Bed and Breakfast.** 168 Lighthouse Dr., at Coast Guard Station, off Main Street; (845) 247-0656; www .saugertieslighthouse.com. Two rooms with terrific views for a night to remember, plus Wi-Fi, DVD player, kitchen, outdoor grill, and breakfast provided. $$$$

**The Woodbine Inn & Arts Center.** 144 Malden Ave., Palenville; (845) 679-5549; www .thewoodbine.com. Rent the whole inn for up to twelve people, with four guest rooms, a ballroom, a bar with 65-inch cable TV and games, a library, a gourmet kitchen, a patio with barbecue, Internet access, and a "you cook or they cook your meals" option. Individual rooms can be booked as well, and include a family-style breakfast. Lessons, seminars, and workshops in yoga, dance, fitness, film, and fine arts are offered, and cooking classes in Indian, Italian, and Hudson Valley cuisine are taught at the Arts Center. $$–$$$$

# High Falls and Hurley

South on US 9W to US 209W to Hurley, then US 209 and NY 213 to High Falls.

Hurley was first settled in 1661, but incensed Esopus burned it to the ground two years later. In 1669 the Dutch rebuilt their houses, this time out of stones.

**Hurley Museum Heritage Society** (ages 6 and up)
52 Main St., Hurley; (845) 338-1661; www.hurleyheritagesociety.org. Museum open May through Oct, Sat 10 a.m. to 4 p.m., Sun 1 to 4 p.m.; Thanksgiving weekend open Fri, Sat, and Sun 10 a.m. to 4 p.m. $$.

# Fairs and Festivals in the Catskills

**Hurley Heritage Corn Festival.** Hurley Dutch Reformed Church; (845) 338-1661; www.hurleyheritagesociety.org.

**Hudson Valley Garlic Festival.** Cantine Field, Saugerties; (845) 246-3090; www.hvgf.org.

**Ulster County Fair.** Libertyville Road, New Paltz; (845) 255-1380; www.ulster countyfair.com.

**Greene County Youth Fair.** Angelo Canna Town Park, Cairo; (518) 239-6159.

**Delaware County Fair.** NY 206, Walton; (800) 585-3737; www.delawarecounty fair.org.

**Railway Festival.** 7 Railroad Ave., Roscoe; (607) 498-4346 or (607) 498-5289; www.nyow.org.

**Little World's Fair.** Town Fairgrounds, Grahamsville; (845) 985-7367; www .grahamsvillefair.com.

**Riverfest.** Main Street, Narrowsburg; (845) 252-7576; www.artsalliancesite .org.

**Lumberjack Festival.** Borden Street, Festival Field, Deposit; (607) 746-2281; www.depositchamber.com.

**Catskill Center Festival.** D&U Railroad Grounds, Arkville; (845) 586-2611; www.catskillcenter.org.

**Belleayre Mountain Fall Festival and Craft Fair.** 181 Galli Curci Rd., NY 28, Highmount; (845) 254-5600.

**German Alps Festival.** NY 23A, Hunter; (518) 263-4223; www.huntermtn.com.

**International Celtic Festival. Hunter Mountain;** (518) 263-4223; www.hunter mtn.com.

**Mountaintop Pumpkin Festival and Suzmmer Festival.** Bear Creek Recreational Park; NY 23A and NY 214, Hunter; (518) 263-3839.

**Catskill Mountain Ginseng/Medicinal Herb Festival.** Catskill Point, Catskill; (518) 622-9820 or (518) 943-0989.

**Grey Fox Bluegrass Festival.** 1 Poultney Rd., Oak Hill; (315) 724-4473; www .greyfoxbluegrass.com.

Historical artifacts and memorabilia are displayed at this small museum, and **free** maps are available to guide visitors through several dozen stone colonial houses in the area.

### The New York Conservancy For The Arts  (ages 4 and up)

**120 Schildknecht Rd., Hurley; (845) 339-4340; www.nyca.org. Open year-round with breaks for holidays and school vacations. $$$$.**

Catch a rising star at this family-friendly performing arts center, offering comedies, dramas, musicals and concerts for all ages, as well as formal classes in acting, dance, and music for kids seven and up. The Summer Performing Arts Camp is geared for folks ages seven to twenty-four, but there's a special Fairy Princess or Brave Knight program for kids four to six, complete with take-home tiara, tutu, and wand, or play armor.

### D&H Canal Museum  (all ages)

**23 Mohonk Road, High Falls; (845) 687-9311; www.canalmuseum.org. Open May through Oct, Sat and Sun 11 a.m. to 5 p.m. $.**

With dioramas, artifacts, and photographs, this museum highlights the history of the 108-mile Delaware and Hudson Canal, the country's first million-dollar private enterprise. Take the self-guided Five Locks Walk past one of the four aqueducts built by Brooklyn Bridge builder John Roebling, several original canal locks, and the Central Hudson Canal Park for views of the town waterfalls.

### Canal Forge  (all ages)

**US 6 and Towpath Road, High Falls; (845) 687-7130; www.iloveny.com. Open year-round daily 9 a.m. to 5 p.m.**

May the forge be with you at this working blacksmith shop overlooking the Rondout Creek next to the D&H Canal.

## Where to Eat

**Depuy Canal House Restaurant.** NY 213, High Falls; (845) 687-7700; www.depuycanalhouse.net. There are actually three restaurants housed in this historic landmark tavern. The Canal House specializes in eclectic American cuisine, the Chefs On Fire Bistro makes great wood-fired pizzas and paninis, and Amici serves sushi and sashimi, with special rolls for children. $$–$$$$

## Where to Stay

**The Inn at Stone Ridge.** 3805 US 209, Stone Ridge; (845) 687-0736; www.innatstoneridge.com. Set on 150 acres of gardens, orchards, and forest, this mid-eighteenth-century Dutch Colonial mansion has several rooms and suites in the Main House, a two-bedroom apartment in the Carriage House, and a tavern and gourmet restaurant on-site. $$$$

**Pinegrove Resort Ranch.** 30 Cherrytown Rd., Kerhonkson; (845) 626-7345 or (800) 346-4626; www.pinegroveranch.com. Reservations required. Open year-round. For city slickers seeking the "best of the West in the East," this is a terrific all-inclusive, award-winning dude-ranch resort. With 126 rooms, fitness center and spa, cable TV, trail rides, cattle drives, nature hikes, hayrides, pro golf and mini-golf, tennis, swimming, archery, laser tag, bingo, a video arcade, cookouts, and more, your family will not be bored. For the youngest rustlers, starting at six months, there's a Day Camp of supervised games and arts and crafts; for slightly older dudes, the Junior Wrangler program offers instruction in basic horsemanship and trail riding; and kids twelve to sixteen can be a stable hand for a day in the new Barn Brats program. Nightly entertainment includes a kids' party complete with DJ, marshmallow roasts, and sing-alongs. The restaurant serves three all-you-can-eat hot meals a day and features a special kids' menu, or you can grab a pizza or burger at the Chuckwagon Snack Bar or the Food Court. $$$$

# New Paltz

Head east on NY 213 to NY 32 south.

Nestled between the spectacular Shawangunks and the Hudson River, New Paltz was settled in the seventeenth century by French Huguenot Protestants seeking religious freedom. Several of their 300-year-old stone houses are still there to explore on Huguenot Street, the "oldest street in America."

**Huguenot Historical Society**  (all ages)

18 Broadhead Ave.; (845) 255-1660; www.huguenotstreet.org. Deluxe and standard tours are given May 1 through Oct 31, 11 a.m. to 4 p.m. every day except Wed, and on weekends in Dec and Nov. Adults, seniors, and students $$, ages 6 to 17 $, children under 6 free.

## Rails to Trails in **Ulster County**

**Catskill Scenic Trail.** P.O. Box 310, Railroad Avenue, Stamford 12167; (607) 652-2821 or (800) 225-4132; www.catskillscenictrail.org.

**Hudson Valley Rail Trail.** 101 New Paltz Rd., Highland; (845) 483-0428, (845) 691-8666, or (800) DIAL–UCO; www.hudsonvalleyrailtrail.com.

**Wallkill Valley Rail Trail.** P.O. Box 1048, New Paltz 12561; www.gorailtrail.org.

## Horsing around **Ulster County**

**Frost Valley Equestrian Center.** 2000 Frost Valley Rd., Claryville; (845) 989-2291; www.frostvalley.org.

**Nevele Saddle Club.** Nevele Road, Ellenville; (845) 647-7556; www.nevele.com.

**Pinegrove Dude Ranch.** 30 Cherrytown Rd., Kerhonkson; (800) 346-4626 or (845) 626-7345; www.pinegroveranch.com.

**Mohonk Stables.** Mohonk Mountain House, 1000 Mountain Rest Rd., New Paltz; (845) 255-1000; www.mohonk.com.

**Payne Farm Too.** 125 Dubois Rd., New Paltz; (845) 255-0177; www.paynefarm too.com.

**Rocking Horse Ranch.** 600 US 44/NY 55, Highland; (800) 647-2624 or (845) 691-2927; www.rockinghorseranch.com.

**Coyote Ridge Stables.** 583 Lattintown Rd., Marlboro; (845) 236-1136; www.coyoteridgestablesny.com.

Huguenot Street, a National Historic Landmark, is the site of a collection of colonial and early national period stone houses. Three of the houses are furnished as they would have appeared in the eighteenth century. Special programs for children include Colonial Overnights, in which kids cook a colonial-era dinner over an open fire, play colonial games, make classic crafts, tour the stone houses (some are said to be haunted!) at night, then camp out on straw mattresses on the floor of Fort DuBois. Weeklong archaeology camps as well as drop-in activities are offered, from seasonal Easter Egg and Halloween Hunts to the arrival of Santa Claus at the Dutch winter holiday of Sinterklaas.

## Mohonk Preserve (all ages)

3197 US 44/NY 55, Gardiner; (845) 255-0919; www.mohonkpreserve.org. **Visitor center open daily year-round 9 a.m. to 5 p.m.; closed Thanksgiving, Christmas Eve after noon, Christmas Day, and New Year's Day.** Free. **Preserve open 365 days a year, sunrise to sunset. Day passes (purchased at visitor center or from a ranger on the trails) adult $, children 12 and under** free.

This 6,500-acre preserve, home to more than 1,400 species, provides 65 miles of trails for hiking, running, mountain biking, horseback riding, cross-country skiing, and snowshoeing. It's also a "living laboratory" in the studies of climate change, wildlife management, and water quality at the on-site Daniel Smiley Research Center. The award-winning "green design" visitor center has exhibits on local wildlife and geology, a 3-D model of the

Shawangunk Ridge, an interactive Weather Learning Station, a Kid's Discovery Corner, and a Nature Store. Outside, there are three short, child-friendly self-guiding trails to give you a unique perspective of this area. Programs for families are offered year-round, from learning about the Lenape to owl prowls. For maps, directions, and suggestions about other trails to explore, ask at the visitor center.

### Minnewaska State Park Preserve  (all ages)

5281 US 44/NY 55, Kerhonkson; (845) 256-0579; www.nysparks.com. **Open daily year-round, dawn to dusk. Be aware that deer hunting is allowed in some sections in season. Free.**

Once the site of two grand Catskill hotels, the preserve's 11,630 acres, cradled by the Shawangunks, include two crystal-clear lakes framed by white conglomerate cliffs and many miles of wide carriage paths, perfect for hiking and biking, that lead to numerous scenic overlooks. Swimming is permitted near the sandy beach at Lake Minnewaska, but if you're willing and able to hike a few miles farther into the woods, you'll find Lake Awosting a bit more primeval and private.

### Sam's Point Dwarf Pine Ridge Preserve  (all ages)

Sam's Point Road, off NY 52, Cragsmoor; (845) 647-7989. **Preserve open daily in summer 8 a.m. to 8 p.m., in winter 8 a.m. to 5 p.m. Conservation Center open Fri, Sat, and Sun 9 a.m. to 5 p.m. $ parking.**

This spectacular 5,400-acre National Natural Landmark, home to almost forty rare plant and animal species, has been designated one of Earth's "Last Great Places" by the Nature Conservancy. Seven trails wind through the rugged rock formations and scenic canyons of the Shawangunks, and on a clear day you can see breathtaking views of the Hudson Valley and Catskills. The Sam's Point Conservation Center offers information about the area, from the history of the huckleberry pickers to suggestions for trail treks.

## Where to Eat

**Main Course.** 232 Main St.; (845) 255-2600; www.maincourserestaurant.com. International creative cuisine, with homemade soups, pastas, grilled seafood, specialty salads, organic burgers, and fabulous desserts.

**Main Street Bistro.** 59 Main St., New Paltz; (845) 255-7766; www.mainstreetbistro.com. Eclectic American and Vegetarian cuisine, breakfast served all day, with freshly baked breads, muffins, brownies, pies, and vegan desserts. $

**Pasquale's Pizza & Restaurant.** 248 Main St.; (845) 255-0400. Best pizza in New Paltz, plus pasta with homemade sauce, salads, Stromboli, calzones, and chicken parmesan, $–$$

## Where to Stay

**Econo Lodge.** 530 Main St.; (845) 255-6200 or (800) 424-4777; www.econolodge.com. Thirty-two rooms, outdoor pool and playground area, free continental breakfast. $$

**Minnewaska Lodge.** 3116 US 44/NY 55, Gardiner; (845) 255-1110; www.minewaska lodge.com. Set on seventeen acres at the base of the Shawangunk Mountains, this lovely lodge offers twenty-six rooms and suites, with either a forest or cliff view, home-made cookies in the afternoon, cable TV, Internet, a fitness center, and complimentary breakfast. $$–$$$

**Mohonk Mountain House.** 1000 Mountain Rest Rd.; (845) 255-1000 or (800) 772-6646; www.mohonk.com. Open daily year-round. A Victorian castle perched on the edge of a glacial lake, Mohonk Mountain House is magical. Built by the Smiley family in 1870, when mountain resorts were all the rage, Mohonk Mountain House and the nearby Mohonk Preserve encompass more than 8,000 acres of forest and rock, laced with 85 miles of trails and dotted with more than a hundred picturesque gazebos. There are 265 rooms in the castle, and prices include three meals, afternoon tea, and cookies daily, with outdoor barbeques and lobster bakes in summer. Cottages are also available, about 2 miles from the castle, but meals are not included. All overnight guests can enjoy more than forty programs throughout the year, many specifically designed for families. Mohonk's stables offer horseback and carriage rides. There's a full-service spa on-site with a fitness center and heated indoor pool. The resort also offers lots of lake activities, from fishing and swimming to kayaking; lawn games, such as croquet and mini-golf; tennis courts; rock climbing; and a 110-year-old golf course. In winter, cross-country skiing, ice-skating, and snow tubing are available. There's a complimentary Kid's Club for overnight guests' children ages two to seventeen, with unique activities and adventures. Call for a schedule and ask about special times when children stay half-price and sometimes free. $$$$ (meals included); day passes ($$); children under 4 always stay free.

**Nevele Grand.** 1 Nevele Rd., off US 209, Ellenville; (845) 647-6000 or (800) 647-6000; www.nevele.com. This 1,000-acre mega-resort has 432 rooms, indoor and outdoor pools, thirteen tennis courts, an ice rink, pro golf and mini-golf courses, horseback and pony riding, boating, live entertainment, skiing and skating in winter, and a day camp for kids. Meals are included, and special family packages are available. $$$$

# Monticello

Take NY 299 west to NY 55 west, then US 209 into Ellenville and NY 52 west to NY 42 south.

Nicknamed the buckle of the "Borscht Belt," Monticello and the surrounding towns of Liberty, Fallsburg, and Kiamesha Lake are home to several family-owned megaresorts, where legendary comedians Jerry Lewis, Joan Rivers, Milton Berle, Mel Brooks, Jerry Seinfeld, and others springboarded to stardom.

# Also in **the Area**

**Skater's World Roller Rink.** 1234 Old Route 17, Ferndale; (845) 292-3288; www.skatersworldrollerrink.com.

**Accord Speedway.** 299 Whitfield Rd., Accord; (845) 626-3478; www.accord speedway.com.

### Holiday Mountain Ski and Fun Park  (all ages)

99 Holiday Mountain Rd.; (845) 796-3161; www.holidaymtn.com. Fun Park open Memorial Day through Labor Day; ski resort open Oct through Mar. Hours vary and subject to change. $$$$.

This family-oriented ski spot, with nine trails, four lifts, and a vertical drop of 400 feet, offers an expanded children's program, including child care for ages four to six; a ski, skate, and snowboard school for all levels; and sleigh rides in winter. In summer, the park offers an array of activities, from bumper boats and batting cages to mini-golf and a mean mechanical bull. Drive a go-kart, kiddie-kart, bumper car or the Choo Choo Charlie train, then climb up a rock wall or slip down the 30-foot Potato Sack Slide. Tickets are $2 and can be purchased in booklets of forty or sixty; attractions vary in price.

### The Petting Zoo at Breezeway Farms  (all ages)

161 Anawana Lake Rd.; (845) 794-4543; www.breezewayfarmpettingzoo.com. Open seasonally 10 a.m. to 6 p.m. $–$$.

A plethora of petting pals, from donkeys and ducks to lambs and llamas, plus pony rides.

## Where to Eat

**Albella Pizza & Restaurant.** 30 Jefferson St.; (845) 794-8866. Friendly family-run restaurant, with delicious Italian specialties and great pizza. $–$$

**Mr. Willy's.** 3695 NY 42; (845) 794-0888; www.mrwillys.com. A family favorite for over forty years, serving steak, seafood, ribs, chicken, pasta, summer deck specials of shrimp on the barbie and buckets of steamed clams, plus mid-week specials when children under eleven eat free from the kids' menu. $$$

## Where to Stay

**All Seasons Campsite on Autumn Lake.** Fraser Road, off NY 42, Kiamesha; (845) 794-0133 or (845) 794-1698. On 375 acres with campsites, lake swimming, fishing and boating, pool table, video games, and a small playground. $

**Kutsher's Country Club.** Kutsher Road, off NY 42; (845) 794-6000 or (800) 431-1273; www.kutshers.com. Wonderful, friendly, 228-room mega-resort with nonstop activities, including pro golf and mini-golf, a driving range, boating, swimming (indoor and outdoor pools), indoor ice-skating, tennis, volleyball, basketball, and bocce courts, a game room, fitness center and spa, and nightly entertainment. Horse-drawn sleigh rides and snow-tubing are offered in winter, and nursery and toddler care, a day camp, and a teen program are offered year-round. Meal plan is optional. $$$$

# Livingston Manor

Take NY 17 north.

A river runs through it, and between here and Roscoe, the American art of fly-fishing was born. This is trout territory, big time, and somewhere in the Willowemoc or the nearby Beaverkill, there's a fish with your name on it.

### Catskill Fly-Fishing Center and Museum (ages 8 and up)

1031 Old Route 17; (845) 439-4810 or (845) 439-3387; www.cffcm.net. Open Apr through Oct, daily 10 a.m. to 4 p.m.; Nov through Mar, Sat 10 a.m. to 4 p.m., Tues through Fri 10 a.m. to 1 p.m., except holidays. $.

Learn about the lore, legends, and lures of the Catskill creeks at this charming museum honoring famous fisher folk and their fly-tying folk art. Special fly-fishing programs for kids 8 and older are offered in July and Aug, and nature trails meander over thirty-five lush acres along a catch-and-release section of the Willowemoc.

## Catskill Park and Forest Preserve

In 1885, prompted by the decimation of the forests for timber, and the depletion of topsoil from subsequent erosion, the preserve was created by carving out about 34,000 acres for "forever wild" protection. Today it has grown to encompass almost 300,000 acres, a mix of public and private land, and includes ninety-eight mountains over 3,000 feet, 300 miles of trails traversing a variety of habitats, and more than forty campgrounds. Camping with children is not without challenges, but the benefits of watching your child chase fireflies at dusk or toasting marshmallows with them over a campfire can be oh so worth it. Give it a try, all you too-timid types—the woods are wonderful, and the Catskills are magical. For more information contact the New York State Department of Environmental Conservation at (518) 473-9518; www.dec.ny.gov; or the New York State Office of Parks, Recreation and Historic Preservation at (518) 474-0456; www.nysparks.state.ny.us/recreation.

### Catskill Fish Hatchery (all ages)

Hatchery Road, DeBruce; (845) 439-4328. Open year-round, Mon through Fri 8:30 a.m. to 4 p.m., Sat and Sun 8:30 a.m. to noon. **Free.**

More than a million rainbow, brown, brook, and lake trout, salmon, walleye, and muskellunge are raised in a dozen state hatcheries across New York every year, to be released in 1,200 rivers and lakes throughout the state. This hatchery specializes in brown trout, with a brood stock capable of producing two million eggs.

### Roscoe O&W Railway Museum (ages 3 and up)

7 Railroad Ave., Roscoe; (607) 498-5500 or (607) 498-5289; www.owrhs.org. Open Memorial Day through Columbus Day, Sat and Sun 11 a.m. to 3 p.m. **Free.**

Artifacts and memorabilia from the Ontario and Western Railway are displayed here, from a Beaverkill Trout car to a red caboose.

### Apple Pond Farm and Renewable Energy Education Center (all ages)

80 Hahn Rd., Callicoon Center; (845) 482-4764; www.applepondfarm.com. Open year-round 10 a.m. to 5 p.m. Reservations required for some programs. $$.

Using the latest renewable energy technology, from photovoltaic to geothermal, this fascinating farm of the future teaches traditional pioneer-style organic agronomy. Special farm tours for families give kids the chance to collect eggs, milk goats, plant or pick some veggies, or help drive the horses. Hayrides and wagon and carriage rides are offered in summer, sleigh rides in winter, and a variety of victuals are for sale at the farm's roadside stand.

## Where to Eat

**The New Robin Hood Diner.** Old Route 17, exit 96; (845) 439-4404; www.robinhood diner.com. European and American home-style specialties, from Hungarian goulash and sauerbraten to spaghetti and meatballs. $

**Peez Leweez.** 2 Pearl St.; (845) 439-3300; www.peezleweez.co. Charming cafe serving homemade soups, sandwiches, and desserts, with an outdoor seating area, a view of the Little Beaverkill, and live music events.

# Horsing Around **Sullivan County**

**Maple Grove Horse Farm.** 222 Muthig Rd., Hurleyville; (845) 866-3990; www .maplegrovehorsefarm.com.

**Bridle Hill Farm.** 190 Hemmer Rd., Jeffersonville; (845) 482-3993.

**Little Pond Farms at Villa Roma Resort.** 356 Villa Roma Rd., Callicoon; (845) 887-4880 or (845) 794-8021.

# The Bridges of **Sullivan County**

Sullivan County has several scenic covered bridges, all reachable on an afternoon drive. For more information go online to www.coveredbridgesite.com/ny or www.dalejtravis.com.

**Van Tran Flat Covered Bridge.** Covered Bridge Road, Livingston Manor.

**Beaverkill Covered Bridge.** Beaverkill Camp Road, Beaverkill.

**Bendo Covered Bridge.** Conklin Hill Road, DeBruce.

**Halls Mills Covered Bridge.** Hunter Road, Curry. Chestnut Creek Covered Bridge. NY 55, Grahamsville.

## Where to Stay

**Beaverkill Valley Inn.** 7 Barnhart Rd., Lew Beach; (845) 439-4844; www.beaverkill valleyinn.com. Formerly a nineteenth-century fishing lodge, today this beautiful B&B has twenty rooms, a wraparound porch overlooking the Beaverkill, an indoor pool, a gym, tennis courts, billiards, Ping-Pong, hiking trails, a winter ice rink, a children's play room, fireside afternoon tea, and an optional meal plan. $$$

**Frost Valley YMCA.** 2000 Frost Valley Rd., Claryville; (845) 985-2291; www.frostvalley .org. More than 5,000 acres to explore, with cross-country skiing, snowshoeing, tubing, tobogganing, ice fishing, and maple sugaring in winter; canoeing, hiking, and horseback riding in summer; and seasonal nature activities and arts and crafts for families on weekends throughout the year. A variety of cabins, lodges, and motel rooms, plus platform tents, are available, with meals included. Ask about family rates. $$–$$$

**Magical Land of Oz.** 753 Shandelee Rd.; (845) 439-3446; www.ozbandb.net. Perched on a mountaintop, this century-old farmhouse B&B on ten acres is enchanting. With Poppy Fields to play in and Emerald Gardens to explore, you won't believe you're in Kansas anymore. $

# Narrowsburg

Head south on scenic NY 97.

Located at a strategic bend in the Delaware, the town of Narrowsburg is another favorite place to be sent down the river with a paddle.

## Fort Delaware Museum of Colonial History (all ages)

6615 NY 97; (845) 252-6660 or (845) 807-0261; www.co.sullivan.ny.us. Open weekends from Memorial Day through June; open Fri through Mon, from the last Fri of June through Labor

Day; Fri, Sat, and Mon 10 a.m. to 5 p.m., Sun noon to 5 p.m. Adults $, children under 5 **free.**

This authentic, rustic re-creation gives kids the chance to experience eighteenth-century family life pioneer style, as costumed guides demonstrate the skills and crafts necessary for survival in the New York frontier.

## Where to Eat

**Main Street Café.** 40 Main St.; (845) 252-7222. Good American food. $–$$

**The Whistle Stop Cafe.** 117 Kirk Rd.; (845) 252-3355; www.whistlestopcafe.net. Family-friendly delicious diner cuisine, serving breakfast, lunch, and dinner, with a $4 kiddie "caboose" menu. $

## Where to Stay

**Lander's Campground.** 5666 NY 97, Narrowsburg; (800) 252-3925; www.landersrivertrips.com. Riverfront, lean-to, and open-field sites, with hot showers, camp store, and snack bar. Campground is within walking distance to Fort Delaware and local shopping. $

**Lander's Ten Mile River Lodge.** NY 97; (800) 252-3925; www.landersrivertrips.com. Motel and efficiencies, cable TV, restaurant, swimming pool, and package deals. $$$

# Eagle **Eyeing**

Bald eagles like to vacation in the Catskills, too. From December through March, southern Sullivan County attracts the largest population of migrating eagles in the Northeast. The Eagle Institute sponsors seasonal festivals featuring eagle dances, art projects, workshops, and watches. Child-size binoculars and telescopes are provided at these recommended spotting sites:

**Mongaup Falls Reservoir,** Observation Hut, Forestburgh.

**Rio Reservoir,** Forestburgh.

**Basha Kill Wildlife Management Area,** Wurtsboro.

**Rondout Reservoir,** Grahamsville.

**Delaware River,** Hawks Nest to Narrowsburg, NY 97.

For more information contact the institute at P.O. Box 182, Barryville 12719; (845) 557-6162 or (570) 685-5960; www.eagleinstitute.org; the DEC Endangered Species Unit at (518) 439-7365; or the Upper Delaware Scenic and Recreational River National Park Service at (570) 729-8251.

## Delaware River **Canoe Trips and Rentals**

**Lander's River Trips.** 5666 NY 97, Narrowsburg; (800) 252-3925; www.landers rivertrips.com.

**Kittatinny Adventure Center and Paintball.** 3854 NY 97, Barryville; other location, 2389 NY 97, Pond Eddy; (800) FLOAT–KC or (800) 356-2852; www .kittatinny.com.

**Indian Head Canoes and Campground.** 3883 NY 97, Cedar Rapids Inn, Barryville; (845) 557-8777 or (800) 874-2628; www.indianheadcanoes.com.

**Wild and Scenic River Tours and Rentals.** 166 NY 97, Barryville; (845) 557-8783 or (800) 836-0366; www.landersrivertrips.com.

**Cedar Rapids Kayak and Canoe Outfitters.** Barryville; (845) 557-6158 or (877) 557-6158; www.cedarrapidsrafting.com.

**Jerry's Three River Campground.** 2333 NY 97, Pond Eddy; (845) 557-6078; www.jerrys3rivercampground.com.

**Silver Canoe Rentals.** 37 S. Maple Ave., Port Jervis; (845) 856-7055 or (800) 724-8342; www.silvercanoe.com.

**Whitewater Willie's.** 37 S. Maple Ave., Port Jervis; (845) 856-7055 or (800) 724-8342; www.whitewaterwillies.com.

# Barryville

Continue south on NY 97.

The gateway to a particularly pretty part of the Delaware River, Barryville has numerous outfitters supplying a variety of vessels to float your family.

## Eldred Preserve (all ages)

1040 NY 55, Eldred; (845) 557-8316 or (800) 557-3474; www.eldredpreserve.com. Open daily year-round 8 a.m. to 4 p.m. $.

If you're hankering to hook a fish or the big one got away, head for the trout ponds at this private 3,000-acre resort. You're almost guaranteed to catch something, and your charge is calculated by the weight of the catch. All trout caught must be kept, and all bass caught must be released. Kids are encouraged to join the **free** "Lord of the Trout" Fan Club and be a "Troutling," thereby giving them **free** admission to the trout ponds for a year, among other "perchs." There is a wonderful restaurant on-site serving trout twelve

## Suggested **Reading**

*Rip Van Winkle*, by Washington Irving

*The Red Badge of Courage*, by Stephen Crane

*The Matchlock Gun*, by Walter D. Edmonds

*The Deerslayer*, by James Fenimore Cooper

*My Side of the Mountain*, by Jean Craighead George

*John Burroughs: The Sage of Slabsides*, by Ginger Wadsworth

*Catskill Eagle*, by Thomas Locker

*Treasure of Watchdog Mountain*, by Alf Evers

*Buzzy and the River Rats: Tales of a Catskill Mountain Boyhood*, by John Clarke Hoffman

terrific ways, with outdoor deck dining in summer. If you'd like to spend the night, there are twenty-five log cabin–style motel rooms available, all with cable TV. A midweek special, the "Bass-N-Crash" package, is an economical boat/room combo, and fishing-guide services may be reserved.

### Minisink Battleground Park  (all ages)

**6615 NY 97, Minisink Ford; (845) 794-3000; www.co.sullivan.ny.us. Open daily mid-May to mid-Oct 8 a.m. to dusk. Free.**

The Battle of Minisink was one of the bloodiest battles of the Revolutionary War and the only one fought in this area. Colonial Americans were defeated by Iroquois working for the British, and the area was so remote it was nearly fifty years before the bodies were discovered and buried. Pick up a map at the interpretive center and explore the Battleground, Woodland, or Old Quarry Trails, which meander through this historic fifty-seven-acre wooded wetland park.

## Where to Stay

**All Breeze Guest House.** 227 Haring Rd.; (845) 557-6485; www.bedandbreakfast.com. This friendly bed-and-breakfast offers three rooms, plus a swing set, a rowboat for the pond, croquet, horseshoes, VCR, full breakfast, and low rates for children and groups. $

**The Spring House Commons.** 54 River Rd., Barryville; (845) 557-8189; www.thespringhouse.com. Formerly a Victorian farmhouse, classic B&B has three guest rooms and three apartments, Internet, a country breakfast basket, and a restaurant, the Chocolate Mousse Cafe, famous for its, well, chocolate mousse. $$$–$$$$

# Other Things to See and Do
## in the Catskills

**Forestburgh Playhouse.** 39 Forestburgh Rd., Forestburgh; (845) 794-1194; www.fbplayhouse.com.

**Esopus Meadows Environmental Center.** 275 River Rd., Ulster Park; (845) 331-5771, (845) 454-7673, or (845) 473-4440; www.clearwater.org.

**Fins and Grins Fishing & Scenic Charters.** 5571 Cauterskill Rd., Catskill; (518) 943-3407.

**Cohatate Preserve.** NY 385, Athens; (518) 622-3620.

**Four Mile Point Preserve.** NY 385, Coxsackie; 8 miles north of the Rip Van Winkle Bridge.

**Little Pond State Park.** Barkaboom Road, Andes; (845) 439-5480.

**East Sidney Lake Recreation Area.** 4659 NY 357, Franklin; (607) 829-3528.

**Cortina Mountain Resort.** 227 Clum Hill Rd., Haines Falls; (518) 589-6378; www.cortinamountain.com.

**Bobcat Ski Center.** Gladstone Hollow Road, Andes; (845) 676-3143.

## For More Information

**General Information.** www.iloveny.com and (800) NYS–CATS.

**Delaware County Chamber of Commerce.** (607) 746-2281 or (800) 642-4443; www.delawarecounty.org.

**Greene County Tourism.** (518) 943-3223 or (800) 355–CATS; www.greenetourism.com.

**Sullivan County Tourism.** (845) 794-3000 or (800) 882–CATS; www.scva.net.

**Ulster County.** (845) 340-3566 or (800) 342-5826; www.ulstertourism.info.

# The
# Mohawk Valley
## Region

H ome to the Iroquois for thousands of years, the Mohawk Valley was an important route between the Great Lakes and the Atlantic Ocean and the easiest
path through the Appalachians. The Dutch and the English were drawn here by
the lucrative fur trade at the beginning of the seventeenth century, many of the battles
that won America's independence were fought here, and the Erie Canal transformed the
Mohawk into an industrial and transportation mecca. The mystery, romance, and passion
of James Fenimore Cooper's stories still reside in the breathtaking scenery and enchanting villages of this ancient river plateau. Whether your family seeks carousels or crystal
caverns, history of times gone by or history in the making, baseball diamonds or Herkimer
diamonds, there is something here to please children of all ages.

## DRIVING TIPS
After the Revolutionary War, settlers headed across the Mohawk Valley toward the Great
Lakes area by way of the Great Western Turnpike, now known as US 20. Running parallel
to that and the Mohawk River is I-90, the New York State Thruway. Cutting diagonally from
Albany to Binghamton is I-88, while I-81 and NY 12 run north and south across the valley.

## Albany

Accessible via I-87, I-787, and I-90.

Henry Hudson sailed the *Half Moon* as far as Albany in search of the Northwest Passage
and claimed this area for the Dutch. Known as Fort Orange when it was a seventeenth-
century Dutch trading post, Albany is New York's capital and its oldest city. While the
theme here is business, politics are the lifeblood of the city, and the roots are still very
Dutch. Visit in springtime, when the tulips are in bloom and the town transforms itself into
a Dutch village at Pinksterfest.

THE MOHAWK VALLEY REGION

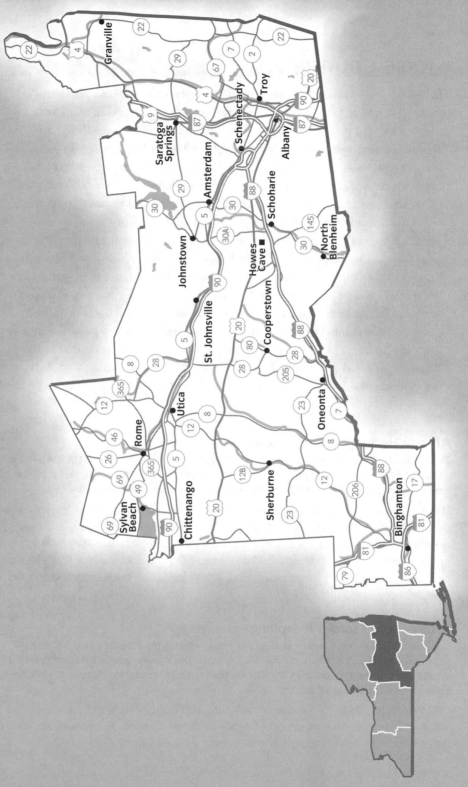

# Apple **Country**

In 1647, when New York governor Peter Stuyvesant planted an apple tree from Holland on the corner of 13th Street and Third Avenue in Manhattan, he was a prescient pomologist. More than a century later another New Yorker, John Chapman, better known as "Johnny Appleseed," planted apple trees on his farm in Olean, and land companies began requiring settlers to plant orchards to support their land claims. By the 1850s, more than 500 varieties of apples had originated in New York. In 1866 Peter Stuyvesant's apple tree was knocked down by a cart, but by the turn of the century the state was producing over 50 million bushels per year, with more than 1,000 varieties available. In the 1930s, when jazz clubs opened in New York City, it became known as the "Big Apple," meaning there were lots of places to play music, or "lots of apples on the tree." Today, New York is the second largest apple producing state in the country, producing about 25 million bushels annually, grown on 694 family farms. The most popular apple varieties grown in New York are McIntosh, Empire, Red Delicious, Cortland, Golden Delicious, Red Rome, Idared, Crispin, Paula Red, Gala, Jonagold, and Jonamac. For more information check out www.nyapplecountry.com.

### Albany Heritage Area Visitors Center (all ages)

25 Quackenbush Sq., at intersection of Broadway and Clinton Avenues; (518) 434-0405 or (800) 258-3582; www.albany.org. Open year-round Mon through Fri 9 a.m. to 4 p.m., Sat 10 a.m. to 3 p.m., Sun 11 a.m. to 3 p.m. Albany Riverfront Park (518) 4342032. **Free.**

Make this your first stop upon arriving in Albany, for along with an orientation show, the center offers seasonal guided walking tours, **free** self-guided walking tour maps, and audiotape guides. Take a stroll down to the water via the Hudson River Way pedestrian bridge near the visitor center, to the Albany Riverfront Park at the Corning Preserve. Scenic walking and biking trails hug the Hudson, and **free** concerts are offered in summer at the 800-seat amphitheater.

### Albany Aqua Ducks & Trolleys (all ages)

Departs from the visitor center at 25 Quackenbush Sq.; (518) 462-DUCK (462-3825); www .albanyaquaducks.com. Open mid-Apr through Oct. Duck tours, adults $$$$, children 4 to 12 $$$, kids under 3 on parent's lap **free.** Trolley tours, adults $$, children $, children under 4 on parent's lap **free.**

See the Albany area by land and water with this amphibious vehicle that offers a guided ninety-minute tour of the region. Trolleys take tourists on a one-hour historical sightseeing trek about town, with hop-on, hop-off options at twenty stops.

### Henry Hudson Planetarium (all ages)

25 Quackenbush Sq., next to visitor center; (518) 434-0405 or (800) 258-3582; www.albany
.org. Open daily 10 a.m. to 4 p.m. $.

For a tour of the celestial sort, special children's star shows take place on Sat, and a historical puppet show about Henry Hudson is performed on occasional Weds throughout the year.

### Empire State Plaza (all ages)

Located between Madison Ave. and State St., and Swan and Eagle Streets. Plaza Visitor's
Center and Capitol Tours, Concourse Level, Room 106 (518) 474-2418; www.ogs.state.ny.
us. Capitol tours offered hourly weekdays 9 a.m. to 4 p.m., Sat and Sun 10 a.m. to noon
and 2 to 4 p.m. The Egg box office (518) 473-1845 or (518) 473-1061; www.theegg.org. New
York State Museum, 3140 Cultural Education Center; (518) 474-5877; www.nysm.nysed.gov.
Museum open daily year-round 9:30 a.m. to 5 p.m., closed major holidays. Corning Tower
observation deck (518) 474-2418; open Mon through Sat 10 a.m. to 4 p.m.; closed Sun and
holidays. **Free.**

A vast complex of ten buildings covering almost one hundred acres, this is the heart of
the city. Take a **free** tour of the **State Capitol,** designed by five different architects,
where you can view the senate chambers and the "Million Dollar Staircase, famous for its
300 carved faces of famous and not-so-famous people. At the opposite end of the plaza
is the **New York State Museum,** the largest and oldest state museum in the country.
Chock-full of interesting artifacts and specimens, it features exhibits highlighting New
York's culture, history, and environment. With more than four million archaeological artifacts, two million plants and animals, at least a million rocks and fossils, and an array of
art and furniture from all over the state, there's a lot to see. While at the museum, stop
by Discovery Place, a special area designed just for kids. A new addition is the recently
restored full-size, forty-animal carousel, making merry going around daily 10 a.m. to 4:30
p.m. Also nearby is the **Plaza Art Collection,** featuring work from "New York School"
artists. For a bird's-eye view of the area, take the elevator to the observation deck at the
nearby Corning Tower. And speaking of birds, you can't miss the giant **Egg** nesting on the
Plaza, a futuristic performing-arts arena that hosts many special events for families.

# Family **Fun Playspaces**

**Jeepers!** 161 Washington Ave. Extension No. 9, Albany; (518) 452-0103; www
.jeepersalbany.com.

**Hoffman's Playland.** 608 New Loudon Rd., Latham; (518) 785–3842; www
.hoffmansplayland.com.

**Sunset Lanes.** 1160 Central Ave.; (518) 438-6404; www.bowlsunset.com.

# Albany's **Parks and Playgrounds**

Albany isn't all architecture and government. The capital city has over three dozen playgrounds and parks to explore, too. Contact the Albany Department of Parks and Recreation at (518) 434-5699 or www.albanyny.org for more information.

**Bayhill Park.** Sheridan Avenue and Dove Street.

**Beverwyck Park.** 640 Washington Ave.

**Buckingham Lake Park.** Berkshire Boulevard and Colonial Avenue.

**Colby Park.** 19 Colby St.

**Hackett Park.** North Pearl Street and North Pearl Avenue.

**Lincoln Park (lower).** Eagle Street and Morton Avenue.

**Lincoln Park (upper).** Morton Avenue and Delaware Avenue.

**Livingston and Lake Playground.** Livingston Avenue and Lake Avenue.

**Madison Avenue Playground.** Madison Avenue and Ontario Street.

**Mater Christi Playground.** New Scotland Avenue.

**Mount Hope Playground.** Mount Hope Drive.

**Mullens Park.** 41 N. 1st St.

**Oak Street Playground.** Oak Street and Second Street.

**Philip Street Park.** 77 Phillip St.

**Ridgefield Park.** 316 Partridge St. at Ridgefield Street.

**Rosemont Playground.** 92 Rosemont St.

**Shaker Park.** Shaker Park Drive and Rosemary Drive.

**South Allen Street Playground.** South Allen Street.

**Swinburne Park.** Clinton Avenue and Manning Boulevard

**Washington Park.** State and Willet Streets.

**Westland Hill Park.** Central, Colvin, Lincoln, and Austin Avenues.

**Whitehall Park.** Colonie and Lark Streets.

**Woodlawn Park.** Woodlawn Avenue and Partridge Street.

# Nature Conservancy **Preserves and Sanctuaries**

For more than half a century, this conservation organization has protected ecologically fragile but important land and water areas, partnering with people and communities in a nonconfrontational, science-based approach. To date, they have protected more than a million acres of land, 5,000 miles of rivers worldwide, and planned over one hundred global marine projects. In the Albany area there are eleven of their protected places, each a unique and rare habitat. While there are no gifts shops, there are treasures on every trail, at some of the last great places on Earth. For more information contact the Eastern New York Conservation Office at (518) 690-7878 and www.nature.org.

**Lisha Kill Natural Sanctuary**

**Hannacroix Ravine Preserve**

**Whitbeck Memorial Grove**

**Limestone Rise Preserve**

**Moccasin Kill Sanctuary**

**Bear Swamp Preserve**

**Christman Sanctuary**

**Lake Julia Preserve**

**Kenrose Preserve**

**Stewart Preserve**

**Barberville Falls**

## Albany Pine Bush Preserve  (all ages)

195 New Karner Rd.; (518) 456-0655; www.albanypinebush.org. Center is open year-round Tues through Fri 9 a.m. to 4 p.m., Sat and Sun 10 a.m. to 4 p.m.; open most Monday holidays, closed Thanksgiving, Christmas, and New Year's Day. **Free.**

This globally unique inland pine barrens is one of only twenty in the world, and at 3,100 acres, one of the largest. Carved clean by a retreating glacier almost 20,000 years ago, this former sandy delta is home and habitat to twenty rare plants and animals and two rare natural communities, Visit the very green photovoltaic-powered Discovery Center for interactive exhibits that may include building a sand dune or touching a snake skin, and for special programs for families, including insect investigations, animal tracking, and a wild edibles walk. Outside are 20 miles of trails branching out across the bush, where you could be fortunate enough to spot the federally endangered Karner blue butterfly or a spadefoot toad. On the easternmost boundary of the preserve is the Pine Bush Field Station and recently restored Rensselaer Lake, Stop at the open-air Satellite Interpretive Center for natural history information, go fishing on the two new docks, walk the wetlands atop a viewing platform, or take a hike along the nature trail at the lake.

### Dutch Apple Cruises  (all ages)

137 Broadway; (518) 463-0220; www.dutchapplecruises.com. Sailing daily 10 a.m. to 10 p.m. Apr through Oct. Adults $$$, children $$.

Choose a cruise on the Hudson. Brunch, lunch, locks, and sunset and moonlight sightseeing itineraries offered.

### John Boyd Thatcher State Park  (all ages)

NY 157 (off NY 85), Voorheesville; (518) 872-1237; www.nysparks.state.ny.us. Open daily year-round 8 a.m. to dusk. Summer parking fee $$. Call ahead to confirm changes to hours, activities available, and possible closures due to pending state budget cuts.

This 2,300-acre park features rich fossil-bearing limestone cliffs and panoramic views of the Mohawk-Hudson Valley. Explore the 0.5-mile Indian Ladder Trail, the Escarpment Trail, or the Nature Trail. Be sure to hold little folks by the hand on narrow footpaths around the ledges. There are playgrounds, ball fields, and picnic shelters, and in winter the trails are open for cross-country skiing.

### Thompson's Lake State Park  (all ages)

68 Thompson's Lake Rd., East Berne; (518) 872-1674; www.nysparks.state.ny.us. Open year-round dawn to dusk; beach open mid-May through Columbus Day.

Four miles from the Helderberg Escarpment is this popular camping and recreation park. Along with 140 campsites, there are swing sets, a sandy beach for swimming, fishing, volleyball courts, a playing field, nature trails, and rowboats to rent. By the lake is the Emma Treadwell Thatcher Nature Center, displaying geologic models, a honeybee hive, and lots of hands-on exhibits, including fossils and furs, and interpretive programs during summer. $.

### Schodack Island State Park  (all ages)

1 Schodack Way, Schodack Landing; (518) 732-0187; www.nysparks.state.ny.us. Open year-round, dawn to dusk. $. Call ahead to confirm changes to hours, activities available, and possible closures due to pending state budget cuts.

Seven miles of shoreline hem this 1,052-acre park, designated a State Estuary and a Bird Conservation Area. Bald eagles, blue herons, and cerulean warblers nest in the cottonwood trees, and 8 miles of multiuse trails wind through a variety of habitats.

### Hudson River Islands State Park  (all ages)

c/o Schodack State Park, 1 Schodack Way, Schodack Landing; (518) 732-0187; www.nys parks.com/parks. Open Memorial Day through Columbus Day, dawn to dusk. $. Call ahead to confirm changes to hours, activities available, and possible closures due to pending state budget cuts.

Although accessible only by boat, these islands in the stream are the habitat of many rare and endangered plants and animals. Most of the park facilities are on Gay's Point and Stockport Middle Ground islands, with nature trails, picnic areas, and good fishing spots.

# Albany Area Athletics

**Hockey: Albany River Rats.** 51 Pearl St.; (518) 487-2244; www.albanyriverrats.com.

**AF2 Football: Albany Firebirds.** 51 S. Pearl St.; (518) 487-2244; www.albanyfirebirds.com.

**Baseball: Tri-City Valley Cats.** 80 Vandenburgh Ave., Troy; (518) 629-2287; www.tcvalleycats.com.

## Five Rivers Environmental Education Center (all ages)

56 Game Farm Rd., Delmar; (518) 475-0291; www.dec.ny.gov. Located about 5 miles south of Albany off NY 443. Grounds open year-round sunrise to sunset; interpretive center open Mon through Sat 9 a.m. to 4:30 p.m., Sun 1 to 5 p.m. **Free.**

This 446-acre preserve has 12 miles of easy trails and roads that wander through wetlands, forests, and fields, and past sixteen ponds. Seasonal interpretive brochures are available at trailheads, family campouts and programs are held in summer, and workshops in wildflower sketching, butterfly counting, and animal tracking are offered in season.

## Hollyhock Hollow Sanctuary (all ages)

46 Rarick Rd., Selkirk, off New York State Thruway, exit 22; (518) 767-9051; www.townofbethlehem.com. Open daily dawn to dusk year-round. **Free.**

Six trails snake through 138 acres of meadows and woodlands, past a pond, and along Onesquethaw Creek. Wildflowers and wildlife thrive here, from flying squirrels to wood frogs, and more than sixty species of birds nest here. Special gardens are grown just for butterflies and hummingbirds, and the May migration of songbirds fills the forest with music.

## Where to Eat

**Carmine's Restaurant.** 818 Central Ave.; (518) 458-8688; www.carminesrestaurant.com. Great gourmet Italian cuisine, with a cable TV cooking show, *Carmine's Table,* hosted by owner and chef Carmine Spiro and taped in the restaurant. If you'd like to be part of the process of creating his show, contact the Web site for filming schedules, and make a reservation for lunch or dinner. $$$–$$$$

**Miss Albany Diner.** 893 Broadway; (518) 465-9148; www.missalbanydiner.com. A real classic, featured in the movie *Ironweed,* serving excellent diner favorites and an interesting brunch. $

**Tess' Lark Tavern.** 453 Madison Ave.; (518) 463-9779; www.albany.com. Irish pub serving seven chicken sandwiches, ten flavors of buffalo wings, a dozen kinds of burgers, paninis, pasta, salads, fish-and-chips, and live music on weekends. $–$$.

## Where to Stay

**The Desmond Hotel.** 660 Albany Shaker Rd.; (800) 448-3500 and (518) 869-8100; www .desmondhotelsalbany.com. Elegant place with 323 rooms and suites, two indoor pools, hot tub, fitness center, billiard room, free wireless Internet, cable TV, in-room pay-per-view video games and movies, room service, and three restaurants. $$$

**Mansion Hill.** 115 Philip St.; (518) 465-2038; www.mansionhill.com. Conveniently located in the downtown area close to many attractions, this friendly B&B also has a fabulous four-star restaurant. $$$

# Troy

Head north on I–787.

Known as the birthplace of "Uncle Sam," Troy was once the country's leading producer of brushes, bells, stoves, surveying instruments, horseshoes, collars, and shirts.

## Riverspark Troy Visitor Center (all ages)

**251 River St. at Broadway; (518) 270-8667; www.troyvisitorcenter.org. Open year-round May through Sept, Tues through Sat 10 a.m. to 5 p.m.; Oct through May, Tues through Sat 11 a.m. to 5 p.m., some Fridays to 8 p.m. Free.**

Stop at this great information center first to get oriented. A film of historical highlights, electronic map printouts, and labor and industry exhibits will help you explore the area.

## The Children's Museum of Science and Technology (all ages) 🖴 🍽

**250 Jordan Rd.; (518) 235-2120; www.cmost.org. Open year-round; summer, Mon through Sat 10 a.m. to 5 p.m.; Sept through June, Thurs through Sun 10 a.m. to 5 p.m. $.**

Explore the environment of the Hudson River, interact with exotic animals, produce and broadcast your own weather forecast, learn about green technology at the new Solar House, manipulate virtual water or an entire solar system at the Play Motion exhibit, make and take your own invention created from recycled materials, and then do some star searching at one of the four animated space shows inside the Lally Digital Dome Planetarium. The Eatery Cafe offers full meals, and the gift shop has fun educational toys and souvenirs.

## Rolling on **the River**

**Captain J. P. Cruise Line.** 278 River St.; (518) 270-1901; www.captainjp.home stead.com. Have lunch, brunch, dinner, or a DJ-hosted dance cruise aboard the four-deck *Capt. JP II*, which accommodates 600 people.

# Empire State **Officials**

**State flower:** rose (1955)

**State tree:** sugar maple (1956)

**State gem:** garnet (1969)

**State bird:** red-breasted bluebird (1970)

**State freshwater fish:** brook trout (1975)

**State animal:** beaver (1975)

**State fruit:** apple (1976)

**State beverage:** milk (1981)

**State fossil:** sea scorpion (1984)

**State muffin:** apple muffin (1987)

**State shell:** bay scallop (1988)

**State insect:** ladybug (1989)

**State reptile:** snapping turtle (2006)

**State bush:** lilac (2006)

**State saltwater fish:** striped bass (2006)

**State motto:** *Excelsior* (Ever Upward)

## Crailo State Historic Site  (all ages)
9½ Riverside Ave., Rensselaer; (518) 463-8738; www.nysparks.state.ny.us. Open Apr through Oct, Mon through Fri 11 a.m. to 4 p.m. $.

Built in 1704, the Crailo mansion is the home of the Museum of Hudson Valley Dutch Culture and is furnished with antiques and historical artifacts. The song "Yankee Doodle" was reportedly written here. Outside are fragrant herb gardens, and in summer concerts are held on the grounds.

## Grafton Lakes State Park  (all ages)
Long Pond Road, Box 163, NY 2, Grafton 12082; (518) 279-1155; www.nysparks.com/parks. Open daily year-round 8 a.m. to dusk. Free, except for parking fee in summer $ and boat rentals $$.

This popular 2,357-acre park has five small ponds (some with beavers), a large sandy beach, a snack bar, rowboat rentals, year-round fishing, ball fields, a playground, a nature center, and 25 miles of trails to explore. In winter the activities shift to ice-skating, sledding, and cross-country skiing.

## Berkshire Bird Paradise  (all ages)
43 Red Pond Rd., Petersburg, off NY 2 (3 miles past Grafton Lakes); (518) 279-3801 or (800) 349-7150; www.birdparadise.org. Open daily Memorial Day weekend through Oct, 9 a.m. to 5 p.m. $.

From emu to eagle, more than 1,200 birds from almost a hundred species live in this sanctuary for injured or adopted avians. Visitors can walk through an evergreen and hardwood forest seeking spotted owls, snowy egrets, and perhaps newly hatched eaglets.

## Also in **the Area**

**Oasis Park Miniature Golf.** 97 North Greenbush Rd., Troy; (518) 283-3646; www.oasispark.net.

**Funplex Mystic Lagoon.** 589 Colonial Turnpike, East Greenbush; (518) 477-2651; www.funplexfunpark.com.

**Gardener's Ice Cream & Miniature Golf.** NY 22, Stephentown; (518) 733-6700.

### Dyken Pond Environmental Education Center  (all ages)
475 Dyken Pond Rd., Cropseyville; (518) 658-2055; www.dykenpond.org. About 14 miles east of Troy. Open daily year-round during daylight hours. $.

This lovely preserve has nature trails winding through thirty-three ecological communities, excellent for wildlife watching, with programs offered throughout the year ranging from owl prowls and full-moon canoe trips to family camp staycations.

### Peebles Island State Park  (all ages)
Delaware Avenue to Peebles Island Bridge; (518) 237-7000; www.nysparks.state.ny.us. Open year-round, dawn to dusk. Visitor center open Wed to Sun. $.

Miles of trails at this park, located at the confluence of the Hudson and Mohawk Rivers, reveal river rapid views and peaceful picnic places. Seasonal programs may be about birds, beavers, and butterflies, or the history of the Hudson.

## Where to Eat

**Brown's Brewing Company.** 417 River St.; (518) 273-2337; www.brownsbrewing.com. Riverfront Park place that brews its own soda and beer, and has great burgers, sandwiches, salads, pasta, chicken, seafood, and a children's menu. $$

**Holmes and Watson, Ltd.** 450 Broadway; (518) 273-8526. Historic British pub with Sherlock Holmes theme, with unusual sandwiches, burgers, homemade meat loaf, chicken 'n' biscuits, great desserts, and a children's menu. $

## Where to Stay

**Olde Judge Mansion Bed & Breakfast.** 3300 Sixth Ave.; (518) 274-5698; www.olde judgemansion.com. Family friendly with comfortable rooms, a parlor with a piano, books, and toys, and a hearty breakfast. $$

**Franklin Square Inn & Suites.** 1 Fourth St., Troy; (518) 274-8800 or (866) 708-2233; www.franklinsquareinn.com. Sixty-three rooms and five suites with Jacuzzis, premium cable, high-speed Internet, and a lounge, within easy walking distance to the Hudson River. $$–$$$

# Granville

Head north on NY 40 to NY 149.

Settled by Quakers in the late eighteenth century, the town's chief resource was its abundance of blue, green, and maroon slate, thereby earning it the nickname of the Colored Slate Capital of the World.

### Pember Museum of Natural History (ages 7 and up)

**33 W. Main St.; (518) 642-1515; www.pembermuseum.com. Open year-round Tues through Fri 1 to 5 p.m., Sat 10 a.m. to 3 p.m. $.**

Franklin T. Pember and his wife, Ellen, wanted to build a library and museum for their town. In 1909 the Pembers amassed a collection of more than 10,000 regional and exotic natural-history objects, from bears and butterflies to fossils and frogs. Children will enjoy the "Please Touch" naturalist's cabinets, with all sorts of shells, bones, and pelts to examine. Special programs may include nature hikes and scavenger hunts.

### Pember Nature Preserve (all ages)

**NY 22, Hebron; (518) 642-1515; www.pembermuseum.com/preserve. Eight miles south of Granville. Open daily year-round dawn to dusk. $, children under 3 free.**

Affiliated with the Pember Museum, this is a great place to explore a variety of natural habitats with children. Seven easy nature trails lace through this 125-acre preserve, and an observation deck offers the chance to spot the waterfowl, beavers, muskrats, and deer that reside here. Nature hikes, owl prowls, and other activities are offered at the one-room Porter Schoolhouse nature education center throughout the year.

### Slate Valley Museum (all ages)

**17 Water St.; (518) 642-1417; www.slatevalleymuseum.org. Open Memorial Day through Columbus Day weekend, Tues through Sat 10 a.m. to 5 p.m., Sun 1 to 4 p.m.; winter hours mid-Oct through May, Tues through Fri 1 to 5 p.m., Sat 10 a.m. to 4 p.m. Closed some major holidays. $.**

## More to Do **around Granville**

**Granville Lanes & Fun Center.** 17 E. Main St., Granville; (518) 642-9855.

**Log Village Grist Mill.** 5499 CR 30, Granville; (518) 632-5237;

**Hick's Orchard.** 18 Hicks Rd., Granville (518) 642-1788; www.hicksorchard .com.

**Hillbilly Fun Park.** 10375 NY 149, Fort Ann; (518) 792-5239.

Queries about quarries can be answered at this informative museum specializing in slate and the settlers that mined it. The Welsh were the first to arrive in the area, then came the Polish, Irish, Italians, and Slovakians. Special programs explore the effect of immigration to the area, from folk art exhibits to polka barn dances, and you mustn't miss the marvelous mural of slate workers painted by Martha Levi for the Works Project Administration in 1939.

### Skenesborough Museum & Urban Cultural Park Center (all ages)

Skenesborough Drive, Whitehall; (518) 499-0716 or (518) 499-1155; www.museumsusa.org and www.washingtoncounty.org. Open mid-June to Labor Day, Mon through Sat 10 a.m. to 4 p.m.; Labor Day to mid-Oct, Sat 10 a.m. to 3 p.m., Sun noon to 3 p.m. $.

Located along the Champlain Canal, this is the birthplace of the American Navy during the Revolutionary War. More than 4,000 artifacts, from farm tools to ship models are displayed, most donated by local residents.

## Where to Eat

**Rathbun's Maple Sugar House.** 1208 Hatch Hill Rd., North Granville; (518) 642-1799. www.rathbunsmaple.com. Fabulous breakfasts year-round, plus springtime maple-sugaring demonstrations, blueberry picking in summer, hot apple cider and homemade doughnuts in winter, and seasonal rides in Clydesdale-drawn wagons. $

**Scarlotta's Car Hop & Diner.** 45 Quaker St.; (518) 642-2445. Flash back to the '50s at this classic diner, serving burgers, fries, milk shakes, chicken dinners, twenty-four flavors of ice cream, and a kids' menu. $

## Where to Stay

**Finch & Chubb Inn, Restaurant, and Marina.** 82 N. Williams St., Whitehall; (518) 499-2049; www.visitwhitehall.com. Located on the water at Lock 12, with rooms and suites, a swimming pool, a playground, a picnic and barbecue area, free canoe rentals, a gift shop, full service marina and a great restaurant. $–$$

**Panorama Motel.** 2227 NY 22A, Hampton (6 miles north of Granville); (518) 282-9648 or (888) 423-9648; www.panoramamotelny.com. Thirteen rooms, each with a private patio, and a three-room bungalow, set on a hillside with nice views.

# Fort Edward and Rogers Island

Take NY 149 west and then head south on US 4.

Once the third largest city in colonial America, this area was a strategic stronghold for the British during the French and Indian Wars.

### Rogers Island Visitors Center (all ages)

11 Rogers Island Dr., Fort Edward; (518) 747-3693; www.rogersisland.org. Open Wed through Sat 10 a.m. to 4 p.m., Sun 1 to 4 p.m., and daily June through Aug. Free.

Native Americans hunted and fished on this island as long ago as 4,000 B.C. The British built Fort Edward, one of their largest fortifications in North America, and it became the base camp for Major Robert Rogers and his irregular fighting force of Rangers.

## Where to Eat

**The Anvil Inn.** 67 Broadway, Fort Edward; (518) 747-0556; www.theanvilinn.com. Once a nineteenth-century blacksmith shop, this historic and reportedly haunted restaurant serves American classic cuisine, with terrific homemade desserts. $$

## Where to Stay

**The Historic Inn of Fort Edward.** 215 Broadway; (518) 747-0778; www.historicinnfe .com. Eight rooms, each decorated with a different theme, with Wi-Fi and cable TV. $

# Saratoga Springs

South on NY 22 to NY 29 west.

Whether you come to take the waters at the "Queen of Spas" or visit the racetrack to watch the "Sport of Kings," Saratoga Springs will reward your family royally with a treasury of fun things to see and do. For foodies, the potato chip and club sandwich were invented here!

### Saratoga Springs Heritage Area Visitor Center  (all ages)

**297 Broadway; (518) 587-3241; www.saratogaspringsvisitorcenter.com. Open daily May through Oct, 9 a.m. to 4 p.m.; Nov through Apr, Mon through Sat 9 a.m. to 4 p.m. Free.**

To start your exploration of Saratoga, stop here to check out the exhibits and the orientation video, and for self-guided tour maps and a schedule of seasonal special events. Across the street is Congress Park, one of the oldest parks in the country and the site of the beautiful 1870s Canfield Casino. No longer used for gambling, it houses the Saratoga Springs History Museum, displaying artifacts of the area. Outside, take a whirl on a wonderful wooden carousel with twenty-eight horses, then find the four fountains featuring the fabled mineral waters of Saratoga Springs.

### Bog Meadow Trail  (all ages)

**Meadowbrook Road or Weibel Avenue, Saratoga Springs; (518) 587-5554; www.saratoga plan.org. free**

Created from a converted railroad bed between the downtown area to Saratoga Lake, this 2-mile trail connects Meadowbrook Road with NY 29 and winds through three different wetlands, with interpretive signs along the extensive boardwalk path.

### Saratoga Race Course  (all ages)

267 Union Ave., Saratoga; (518) 584-6200; www.nyra.com. Season runs late July to Labor Day; $$$, children under 12 **free.** Breakfast buffet on racing days 7 to 9:30 a.m.; adults $$, children 3 to 12 $. Trams filled on a first-come, first-served basis.

This is the oldest thoroughbred racetrack in the country, and one of the most accessible to children. Watch the morning workouts of these amazing animals while you eat breakfast on the Porch of the Clubhouse. Afterward, **free** behind-the-scenes tram tours of the Backstretch Area are offered, with a Paddock Show and a Starting Gate demonstration. Five other restaurants are on-site as well, and frequent family festivals, contests, and T-shirt and hat giveaways are scheduled in season.

### Children's Museum at Saratoga Springs  (7 and under)

69 Caroline St.; (518) 584-5540; www.childrensmuseumatsaratoga.org. Open July through Labor Day, Mon through Sat 9:30 a.m. to 4:30 p.m.; Labor Day through June, Tues through Sat 9:30 a.m. to 4:30 p.m., Sun noon to 4:30 p.m.; closed most major holidays. $.

Walk through a toddler-size replica of Congress Park, climb into a tree house, pretend to be a bank teller, grocery clerk, construction worker, chef, actor, or fireman (all props provided), create giant bubbles, or construct a Lego village at this imaginative interactive museum.

### Petrified Sea Gardens  (all ages)

42 Petrified Sea Gardens Rd.; (518) 584-7102; www.petrifiedseagardens.org. Hours vary by season. $, children under 6 **free.**

Stroll among the stromatolites, or Cambrian sea cabbage fossils, formed when Saratoga Springs was at the bottom of the ocean about 500 million years ago. There are two trails and a sundial garden to explore, a small rock-and-mineral museum, and Native American activities and workshops for children.

### National Museum of Racing and Hall of Fame  (all ages)

191 Union Ave.; (518) 584-0400 or (800) JOCKEY-4; www.racingmuseum.org. Open Mon through Sat 10 a.m. to 4 p.m., Sun noon to 4 p.m. Closed Mon and Tues, Jan through Mar. Adults $$, children $, children under 5 **free.**

For the equine enthusiast, this is a winning bet. Three centuries of horse racing are highlighted here, with exhibits of thoroughbred anatomy, art, artifacts, racing silks, betting boards, and Hall of Famers. The Horseplay! Gallery provides kid-size pretend play activities, from dressing up as a jockey to shoeing a horse. For jockeys over 48 inches tall, hop on and hold tight on the new Ready to Ride mechanical horse, synchronized with jockey-cam videos. Documentary movies about horses are screened daily, and races are simulcast inside the Hall of Fame in season.

### Saratoga Spa State Park  (all ages)

19 Roosevelt Dr. (between US 9 and NY 50); (518) 584-2000 or (518) 584-2535; www.saratoga spastatepark.org. Park open year-round, dawn to dusk. Roosevelt Baths & Spa (518) 226-4790; www.gideonputnam.com; open daily year-round 9 a.m. to 7 p.m. Swimming pools

# More Fun around **Saratoga Springs**

**Saratoga Strike Zone.** 32 Ballston Ave., Saratoga; (518) 584-6460; www.saratoga
strikezone.com.

**Saratoga Mini-Golf.** 54 Vista Dr., Saratoga; (518) 581-2841.

**Saratoga Biking.** Various locations around Saratoga; (518) 587-0286; www
.healthytransportation.org/tourism.

**Saratoga Boat Works.** 549 Union Ave., Saratoga; (518) 584-2628; www.saratoga
boatworks.com.

**Saratoga Harness Hall of Fame.** Jefferson Street, Saratoga; (518) 587-4210;
www.saratoga.org.

**Saratoga Polo.** Whitney Field, corner of Bloomfield and Denton Roads, Saratoga; (518) 584-8108; www.saratogapolo.com.

**Moreau Lake State Park.** 605 Old Saratoga Rd., Gansevoort; (518) 793-0511;
www.nysparks.state.ny.

**Ellms Family Farm.** 468 Charlton Rd., Ballston Spa; (518) 884-8168; www.ellms
farms.com.

**Extra Innings.** One McCrea Hill Rd., Ballston Spa; (518) 885-1100; www.extra
innings-saratoga.com.

open 10 a.m. to 6 p.m. daily July through Labor Day except Tues; $. Saratoga Automobile
Museum (518) 587-1935; www.saratogaautomuseum.org; open year-round 10 a.m. to 5
p.m.; closed Mon fall and winter; $. Spa Little Theater (518) 587-4427; www.homemade
theater.org; call for tickets. National Museum of Dance (518) 584-2225; www.dance
museum.org; open year-round Tues through Sun 10 a.m. to 4:30 p.m.; $. Saratoga Perform-
ing Arts Center (518) 587-3330; www.spac.org; call for tickets.

Pamper yourselves with a stop at the spas for a mineral bath, or take the kids swimming at
the ornately tiled Victoria Pool or the larger Peerless Pool. This lushly manicured 2,200-acre
park also has two golf courses, six tennis courts, six hiking trails, the grand Gideon Putnam
Hotel, the Saratoga Automobile Museum, the Spa Little Theatre, the National Museum of
Dance, and the Saratoga Performing Arts Center to keep you entertained in high style.

### Saratoga National Historic Park (all ages)
648 NY 32 (at US 4), Stillwater; (518) 664-9821, ext. 224; www.nps.gov/sara. Open year-
round 9 a.m. to dusk; visitor center closes at 5 p.m. $.

Possibly the most decisive battles of the American Revolution were fought here in the
autumn of 1777. Led by generals Horatio Gates and Benedict Arnold, the American troops

routed British general John Burgoyne's army in two savage assaults, effectively bringing about the beginning of the end of British rule in America. The visitor center offers interpretive exhibits, an orientation film, and a ten-stop auto tour map of the battlefields. History comes to life dramatically at battle reenactments and military encampments that occur here throughout the year.

### Brookside Museum (ages 6 and up)

**6 Charlton St., Ballston Spa; (518) 885-4000; www.brooksidemuseum.org. Open year-round Tues through Sat 10 a.m. to 4 p.m. $.**

This interesting museum offers permanent and changing exhibits of cultural and social history, with a hands-on history room, a costume display, interactive computers, and classes for kids in painting and knitting.

### Camp Saratoga (all ages)

**Scout Road, Wilton; www.saratoga.com.**

Once a Boy Scout camp and now the habitat of the endangered Karner blue butterfly, this 310-acre preserve has five miles of easy paths that wander through woodlands and wetlands in summer and morph into cross-country ski trails in winter.

### Yaddo (all ages)

**Union Avenue, Saratoga; (518) 584-0746; www.yaddo.org. Gardens open seven days a week, from 8 a.m. to dusk. Free.**

At the turn of the century, Financier Spencer Trask and his wife Katrina built a magnificent mansion on 400 beautifully landscaped acres for their family of four children. The name *Yaddo* was invented by one of the young daughters, because it rhymed with shadow. When all the children died young, the Trasks decided to bequeath their home to future generations of writers, composers, choreographers, filmmakers, painters, and other creative artists, by providing a supportive environment without interruptions. Over the years more than 4,000 artists have come here to amuse their muse, and sixty-four Pulitzer Prizes, sixty National Book Awards, and a Nobel Prize have been awarded to people who resided here. Some say the place has a mystical creative power, and although visitors may not enter the mansion except on special occasions, the romantic rose and rock gardens are open to the public, and are a wonderful place to walk.

## Where to Eat

**Circus Cafe.** 392 Broadway; (518) 583-1106. Wonderfully whimsical, this circus-themed restaurant serves classic comfort food like Yankee pot roast, chicken potpie, lasagna, fish-and-chips, huge salads, a fun kids' menu, and homemade cotton candy. $$

**Hattie's Restaurant.** 45 Phila St.; (518) 584-4790; www.hattiesrestaurant.com. Serving southern and Louisiana cuisine since 1938; specializing in fabulous fried chicken, marvelous mac and cheese, gumbo, jambalaya, and pecan pie. $$$

**Lakeside Cider Mill & Farm.** 336 Schauber Rd., Ballston Lake; (518) 399-8359; www.lakesidefarmscidermill.com. This seasonal cider mill also serves year-round country-fresh breakfasts, apple-cider doughnuts, and deli-style lunches. $

**Saratoga Diner.** 153 S. Broadway; (518) 584-4044. Open twenty-four hours, serving diner classics. $

## Where to Stay

**Gideon Putnam Resort.** 24 Gideon Putnam Rd.; (866) 890-1171; www.gideonputnam .com. Located inside the Saratoga Spa State Park, this historic Georgian Revival inn has 120 rooms, eighteen suites, high-speed Internet, laundry service, room service, two restaurants, and all the amenities of the park that surrounds it. $$$–$$$$

**The Inn at Saratoga.** 231 Broadway; (518) 583-1890 and (800) 274-3573; www.theinn atsaratoga.com. Victorian-style rooms and suites, complimentary buffet breakfast, Wi-Fi, use of bicycles, use of the Victoria Pool, and nightly horse-drawn carriage shuttles to the downtown area during racing season.

# Schenectady

South on NY 50.

Schenectady, the site of the earliest European settlement in the Mohawk Valley, was once referred to as the City that Lights and Hauls the World. The theme here is still labor and industry, but it's the architectural treasures of the Stockade District that make Schenectady special.

## Schenectady County Historical Society Museum (all ages)

32 Washington Ave.; (518) 374-0263; www.schist.org. Open Mon through Fri 9 a.m. to 5 p.m., Sat 10 a.m. to 2 p.m. $.

Located inside the Stockade District, this lovely nineteenth-century Georgian–Greek Revival museum has many artifacts and antiques of the area, but it's the large, fourteen-room dollhouse filled with miniature period furniture that will enchant your children. It was built for Governor Yates's granddaughter in 1834, and it's the only one of its era in the state. The museum also has walking-tour maps of the Stockade District, one of the oldest neighborhoods in the country. Named for the succession of wooden walls built in the seventeenth century to protect the early Dutch settlers, the area encompasses the largest collection of prerevolutionary buildings in the country.

## Schenectady Museum and Suits-Bueche Planetarium (all ages)

15 Nott Terrace Heights; (518) 382-7890; www.schenectadymuseum.org. Open year-round Tues through Fri 10 a.m. to 5 p.m. $. Planetarium open Tues through Sat; call for show hours. $.

This Tech Valley science center offers interactive science and industry exhibits, plus fun experiment labs with PBS's Fetch, the animated canine spokesdog for the National Science

# Mohawk Valley **Fairs and Festivals**

Country fairs are the original family fun fests, and almost every county in New York has one. Here are some of the main Mohawk Valley county fairs.

**Albany:** NY 146, Altamont Fairgrounds, Altamont; (518) 861-6671; www .altamontfair.com. (mid-Aug)

**Rensselaer:** Schaghticoke Fair; (518) 753-4411 or (518) 369-7779; www .schaghticokefair.com. (Labor Day weekend)

**Schoharie:** South Grand Street. Fairgrounds, Cobleskill; (518) 234-2123; www .cobleskillfair.com. (early Aug)

**Otsego:** Fairgrounds, Morris; (607) 263-5289; www.otsegocountyfair.org. (early Aug)

**Montgomery and Fonda:** 21 South Bridge St., Fonda; Montgomery County Fairgrounds, NY 30A; (518) 853-3313; www.fondafair.com. (early Sept)

**Saratoga:** 162 Prospect St., Ballston Spa; (518) 885-9701; www.saratoga countyfair.org. (mid-July)

**Washington:** 392 Old Schuylerville Rd., Greenwich; (518) 692-2464; www .washingtoncountyfair.com. (late Aug)

**Herkimer:** 133 Cemetery St., Frankfort; (315) 895-7465; www.herkimercounty fair.org. (mid-Aug)

**Chenango:** 168 E. Main St., Norwich; (607) 334-9198; www.chenangocounty fair.homestead.com. (mid-Aug)

**Madison:** 1968 Fairgrounds Rd., Brookfield; (315) 899-5867; www.madison county-fair.com. (early July)

**Oneida:** Schuyler Street, Boonville; (315) 942-2251; www.frontiernet .net/~boonvillefair. (late July)`

Foundation. The planetarium has a new GOTO Star Machine, the only one of its kind in the Northeast and one of only twelve in the country. You'll be able to see more than 8,500 stars, constellations, and planets from anywhere on Earth or any place in the solar system.

## Empire State Aerosciences Museum (all ages)

250 Rudy Chase Dr., Glenville; (518) 377-2191; www.esam.org. Open year-round mid-June through Labor Day, Wed through Sat 10 a.m. to 4 p.m., Sun noon to 4 p.m.; Labor Day through mid-June, Fri and Sat 10 a.m. to 4 p.m., Sun noon to 4 p.m. Adults $$, children $.

Lindbergh landed on this field, and rocket research here rivaled that being done in Peenemünde, Germany during World War II. Located on twenty-seven acres next to the Schenectady County Airport, this museum has an extensive collection of incredible aircraft, from zeppelins to lunar landers. Nine buildings and hangars house the more fragile vintage aircraft, artifacts, dioramas, and photographic displays, while outside are parked Tomcats, Tigers, and Trackers. Climb into the cockpit of a 1910 Von Pomer, or rock and roll in a Simulated Reality Vehicle that bounces together video and motion. Special programs for children include rocket building and launching, designing aircraft, and scavenger hunts, and every third Sat (except Dec) ESAM sponsors an all-you-can-eat breakfast for $5.

## Mabee Farm (all ages)

**1080 Main St. (NY 5S), Rotterdam Junction, five minutes west of exit 26; (518) 887-5073 or (518) 374-0263; www.schist.org. Open May through Sept, Tues through Sat 10 a.m. to 4 p.m. $.**

Once the site of a Dutch fur-trading post, this 300-year-old farmhouse is the oldest standing home in the Mohawk Valley. Four gardens grace the grounds, antique furniture and farm equipment are on display, and annual festivals celebrate arts and crafts, music, history, and early technology.

## Vischer Ferry Nature and Historic Preserve (all ages)

**Riverview Road, Clifton Park. Adjacent to Mohawk River; www.dec.ny.gov. Open daily dawn to dusk. Free.**

Recently designated a Bird Conservation Area because of the variety of waterfowl and migratory birds that pass through this wetland complex, the 600-acre park also hugs a historic section of the Erie Canal, Old Double Lock 19. Ten miles of trails are open year-round, for hiking, biking, horseback riding, and cross-country skiing in season.

## Where to Eat

**Canali's Restaurant.** 126 Mariaville Rd.; (518) 355-5323; www.canalisrestaurant.com. Terrific pasta, Italian specialties, and a children's menu. $$

**Jumpin' Jack's Drive-In.** 5 Schonowee Ave., Scotia; (518) 393-6101; www.jumpin jacksdriveininc.com. 1950s-style burgers, chicken fingers, fries, and sundaes. $

## Where to Stay

**The Parker Inn.** 434 State St.; (518) 688-1001; www.parkerinn.com. Located next door to the Procter Theater, with twenty-three rooms and suites, laundry, free Wi-Fi, cable, and continental breakfast. $$–$$$$

**The Stockade Inn.** 1 North Church St.; (518) 346-3400; www.stockadeinn.com. Eighteen rooms and suites in the historic Stockade District, with free Wi-Fi, cable, live jazz in the lounge, and a gourmet restaurant. $$–$$$

# Amsterdam

Head west along NY 5.

This river valley was home to the Mohawks for thousands of years before Dutch and German settlers arrived in the early eighteenth century.

### Walter Elwood Museum (ages 5 and up)

**300 Guy Park Ave.; (518) 843-5151; www.walterelwoodmuseum.org. Open year-round Tues, Wed, and Thurs 9 a.m. to 3 p.m. Donation.**

As a young man, Walter Elwood traveled the world, collecting ethnographic artifacts and natural history specimens. When he returned to Amsterdam as the superintendent of schools, he used his collection of more than 25,000 objects to create a school museum. Interactive eclectic exhibits feature the Mohawk Valley's ethnic and industrial past, the Victorian era, and collections of rocks, fossils, buttons, and handmade doll clothes.

### The Noteworthy Indian Museum (all ages)

**Corner of Church and Prospect Streets; (518) 843-4761; www.greatturtle.net. Open June through Aug; call for times; Donation.**

Trace 12,000 years of Native American life in the Mohawk Valley at this museum with more than 60,000 artifacts and illustrations. Contemporary art is also displayed, and programs include storytelling, poetry readings, and historical presentations.

### Schoharie Crossing State Historic Site (all ages)

**129 Schoharie St.; (518) 829-7516; www.nysparks.com. Visitor center open in May, Wed through Sat 10 a.m. to 5 p.m.; Memorial Day through Oct, Wed through Mon 10 a.m. to 5 p.m. Grounds open dawn to dusk. Free. Call ahead to confirm changes to hours, activities available, and possible closures due to pending state budget cuts.**

Seven arches of an aqueduct that carried the Erie Canal over the Schoharie Creek still stand here, a testament to one of the most amazing engineering feats of the nineteenth century. Storytelling, birdhouse building, and geocaching (treasure hunting with a GPS) are some of the activities offered at the visitor center, and there's an easy 3-mile nature trail on the grounds.

## Where to Eat

**Raindancer Restaurant.** 4582 NY 30; (518) 842-2606; www.raindancerrestaurant.com. Rustic steak and seafood place with salad bar, early-bird specials, and prime rib on the children's menu. $$

**Windmill Diner Restaurant.** 4790 NY 30; (518) 842-0087. Big breakfasts, diner delights and a great dessert selection. $

## Where to Stay

**Americas Best Value Inn.** 10 Market St.; (518) 843-5760; www.americasbestvalueinn

.com. Indoor pool, Internet, cable TV, room service and restaurant. $$

**Halcyon Farm Bed & Breakfast.** 157 Lang Rd.; (518) 842-7718; www.bedand breakfast.com. Formerly a tavern, this lovely eighteenth-century Federal brick B&B is set amidst 300 acres of woods and hay fields near the shore of the Schoharie River. Five beautiful bedrooms have Wi-Fi and flat-screen TVs with DVD players, and the library has a baby grand piano, books, and board games. $$–$$$

# Johnstown

Continue west on NY 5, then north on NY 30A.

This was the birthplace of suffragette Elizabeth Cady Stanton and was once, along with nearby Gloversville, the center of a thriving leather- and glove-manufacturing industry.

### Johnson Hall State Historic Site (ages 7 and up)

**Hall Avenue (between Johnson Avenue and West State Street); (518) 762-8712 or (518) 762-2330; www.nysparks.state.ny.us. Open Memorial Day to Labor Day, Thurs through Mon 10 a.m. to 5 p.m. $, children under 12 free. Call ahead to confirm changes to hours, activities available, and possible closures due to pending state budget cuts.**

The former home of Sir William Johnson, brother-in-law of Iroquois leader Joseph Brant, is now a museum that offers interesting exhibits on the French and Indian War.

### Johnstown Historical Society Museum (ages 8 and up)

**17 North William St.; (518) 762-7076. Open Memorial Day to Labor Day, Sat and Sun 1 to 4 p.m. Free, donations appreciated.**

This restored eighteenth-century cottage houses artifacts from Johnstown's Revolutionary and Civil War past, as well as an exhibit on town native and pioneer for women's rights, Elizabeth Cady Stanton.

### Adirondack Animal Land (all ages)

**3554 NY 30, Gloversville; (518) 883-5748; www.adirondackanimalland.com. Open daily mid-May through Labor Day 10 a.m. to 5 p.m. $$.**

Spread over eighty acres, this wildlife park is home to more than 500 regional and exotic birds and animals. Wildlife propagation of rare and endangered species is a priority here, so stop by the nursery, where possibly 200 babies will be born this year. Pause at the petting zoo, ride a pony, go on an African safari, walk through a nineteenth-century western town, enjoy three animal shows daily, then have lunch at the Country Cafe or plan a picnic on the grounds.

# Native Americans of **New York**

The earliest known humans to settle in the New York region were the "mound people," about 7000 B.C. Later, probably 6,000 to 8,000 years ago, came the tribes of the Lenape (Munsee, Unami, Renneiu, Unalatchtigo, and Esopus), Poospapuck, Delaware, Mohican, Nanticoke, and Wappinger, along with the thirteen tribes of Long Island (Montauk, Shinnecock, Unquachaug, Secatogue, Massapequa, Merrick, Rockaway, Canarsie, Matinecock, Nissequogue, Setaukets, Corchaug, and Manhansset), linked by the similarities of their Algonquin language, and the Iroquois, including the Mohawk, Oneida, Onondaga, Cayuga, Seneca, and, later, the Tuscarora. Most lived in communal homes, called longhouses, made from saplings and bark (some as long as a football field). While many of the Algonquin tribes were wiped out by exposure to European diseases such as smallpox and measles, the Iroquois prospered, mostly due to the fur trade. The more powerful Iroquois tribes formed a confederacy of Six Nations, with rules of social order and government meant to promote peaceful relations. Allied with the Susquehanna, Abenaki, Erie, and Huron to the west, the Iroquois aided the British during the French and Indian War and were a major factor in France's defeat. During the Revolutionary War most of the Native Americans sided with the British again. After that defeat, coupled with the attack Gen. George Washington unleashed on the Iroquois in 1779, the Native American way of life was changed forever.

### The National Shrine of Blessed Kateri Tekakwitha and Mohawk-Caughnawaga Museum (ages 7 and up)

3628 NY 5, Fonda; (518) 853-3646; www.katerishrine.com. Open daily 9 a.m. to 6 p.m. Free.

Known as "the Lily of the Mohawks," Kateri, born in 1656, was the daughter of an Algonquin mother and a Mohawk chief. Stricken with smallpox and orphaned at age four, she suffered failing eyesight and was given the name Tekakwitha, which means "she who bumps into things." Baptized at age twenty, she was known for her courage and compassion for others and is said to have performed many miracles, becoming the first Native American saint. The Mohawks called this area Caughnawaga, and it's the site of the only completely excavated Iroquois village in the country, The museum houses an excellent collection of ancient and modern Native American art, as well as archaeological artifacts from the area.

## Where to Eat

**Fireside.** 320 Steele Ave. Extension, Gloversville; (518) 725-2200; www.firesideny.com. Steaks, seafood, chicken, build-a-burger, specialty salads, and homemade desserts. $$

**Union Hall Inn.** 2 Union Pl.; (518) 762-3210; www.unionhallinnrestaurant.com. Once the favorite tavern for Napoleon's brother Joseph Bonaparte, this post-revolutionary place, guided by chefs from the Culinary Institute of America, serves fabulous seasonal creative cuisine. $$$

## Where to Stay

**Johnstown Holiday Inn.** 308 N. Comrie Ave. (NY 30A); (518) 762-4686; www .holiday-inn.com/johnstownny. Recently renovated, with rooms and suites, free Wi-Fi, heated outdoor pool, and restaurant with patio dining. Children under 12 stay and eat free. $$$

**Peck's Lake Park and Campground.** 180 Peck's Lake Rd., Gloversville; (518) 725-1294. Family fishing resort with fourteen cottages, campsites, boat rentals, and a 1,370-acre lake. $

# St. Johnsville, Canajoharie, and Herkimer

South on NY 30A, then NY 5 west.

Once a major stop on seventeenth- and eighteenth-century fur-trade routes, St. Johnsville later became an important mill town. Nearby Canajoharie is the birthplace of the flat-bottom paper bag and the sleeping car, and hunting for Herkimer diamonds has been a Mohawk pastime for thousands of years.

## Fort Klock (all ages)

**NY 5 (between NY 67 and NY 10, St. Johnsville); (518) 568-7779; www.fortklockrestoration .org. Open Memorial Day to Columbus Day, Tues through Sun 9 a.m. to 5 p.m. $.**

Built in 1750, this fortified stone farmhouse, with walls 2 feet thick, was a fur-trading post along the Mohawk River. A nineteenth-century schoolhouse, a blacksmith shop, and a Dutch barn have been added to the thirty-acre complex. Colonial skills such as smithing, weaving, cooking, and candle making are demonstrated, and craft fairs, concerts, and historical reenactments are scheduled throughout the season. Every Aug, potential pioneers between the ages of nine and thirteen are given the chance to time travel back to the eighteenth century, costumed in period clothes, and given a crash course in colonial life. Those that like that time period may apprentice with some of the on-site artisans and become historical interpreters for future fort events.

## Canajoharie Wintergreen Park and Gorge (all ages)

**Wintergreen Park Road, Canajoharie, near exit 29 off I-90; (518) 673-5508. Open Memorial Day weekend through Labor Day daily 9 a.m. to 9:30 p.m. $.**

Canajoharie is the Iroquois word for "the pot that washes itself," and a spectacular waterfall rushing over geological potholes does just that. Follow nature trails past this unusual phenomenon.

### Herkimer County Historical Society Museum (all ages)

**400 N. Main St., Herkimer; (315) 866-6413; www.rootsweb.com/~nyhchs. Open year-round Mon through Fri 10 a.m. to 4 p.m.; also Sat from July through Aug, 10 a.m. to 3 p.m. Free.**

A restored 1834 jail and a wonderful collection of dollhouses and miniatures grace this 1884 Queen Anne house.

### Herkimer Home State Historic Site (all ages)

**200 NY 169, Little Falls; (315) 823-0398 or (315) 823-0587; www.nysparks.state.ny.us. Call ahead to confirm changes to hours, activities available, and possible closures due to pending state budget cuts.**

Costumed interpreters, colonial crafts, and historical reenactments revive the American Revolution at the Georgian-style mansion that was the home of war hero General Nicholas Herkimer.

### Erie Canal Cruises (all ages)

**880 Mohawk St., Herkimer; (315) 717-0350; www.eriecanalcruises.com. Cruises daily mid-May through mid-Oct, 1 and 3 p.m. Adults $$$, children under 3 free.**

Cruise the canal aboard the sixty-seat *Lil' Diamond II,* on a one-and-a-half-hour "Lock Thru" voyage, complete with a narrated tour of the sights, legends, and "liquid elevator" Lock 18.

## Where to Eat

**Beardslee Castle.** 123 Old State Rd., Little Falls; (315) 823-3000; www.beardsleecastle .com. Fine dining in a 1860 haunted Irish castle, with an international eclectic cuisine serving organic seasonal produce, apple-wood grilled steaks and seafood, fifty beers, and a children's menu. Downstairs in the Dungeon, dinner's more casual, with soups, salads, and bar munchies; afterward, shoot some pool, gaze at the giant glass fish tank of koi, and look out for the ghosts! $$

**Parkside Drive-In.** 7485 NY 5, St. Johnsville; (518) 568-2802; www.parksidedrivein.com. Great diner classics, burgers, hot dogs, fish-and-chips, paninis and wraps, homemade soups and ice cream, and child-size classic cruiser car meals. $

**Waterfront Grille.** 800 Mohawk St., Herkimer; (315) 717-0700; www.waterfrontgrille .com. Sandwiches, salads, steaks, seafood, chicken, pizza, a children's menu, and home-made pie. $–$$$

## Where to Stay

**Herkimer Motel and Suites.** 100 Marginal Rd.; (315) 866-0490; www.herkimermotel .com. Rooms, suites, and efficiencies, heated outdoor pool, fitness room, free Wi-Fi, coin laundry, twenty-four-hour restaurant, free continental breakfast. $–$$

**Portobello Inn Bed & Breakfast.** 5989 NY 5, Herkimer; (315) 823-8612; www.portobello inn.com. Five rooms, cable TV, Wi-Fi, dining rooms with fireplaces, and a gift shop. $$

## Dig for **Diamonds**

The diamonds, called "Herkimer Diamonds," are actually eighteen-faceted, double-terminated quartz crystals formed half a million years ago in pockets of dolomite.

**Herkimer Diamond Mines.** 4601 NY 28, Herkimer; (315) 717-0175, (315) 891-7355, or (800) 562-0897; www.herkimerdiamond.com. Open daily Apr through Oct, 9 a.m. to 5 p.m. Mine, museum, restaurant, gift shop, and campgrounds. Adults $$, children $.

**Ace of Diamonds Mine.** NY 28, Middleville, 8 miles north of I-90, exit 30; (315) 891-3855; www.herkimerdiamonds.com. Open daily Apr through Oct, 9 a.m. to 5 p.m. Mine, gift shop, snack bar, and campground. Adults $$, children $.

**Crystal Grove Diamond Mine.** 161 CR 114, St. Johnsville; (518) 568-2914 or (800) KRY-DIAM; www.crystalgrove.com. Open Apr 15 through Oct 15 daily. Summer hours, 8 a.m. to 8 p.m.; spring and fall hours, 9 a.m. to 7 p.m. Mine, campsites, cabins, picnic area, playground, and gift shop. Adults $$, children $.

**Diamond Acres.** 1716 Stone Arabia Rd., Fonda; (518) 762-7960; www.herkimer history.com. Open daily sunup to sundown, weather permitting. Adults $, children under 13 **free.**

# Utica

Continue west on NY 5.

Home to the Oneida Nation for centuries, Utica evolved into a major trading and manufacturing center after the Dutch and English came to trade and never left. Woolworth opened his first five-and-dime store here in 1879.

### Children's Museum of History, Natural History, Science & Technology (all ages)

311 Main St.; (315) 724-6129; www.museum4kids.net. Open year-round Mon, Tues, and Thurs through Sat 9:45 a.m. to 3:45 p.m. Closed Wed, Sun, Thanksgiving, Christmas, and New Year's. $$.

One of the oldest and best children's museums in the country, and the only one to be adopted by NASA and the Department of Energy, this a fun place to explore. Interactive and hands-on exhibits range from an Iroquois longhouse to a Dinorama and a Weather Room Doppler Radar display. Arts and crafts projects are offered daily for all ages, and your kids will bug you to take them to the live insect zoo on the third floor.

## Utica Zoo  (all ages)

99 Steele Hill Rd.; (315) 738-0472; www.uticazoo.org. Open daily year-round 10 a.m. to 5 p.m. $.

See sea lions, snow leopards, tamarins, and toucans at this century-old zoo. Animal shows are scheduled in summer, there's a separate Children's Zoo with rabbits, sheep, and goats to pet, and the Tot Lot playground provides physical fun for all.

## Munson-Williams-Proctor Arts Institute Museum of Art  (all ages)

310 Genesee St.; (315) 797-0000; www.mwpi.edu. Open 10 a.m. to 5 p.m. Tues through Sat, 1 to 5 p.m. Sun. Free.

This regional fine arts center offers over a hundred musical, theatrical, and cinematic programs annually, and the School of Art gives instruction in all levels to several thousand children, teenagers, and adults every year. For further inspiration, there are more than 25,000 American and European eighteenth-, nineteenth-, and twentieth-century paintings and decorative arts displayed inside the twenty galleries of this award-winning architectural building by Philip Johnson. Works by Picasso, Pollock, Dali, and Kandinsky are here, as well as treasures by Tiffany & Co. inside the restored 1850s mansion Fountain Elms next door.

## Utica Marsh Wildlife Management Area  (all ages)

Barnes Avenue, off NY 5A; (315) 793-2554; www.uticamarsh.org. Open dawn to dusk year-round. Free.

Five minutes from downtown Utica is a unique urban wetland that harbors an enormous variety of plants and wildlife. Boardwalks branch out across the marsh, and a viewing platform and two observation towers overlook the 213-acre floodplain. Several thousand muskrats call this place home, as do 150 species of birds, thirty species of mammals, and a lot of snakes (nonpoisonous) and salamanders. Bring the binoculars.

## Adirondack Scenic Railroad  (all ages)

Union Station, 321 Main St.; (315) 724-0700 or (800) 819-2291; www.adirondackrr.com. Operates May through Oct; call for schedule and events. Adults $$$$, children $$.

Make tracks to this rustic railroad for a ride aboard vintage coaches and open-air cars, traveling from Utica to Old Forge and back. Special excursions range from train robberies that occur with alarming regularity every Wed in July and Aug to a Polar Express in Dec, and the fall foliage rides are spectacular. Trips also originate from the Thendara Station in Old Forge.

# Where to Eat

**Babe's Macaroni Grill & Bar.** 80 N. Genesee St.; (315) 735-0777; www.babesutica .com. Homemade pastas and sauces, pizza, soups, salads, steaks, ribs, chicken, burgers, wraps, and a kids' menu. $$

# Fifteen Miles **on the Erie Canal**

Cruise the waterways of the 524-mile New York State Canal System for a voyage through history and time. Linking more than 2,500 recreational facilities and attractions, the Erie, Champlain, Oswego, and Cayuga-Seneca Canals offer a scenic slice of life not available to landlubbers. For more information, contact the New York State Canal System at 200 Southern Blvd., Albany; (800) 4-CANAL-4 or (518) 436-2700; www.canals.state.ny.us.

**Thornberry's Restaurant.** 1011 King St.; (315) 735-1409; www.thornberrysrestaurant .net. Located directly behind the wonderful Stanley Theater, serving salads, sandwiches, burgers, steaks, seafood, pasta, and a special pre-theater menu. $$–$$$

## Where to Stay

**Hotel Utica.** 102 Lafayette St.; (877) 906-1912; www.hotelutica.com. Beautiful historic hotel with 112 rooms and suites, some with whirlpools, plus free Wi-Fi, cable TV and in-room movies, fitness room, restaurant, refrigerators in most rooms, and complimentary continental breakfast. $$

**Radisson Hotel-Utica Center.** 200 Genesee St.; (315) 797-8010 or (800) 333-3333; www.radisson.com. 162 rooms, refrigerator, cable TV, free Wi-Fi, indoor pool, fitness room, Jacuzzi, restaurant, game room, complimentary continental breakfast. $$–$$$

# Rome

From Utica, take NY 49.

Called De-O-Wain-Sta by local Native Americans, this was an important portage point for travel between the Great Lakes and the Atlantic Ocean. During the Revolutionary War the Stars and Stripes were first flown in battle here, and the settlement was renamed Rome when the British were defeated. The Erie Canal and the railroads that followed soon transformed the town into a major transportation hub.

## Fort Rickey Children's Discovery Zoo  (all ages)

5135 Rome–New London Rd.; (315) 336-1930; www.fortrickey.com. Open mid-May through mid-June, Wed through Fri 10 a.m. to 4 p.m.; mid-June to Labor Day, Sat 10 a.m. to 5 p.m. Open weekends Sept to Nov during Fall Fun Festival. Adults $$, children $, or free with paying adult.

This wonderful wildlife park encourages children to explore, investigate, and interact with a wide variety of animals, from antelopes and eagles to reindeer and reptiles. A large petting area with goats, sheep, and deer offers daily pony rides and animal shows. A playland features geysers and waterfalls, tunnels, slides, and a clubhouse. A recent addition is the Fall Fun Festival, held weekends in autumn, with weaving demonstrations, wagon rides, wolf shows, and the world famous Mrs. Lumpkin the Talking Pumpkin. Children can ride around the festival on pedal tractors, the concession stands serve cocoa and hot apple cider, and each child gets a **free** mini-pumpkin to paint.

### Fort Stanwix National Monument  (all ages)

**100 North James St.; (315) 336-2090 or (315) 338-7730; www.nps.gov/fost. Open daily year-round 9 a.m. to 5 p.m. Closed New Year's Day, Thanksgiving, and Christmas. Guided tours from the Willett Center at 10:30 a.m. and 12:30 and 2:30 p.m., weather permitting. Free.**

This reconstructed log-and-earth fort was strategically important during the Revolutionary War because it protected a major portage point on the route between New York City and Canada. To learn more, stop, at the new Marinus Willett Collections Management and Education Center, which houses an incredible collection of over 450,000 artifacts, and view the video presentation and exhibits. Outside, costumed guides explain life lived behind these logs, and three short trails encircle the fort. Visit in Aug and see the siege of Fort Stanwix dramatically reenacted by eighteenth-century soldiers and their camp followers. Nearby is the site of the Battle of Oriskany, which was the bloodiest battle of the American Revolution and led the Mohawks to stop supporting their British allies.

### Erie Canal Village  (all ages)

**5789 Rome New London Rd.; (315) 337-3999 or (888) 374-3226; www.eriecanalvillage.net. Open Memorial Day through Halloween, Wed through Sat 10 a.m. to 5 p.m., Sun noon to 5 p.m.; weekends only Labor Day through Columbus Day. Adults $$, children $, under 4 free.**

Take a ride back in time aboard a mule-drawn packet boat on the Erie Canal. This nineteenth-century village has been re-created on the spot where the first shovelful of earth was turned for the canal in 1817. The **Erie Canal Museum** exhibits the history of this waterway, the **Harden Museum** houses horse-drawn vehicles of all sorts, and the **New York State Museum of Cheese** tells the story of, well, cheese. Nineteenth-century skills, from blacksmithing to corn shelling, are demonstrated daily; boat, wagon, and train rides are available; and Bennett's 1850s Tavern serves simple snacks. Civil War encampments and subsequent battles occur here as well.

## Where to Eat

**Coalyard Charlie's.** 100 Depeyster St.; (315) 336-9940; www.coalyardcharlies.com. All-you-can-eat soup, salad, and bread bar, steaks, seafood, chicken, burgers, sandwiches, and a li'l Tugboat kid's meal. $–$$

**Savoy Restaurant.** 255 E. Dominick St.; (315) 339-3166; www.romesavoy.com. A century-old place serving wonderful Italian

family recipes, from *zuppa di pesce* to baked ziti, plus family-style dining options for four or more. $$–$$$

**Teddy's.** 851 Black River Blvd.; (315) 336-7839; www.teddysrestaurantny.com. Friendly restaurant serving pasta, pizza, paninis, and pot roast, as well as steak, seafood, salads, and homemade desserts. $–$$

## Where to Stay

**The Beeches Inn.** 7900 Turin Rd., NY 26N; (315) 336-1775; www.thebeeches.com. Located on fifty-two lavishly landscaped acres, this elegant inn offers seventy rooms, including seven extended-stay suites/kitchenettes, a pretty pool, complimentary laundry facility, and two excellent restaurants. $$

**Quality Inn Rome.** 200 S. James St.; (315) 336-4300; www.qualityinnrome.com. 104 newly renovated rooms, free Internet, fitness center, guest laundry, refrigerator, microwave, cable TV, seasonal courtyard pool, and a twenty-four-hour restaurant. $–$$

# Sylvan Beach

On the shores of Oneida Lake; take NY 49 west to NY 13 south.

This is a popular family resort area, where you can ride in a horse-drawn carriage or a roller coaster, reel in a fat bass, or paddle a canoe.

### Sylvan Beach Amusement Park  (all ages)

112 Bridge St., NY 13; (315) 762-5212; www.sylvanbeach.org/amusementpark. **Open May through Sept, Sun through Thurs noon to 10 p.m., Fri and Sat noon to 11 p.m.** Free **admission to walk around, but rides require tickets and there are pay-one-price deals an group rates.**

Twenty-three classic rides rock and roll here each summer, from the tilt-a-whirl to the scrambler, and there's skee ball for all at the arcade. Beyond the midway, explore the 4 miles of cottage-lined beach, or hop aboard a high-performance speedboat, *The Screamer,* for a howling good ride on Oneida Lake.

### Verona Beach State Park  (all ages)

NY 13, Verona Beach; (315) 762-4463; www.nysparks.com/parks. **Off NY 13, 2 miles south of Sylvan Beach. Open year-round; campground open May through mid-Oct. Vehicle fee $.**

The best of both worlds, this 1,735-acre park is part sandy beach and part forest. Sixteen miles of hiking trails wind around a peaceful pond, where wildlife is abundant, and there

## Also in **the Area**

**Shako:wi Cultural Center.** 5 Territory Rd., Oneida; (315) 829-8801; www .oneidaindiannation.com.

**Peterpaul Recreation Park.** 5615 Rome–New London Rd., Rome; (315) 339-2666; www.peterpaulrecreation.com.

are ball fields and courts, picnic areas, a playground, and a concession stand near the campgrounds.

## Where to Eat

**Cinderella's Cafe and Suites.** 1208 Main St.; (315) 762-4280; www.cinderellasrestaurant.com. Serving breakfast, lunch, and dinner, freshly baked pastries, more than forty flavors of ice cream, with an outdoor patio; some days children pay what they weigh. $

**Yesterday's Royal.** 13 Canal St.; (315) 762-4677. Casual place with two dining rooms and a tavern, featuring American cuisine, twenty-five flavors of homemade ice cream, early-bird specials, a children's menu, and live entertainment on weekends. $$

## Where to Stay

**Oneida Lake Inn.** 1509 Main St.; (315) 761-0000; www.oneidalakeinn.com. Twenty-five remodeled rooms and cottages, cable TV, new restaurant and tiki bar, within walking distance of amusement park, canal, and restaurants, plus complimentary coffee and pastries. Available daily or weekly. $–$$$

**Sunset Cottages.** 801 Park Ave.; (315) 762-4093 or (516) 746-4902; www.sylvanbeach.com/sunset.html. Fully-equipped cottages, with two, three, and four bedrooms, on the beach and within walking distance of amusement park, shopping, and restaurants. Weekly rentals. $–$$$

# Chittenango

Continue south on NY 13.

Follow the yellow-brick road and you will come to Chittenango, the birthplace of L. Frank Baum, author of *The Wizard of Oz*. Every spring the town honors its favorite native son by hosting the Oz-stravaganza, with guest appearances by some of the original Munchkins.

### Chittenango Landing Canal Boat Museum  (all ages)

7010 Lakeport Rd.; (315) 687-3801; www.chittenangolandingcanalboatmuseum.com. Open weekends May, June, Sept, and Oct, 1 to 4 p.m.; July through Aug, daily 10 a.m. to 4 p.m. $, children under 5 **free.**

This is an archaeological work in progress, with an interpretive center offering hands-on activities and exhibits, a blacksmith shop, and a restored sawmill. The 36-mile towpath of the Old Erie Canal Park runs through here and serves as an easy hiking and biking path.

## New York **Trivia**

The largest rivers in New York are the Hudson, the Mohawk, the Delaware, the Susquehanna, the Genesee, the Allegheny, and the St. Lawrence.

# Also in **the Area**

**Stone Quarry Hill Art Park.** 3883 Stone Quarry Rd., US 20, Cazenovia; (315) 655-3196; www.stonequarryhillartpark.org.

**Great Swamp Conservancy.** 8375 North Main St. and Pine Ridge Road, Canastota; (315) 697-2950; www.gscincny.tripod.com.

**Muller Hill State Forest.** Muller Hill Rd., Georgetown; (607) 674-4017 and (607) 674-4036; Forest Ranger (315) 655-5643; www.dec.ny.gov.

**Nichols Pond County Park.** Nichols Pond Rd., Canastota; (315) 366-2376; www.madisontourism.com.

**Oxbow Falls County Park.** Oxbow Rd., Canastota; (315) 366-2376; www.madisontourism.com.

**Nelson Swamp Unique Area.** Stone Quarry Rd., Cazenovia; (607) 674-4036; www.dec.ny.gov.

**Stoney Pond State Forest.** Jones Rd., Nelson; (607) 674-4017; www.dec.ny.gov.

## Chittenango Falls State Park  (all ages)

2300 Rathbun Rd.; (315) 655-9620; www.nysparks.com/parks. Off NY 13, 6 miles south of town. Open year-round; campground open mid-May through mid-Oct. Vehicle fee $. Call ahead to confirm changes to hours, activities available, and possible closures due to pending state budget cuts.

Higher than Niagara at 167 feet, the cascades of Chittenango Falls are breathtaking. Hike along the scenic trails of this 192-acre park, formed when the last glaciers retreated about 10,000 years ago.

## Where to Eat

**Auntie Em's Restaurant.** 262 Genesee St.; (315) 687-5704. Breakfast, lunch, and dinner with home-style cuisine, and a lot of Oz decor, too. $

**Emerald City Grill.** 225 Genesee St.; (315) 687-7453. Next door to the Baum Museum. Serving good soups, sandwiches, burgers, fried fish, fried Oreos, a munchkin menu, and lots of Oz decor. $

**Oz Cream Parlor.** 277 Genesee St.; (315) 687-5504. Oz-some soda fountain classics. $

## Where to Stay

**Brae Loch.** 5 Albany St., Cazenovia; (315) 655-3431; www.braelochinn.com. Scottish-style inn with twelve rooms, private bath, cable TV, Wi-Fi, restaurant, and complimentary continental breakfast. $$–$$$

**Lincklaen House.** 79 Albany St., Cazenovia; (315) 655-3461; www.lincklaenhouse.com. Twenty-three rooms and suites in a former stagecoach inn, free Wi-Fi, cable TV, and two restaurants, one casual and one upscale. $$–$$$

# Sherburne

Take NY 13 south to NY 80.

## Rogers Environmental Education Center  (all ages)

2721 NY 80; (607) 674-4017; www.dec.ny.gov/education. Grounds open year-round dawn to dusk; center open weekdays 8:30 a.m. to 4:45 p.m., Sat (and Sun in June through Aug) 1 to 4:45 p.m. Closed state holidays. Free.

The visitor center houses exhibits on native plants and animals, and the upper gallery offers a view of the marsh with live audio piped in. Outside, there are 6 miles of marked trails meandering through the 600 acres of woodlands, wetlands, meadows, and farm fields. A good choice for families is the 2-mile trail starting at the visitor center; it has a companion trail guide booklet explaining the hike highlights. Programs for families are planned throughout the year, and free ranger-guided walks are offered year-round almost every Sat at 1:30 p.m.

## Bowman Lake State Park  (all ages)

745 Bliven Sherman Rd., Oxford; (607) 334-2718 or (800) 456-CAMP; www.nys parks.state.ny.us. Eight miles northwest of Oxford off NY 220. Open year-round; campgrounds open May through mid-Oct. $.

There are several easy but sometimes soggy trails to explore over 660 acres of beautiful hardwood forest, with swimming, rowboating, and fishing opportunities at the thirty-five-acre, trout-stocked artificial lake, and 103 species of birds to spot.

## Wampum

Wampum was made of tiny white and purple beads carved from whelk, clam, and oyster shells, drilled with stone awls, and woven into belts using hemp and deer sinew. Designs were incorporated in the beadwork to record treaties or documents, and it was used for barter among Native Americans for at least 4,000 years before the Europeans arrived. It wasn't that the material wampum was made from was rare—in fact, shells were abundant everywhere. Rather, the value of wampum came from the document itself as well as the labor and craftsmanship put into its creation. The Europeans valued the purple beads at twice the price of the white ones, but the Native Americans used the purple beads on wampum belts to signify sorrow or serious political issues. When the Dutch traders introduced steel awls to the Algonquins, the beads became easier to make, and wampum was devalued as a currency.

## Where to Eat

**D&D Diner.** 47 N. Main St.; (607) 674-9697. Diner fare served for breakfast, lunch, and dinner. $

## Where to Stay

**Sherburne Motel.** 63 Main St.; (607) 674-5511. Eleven rooms. $

# Binghamton

South on NY 12.

The Industrial Revolution boosted Binghamton's fortunes, but it was the paternalistic pride of George F. Johnson, founder of Endicott-Johnson, that really transformed the city. Long before it was required, or even fashionable, Johnson treated his employees like family and provided health care, an eight-hour work day, and company-sponsored picnics and ball games. Named the "Carousel Capital of the World" for the six restored antique merry-go-rounds scattered around town, this was also the boyhood home of *The Twilight Zone* creator Rod Serling.

### Roberson Museum and Science Center (ages 10 and up)

30 Front St.; (888) 269-5325; www.roberson.org. Open Wed, Thurs, Sat, and Sun noon to 5 p.m., Fri noon to 9 p.m.; closed to the public Mon and Tues, and Easter, Thanksgiving Day, New Year's Day, and the first two weeks in Jan. Link Planetarium shows Fri 8 p.m., Sat and Sun 1, 2, and 3 p.m.; adults $$, children $, under 4 free.

This complex offers a wonderful blend of regional art and history as well as a science wing, planetarium, and children's center with interactive and hands-on exhibits. Recent renovations to the Carriage House created a modern pottery studio called Clayworks, and the mansion across the street was acquired to become the home of the Decker Arts and Cultural Center. Near the entrance to the museum is the Binghamton Visitor Center, which houses the Susquehanna Heritage Area exhibits and provides a good introduction to the Triple Cities with a multimedia presentation and maps of the towns.

### Kopernik Observatory & Science Center (all ages)

698 Underwood Rd., Vestal; (607) 748-3685; www.kopernik.org. Open to the public every Fri night at 7:30 p.m. Mar through Nov, and on special weekend event nights Dec through Feb. $.

Considered to be the best sited and best equipped public observatory in the northeast United States for more than a quarter century, this is also the state's first science laboratory facility designed especially for teachers, students in kindergarten through grade 12, and their families.

Twenty acres of darkness surround the domes containing three observatory and twelve portable telescopes, a solar scope, a computer, physics and laser lab, a NASA

## The Carousels of **Broome County**

When George F. Johnson was a boy, he couldn't afford a ticket to ride a carousel. He decided that if he ever became rich, he would make sure no one would be deprived of that joy. Years later, as owner of twenty-two shoe factories, he made good on his promise and commissioned six county fair–style carousels complete with calliopes. The price of a ticket now, as it was then, is one piece of litter, and if you ride all six, you'll receive a special button. Call or check www.gobroomecounty.com.for more information.

**Ross Park.** Morgan Road, Binghamton; (607) 724-5461.

**Recreation Park.** Beethoven Street, Binghamton; (607) 722-9166 or (607) 772-7017.

**George W. Johnson Park.** Oak Hill Avenue, Endicott; (607) 757-2427.

**West Endicott Park.** Page Avenue., Endicott; (607) 786-2970.

**C. Fred Johnson Park.** C. F. J. Boulevard, Johnson City; (607) 797-9098.

**Highland Park.** Hooper Road, Endwell; (607) 786-2970.

Satellite Downlink, a solar-energy array, an earthquake station, and an annual RocketFest, where kids can build and blastoff their handmade missiles.

### Discovery Center of the Southern Tier (all ages)

60 Morgan Rd.; (607) 773-8661; www.thediscoverycenter.org. Open year-round; summer hours Mon through Fri 10 a.m. to 4 p.m., Sat 10 a.m. to 5 p.m.; closed Sun in July and Aug and major holidays. $.

Located in Ross Park, this wonderful interactive museum has thirty hands-on exhibits kids can fly, drive, dig, shop, paint, and perform their way through. Fantasy play is big here, with a pint-size plane, a TV studio, a grocery store, and doctor and dentist offices, all complete with costumes and props. A new exhibit, Pedal Power, is about bicycles, and outside the Story Garden has taken root, with thirteen interactive areas focusing on themes from children's literature.

### Binghamton Zoo at Ross Park (all ages)

60 Morgan Rd.; (607) 724-5461; www.rossparkzoo.com. Open Apr through Nov, daily 10 a.m. to 5 p.m.; June, July, and Aug, until 8 p.m. every Thurs and second Sat of the month. Adults $$, children $, 2 and under free.

Built in the late nineteenth century, this is the fifth-oldest zoo in the country, with more than 180 animals in residence, including big cats, bears, and wolves. Financial problems caused the zoo to lose its accreditation in 2005, but new renovations and refurbishments have brought this beloved menagerie back to life. A new addition is the Wonders of Nature exhibit, featuring snow leopards, cougars, gila monsters and golden lion tamarins. Animal presentations and artifact carts add to the fun, and every Aug you can attend "Feast With The Beasts," a progressive dinner throughout the zoo, featuring food from regional restaurants. Nearby is the beautiful Ross Park Carousel, with sixty jumping horses, four abreast, two chariots with monkeys, and an original fifty-one-key Wurlitzer Military Band Organ.

## Chenango Valley State Park (all ages)

**153 State Park Rd. (off NY 369, 12 miles northeast of town), Chenango Forks; (607) 648-5251; www.nysparks.state.ny.us. Park open year-round; campgrounds and cabins open May through Labor Day. $$.**

At the end of the last ice age, retreating glaciers left behind colossal chucks of ice that melted to form the two kettle lakes of Lily and Chenango. Today, this 1,075-acre park is

# Also in **the Area**

**Game It Family Fun Center.** 225 Harrison Ave., Endicott; (607) 785-7612; www.gameitfun.com.

**Conklin Sports Park.** 942 Conklin Rd., Conklin; (607) 771-7526.

**New Image Roller Dome.** 3116 Lawndale St., Endwell; (607) 785-5012.

**Skate Estate.** 3401 Old Vestal Rd., Vestal; (607) 797-9000; www.skateestate.com.

**Greater Binghamton Sports Complex.** 1500 Airport Rd., Binghamton; (607) 729-5165; www.southerntiersportscenter.com.

**Northgate Speedway.** 1250 Upper Front St., Binghamton; (607) 723-1362; www.na-motorsports.com/Tracks/NY/Northgate.html.

**Chenango Ice Rink.** 614 River Rd., Binghamton; (607) 648-9202; www.chenangoicerink.com.

**Finch Hollow Nature Center.** 1394 Oakdale Rd., Johnson City; www.go broomecounty.com.

**Enchanted Gardens.** 2975 NY 7, Harpursville; (607) 693-2755; www.canoe rental.net.

**Windy Hill Candle Factory & Candy Store.** 5201 NY 79, Port Crane; (607) 693-2429; www.4greatcandy.com.

**Cutler Botanical Garden.** 840 Upper Front St., Binghamton; (607) 584-9966; www.cce.cornell.edu/broome.

a birder's paradise, and the lakes are brimming with bass, bullhead, perch, and trout. Cabins and campsites are available, as well as swimming at a sandy beach, boat rentals, a nature trail, a playground, a picnic area, and an eighteen-hole golf course. In winter, sledding, cross-country skiing, and ice-skating are cool ways to chill out at this glacial gift.

## Where to Eat

**The Lost Dog Café.** 222 Water St.; (607) 771-6063; www.lostdogcafe.net. Innovative, eclectic, fun food, from rigatoni to grilled chicken, with a fried cheesecake topped with chocolate, raspberry, and caramel sauce for dessert. The cafe is named after Clarese, the resident Chihuahua, who looks, um . . . lost.

**Number 5.** 33 S. Washington St.; (607) 723-0555; www.number5restaurant.com. Steak, seafood, chicken specialties, served in a former 1897 fire station, recently renovated. Early-bird specials, a children's menu, lots of fire memorabilia, and live entertainment on weekends. $$$$

## Where to Stay

**Fairfield Inn Binghamton.** 864 Upper Front St.; (607) 651-1000; www.marriott.com. Eighty-two newly renovated rooms, free Wi-Fi, complimentary hot breakfast, indoor pool, and spa. $$

**The Grand Royale Hotel.** 80 State St.; (607) 722-0000; www.clarionhotel.com. Beaux Arts architecture with sixty-one rooms, refrigerator, microwave, complimentary continental breakfast, coffee, and homemade cookies, and convenient to Ross Park. $$–$$$

# Oneonta

From Binghamton, head north along I-88.

Oneonta was a huge railroad town in its day, and the world's largest roundhouse was at the center of it all.

### National Soccer Hall of Fame (all ages)

**Wright National Soccer Campus, 18 Stadium Circle; (607)432-3351; www.soccerhall.org. Open Apr through June, daily 10 a.m. to 5 p.m.; July through Labor Day, daily 9 a.m. to 6 p.m.; after Labor Day through Mar, Wed through Sun 10 a.m. to 5 p.m.; closed Thanksgiving, Christmas, and New Year's Day. Adults $$$, children 6 to 12 $$, 5 and under free.**

Called football by the rest of the world, soccer is played by over 240 million people from more than 200 countries, making it the most popular sport on the planet. This multimillion-dollar, state-of-the-art museum celebrates the national superstars of "the beautiful game" and the powers behind the pitch. More than 100,000 items are amassed here, from trophies and team rosters to uniforms and photographs, chronicling the history of the sport. Get your game on at the Zone, where you can practice power shots and headers, or test your video skills at a Major League Soccer Playstation kiosk. Tournaments, games, and clinics are scheduled throughout the season, and the Hall of Fame inducts new members every summer.

### Science Discovery Center (all ages)

I-88, exit 15, SUNY College, College at Oneonta, Physical Science Building, 108 Ravine Parkway; (607) 436-2011; www.oneonta.edu/academics/scdisc. Open Sept through June, Thurs through Sat noon to 4 p.m.; July and Aug, Mon through Sat noon to 4 p.m. Closed major holidays. **Free,** but donations welcome.

This interactive science museum has more than seventy exhibits kids can get their hands on, ranging from electrical experiments and optical illusions to matter and motion models.

### Oneonta World of Learning (all ages)

Multiple locations; (607) 433-0160; www.oneontaworldoflearning.com and www.oneonta childrensmuseum.blogspot.com. $$.

Founded by three motivated moms, this movable feast of fun known as OWL is a children's museum on the hoof, presently awaiting a permanent home. In the meantime, activities, workshops, concerts, and theatrical experiences are offered at various venues around town. Check out their Web site and blog for current event information.

### Gilbert Lake State Park (all ages)

CR 12, off NY 205, Laurens; (607) 432-2114; www.nysparks.state.ny.us. Park open year-round; campground open May through mid-Oct. Summer parking fee $$.

This popular park 10 miles north of town has three ponds plus the lake for swimming, fishing and boating, as well as 12 miles of trails for hiking in summer and cross-country skiing in winter, thirty-three cabins, and 221 campsites. On the grounds is a small museum chronicling the history of the Civilian Conservation Corps, a work program for unemployed youth during the Great Depression. Much of what you see here, including the roads, trails, cabins, stone fireplaces, picnic shelters, and landscaping, was built by 200 teenagers, the "Tree Army" of President Franklin D. Roosevelt, and many earned their high school diplomas at the same time.

## Where to Eat

**Brooks House of Barbecue.** 5560 NY 7; (800) 498-2445; www.brooksbbq.com. Family owned for three generations, this place has the largest indoor charcoal barbecue pit in the East, and their chicken and ribs are awesome. One of the secrets of their success may be their terrific homemade sauces, which you can watch being bottled on-site, at a rate of 1,400 bottles per hour. $–$$

**The Farmhouse at Emmons.** 5649 NY 7; (607) 432-7374; www.thefarmhouseatemmons.com. Really good regional American cuisine, created by a Culinary Institute of America–trained chef, featuring fresh seafood, steaks, poultry, vegetarian specials, and a children's menu. $$–$$$$

## Where to Stay

**Christopher's Restaurant and Country Lodge.** Southside Oneonta; (607) 432-2444;

www.christopherslodging.com. Unique Adirondack-style lodge rooms, free Wi-Fi and phone, plus a great restaurant with children's menu. $–$$$

**Deer Haven Campground and Cabins.** Chestnut Street; (607) 433-9654; www.oneontacampground.com. Campsites, cabin, RV sites and rentals, Wi-Fi, playground, picnic pavilions, and a new pool. $–$$

# Cooperstown

Northeast on I-88, then NY 28 north.

James Fenimore Cooper's *Leatherstocking Tales* immortalized his Glimmerglass Country, but today it's probably best known for its passion for baseball. If you visit in summer, plan to park your car at one of the three **free** lots around the village, then tour the town on the trolley. An unlimited day pass gives families hassle-free, hop-on, hop-off options at points of interest for a minimal charge, and it's fun!

## National Baseball Hall of Fame & Museum (ages 5 and up)

25 Main St.; (607) 547-7200 or (888) HALL-OF-FAME; www.baseballhall.org. Open daily year-round, Memorial Day weekend through Labor Day, Mon 9 a.m. to 9 p.m.; after Labor Day through the Thurs before Memorial Day weekend, 9 a.m. to 5 p.m. Closed Thanksgiving, Christmas, and New Year's. Adults $$$, children 7 to 12 $, children under 7 **free;** ask about combination tickets.

In 1839 Abner Doubleday chased the cows out of his neighbor's pasture and invented the national pastime of baseball. That's the local legend, anyway, and there's no shortage of legends at this excellent museum. Gloves, bats, uniforms, trading cards, and other memorabilia are on display here, with multimedia presentations of historical footage of the greats of the game, including special exhibits on the "Negro leagues" and women in baseball.

In a successful effort to make the museum more accessible to kids, costumed presenters are around to answer questions, self-guided scavenger hunts are offered, and family-friendly flip-panels are scattered throughout, on topics such as prejudice and forming clubs. An interactive exhibit allows kids to tap out Morse Code for "home run" just as in the early days of sports reporting. A new area for two- to eight-year-olds is the Sandlot Kids' Clubhouse, filled with baseball books, games and toys, set on a rubberized miniature Miracle League field and designed for children with special needs. As they leave, kids can become junior members of the Hall of Fame, receive a personalized membership card, **free** admission to the museum for a year, a poster, and for those who completed the scavenger hunt, a pack of complimentary commemorative cards.

# Also in **the Area**

**Cooperstown Fun Park.** 4850 NY 28, Cooperstown; (607) 547-2767; www
.cooperstownfunpark.com.

**Fly Creek Cider Mill.** 288 Goose St., Fly Creek; (607) 547-9692; www.flycreek
cidermill.com.

**Hogs Hollow Farm.** Basswood Road, off NY 51 north, Burlington Flats; (607)
965-8555.

**Cooperstown & Charlotte Valley Railroad.** Leatherstocking Railway Historical Society, P.O. Box 681, Oneonta 13820; (607) 432-2429; www.lrhs.com.

## Doubleday Field and Batting Range (all ages)
1 Doubleday Court, Doubleday Field, Main Street; (607) 547-2270. Batting range at 2 Doubleday Court; (607) 547-1852; www.cooperstown.org. Season runs Apr through Oct. $.

The oldest baseball diamond in the world, this is the original field of dreams. An average
of 325 games are played here in season, and in Aug the dream teams arrive for the Hall of
Fame's All-Star and Old Timers' games. Just in case the scouts are looking for a midseason
replacement, polish your skills at the batting cages next door.

## Cooperstown Bat Company (ages 7 and up)
118 Main St.; (888) 547-2415; www.cooperstownbat.com. $$

Watch the birth of a bat at their nearby Fly Creek factory, or stop at their shop across
from Doubleday Field and buy a bat laser-blazed with your name, stats, or team logo. A
Wonderboy or Savoy Special could be waiting here for the next "Natural."

## Heroes of Baseball Wax Museum (ages 5 and up)
99 Main St.; (607) 547-1273; www.baseballwaxmuseum.com. Open mid-June through Labor
Day, 9 a.m. to 9 p.m.; after Labor Day, 10 a.m. to 6 p.m. Adults $$, children $.

A block from the Baseball Hall of Fame, this fun museum features faux figures of favorite
ballplayers in historical dioramas, a virtual-reality batting cage, more than a thousand
autographed items, a Baseball Bloopers movie theater, an outdoor cafe, and a gift shop.

## Farmers' Museum (all ages)
5775 NY 80 (Lake Road); (607) 547-1450 or (888) 547-1450; www.farmersmuseum.org. Open
daily mid-May through mid-Oct, 10 a.m. to 5 p.m. Call for fall and spring hours. Ask about
combination tickets. Adults $$$, children 7 to 12 $, children under 7 free.

Founded in 1943, this was one of the first living-history museums in the country. Stroll
past a dozen restored buildings at the Crossroads Village as costumed guides dem-
onstrate nineteenth-century skills and crafts, from spinning and weaving to baking

and blacksmithing. More than 23,000 artifacts of agriculture are displayed, food and medicinal crops are grown, and heritage breed animals roam the pastures. A Children's Barnyard at the Lippitt Farmstead has barnyard babies to pet and sheep shearing shows. The grandest hoax of all time, the Cardiff Giant, resides here, as well. Next door is the Empire State Carousel, a merry-go-round museum menagerie of twenty-five hand-carved animals representing the natural and agricultural resources found in New York. Take a ride in a scallop shell, the state shellfish, or an Erie Canal boat, as you whirl past panels depicting other notable New Yorkers, like Uncle Sam and Susan B. Anthony, and reflect on the diversity of the Empire State, depicted in eleven marvelous mirror frames.

### Fenimore Art Museum  (all ages)

5798 NY 80 (Lake Rd.); (607) 547-1400 or (888) 547-1450; www.fenimoreartmuseum.org. Open daily mid-May through mid-Oct, 10 a.m. to 5 p.m.; call for spring and fall hours; closed Jan through Mar. Adults $$, children 7 to 12 $, under 7 free.

Across the road from the Farmer's Museum, this elegant neo-Georgian mansion houses an amazing assortment of American fine and folk art, plus a photography archive with more than 60,000 images of a changing Cooperstown. The new American Indian Art wing displays over 850 objects from the Thaw Collection, and outside is a full-size reproduction of an eighteenth-century Mohawk Barkhouse.

### Glimmerglass State Park  (all ages)

1527 CR 31; (607) 547-8662; www.nysparks.com. Hyde Hall; 267 Glimmerglass State Park Road; (607) 547-5098; park open year-round; Hyde Hall open 10 a.m. to 4 p.m. $$.

Inspired by beautiful Lake Otsego, this is the "Glimmerglass" of James Fenimore Cooper's *Leatherstocking Tales*. Forest paths lead to a lake lookout, wildflowers and wildlife may be seen along the Woodland and Beaver Pond Nature Trails, and picnic pavilions, a playground, and a sandy beach keep kids busy. Inside the park is the nineteenth-century neoclassical mansion Hyde Hall, an architectural masterpiece currently under restoration. Campgrounds are open May through Sept, and in winter activities include ice-skating, ice fishing, and cross-country skiing.

### Petrified Creatures Museum of Natural History  (all ages)

NYUS 20, Richfield Springs; (315) 858-2868 or (315) 627-6399; www.cooperstownchamber .org/pcm. Open mid-May through mid-Sept 9 a.m. to 5 p.m. $$.

This is the oldest museum in central New York, founded in 1934, but the petrified Devonian sea creatures found here beat that by about 300 million years. Tools are provided for excavating these tiny critters, and you can keep what you find. Kids will definitely enjoy the brightly painted, life-size dinosaur replicas poised to pounce along the nature paths, the hands-on discovery center, and the gift shop filled with fossils, rocks, T shirts, and toys.

## Where to Eat

**Alex & Ika.** 149 Main St.; (607) 547-4070; www.alexandika.com. Innovative international gourmet cuisine with a Swedish flavor, serving hanger steaks, sesame seared wild salmon, coconut curry with cherry carrot salsa, and maple crème brûlée. $$-$$$

**Blue Mingo Grill.** 6098 NY 80; (607) 547-7496; www.bluemingogrill.com. Located at Sam Smith's Boatyard, overlooking Otsego Lake, serving salads, burgers, sandwiches, wraps, steaks, seafood, ribs, poultry, homemade banana bread, and a children's menu. $-$$

**Fly Creek Cider Mill Restaurant.** 288 Goose St., Fly Creek; (607) 547-9692; www.flycreekcidermill.com. Located at a historic 150-year-old cider mill and orchard, this family farm features fresh-baked cookies and pies, homemade soups and chili served in a bread bowl, pulled pork barbecue sandwiches, spiced apple cider, and colossal cinnamon buns. $

## Where to Stay

**Cooperstown Family Campground.** 230 Petkewec Rd., Cooperstown; (607) 293-7766; www.cooperstownfamilycampground.com. Campsites, RV hookups, twin ponds, recreation hall and arcade, swimming pool, playground, nature trail, rental paddleboats, mini-golf, pony, hay, & tractor rides, reindeer, Shetland ponies, and pygmy goats, and cow milking in the morning. $

**The Inn at Cooperstown.** 16 Chestnut St.; (607) 547-5756; www.innatcooperstown.com. Historic nineteenth-century country inn with seventeen spotless rooms, a delicious breakfast buffet, and special package deals, from bat making to brewery touring to an evening of anecdotes told by Babe Ruth's granddaughter. $$-$$$$

**Lake Front Motel, Restaurant & Marina.** 10 Fair St.; (607) 547-9511; www.lakefrontmotelandrestaurant.com. Forty-five rooms, some with private porches overlooking Otsego Lake, cable TV, indoor and outdoor dining at the restaurant, and boat tours on the *Glimmerglass Queen,* departing from the motel dock. $-$$

# North Blenheim

Take NY 28 south toward Oneonta, NY 23 east to Grand Gorge, then NY 30 north.

The longest single-span covered bridge in the country crosses Schoharie Creek here, and the same road (NY 30) will afford great views and access to the natural landmark known as Vroman's Nose.

## Blenheim-Gilboa Pumped Storage Power Project (ages 7 and up)

**1378 NY 30; (518) 827-6121 or (800) 724-0309; www.nypa.gov. Visitor center open daily 10 a.m. to 5 p.m., closed major holidays. Reservations must be made for tours of power plant. Free.**

The dynamics of hydropower are demonstrated here, New York's largest energy storage plant, with state-of-the-art exhibits and interactive displays at the newly renovated visitor center. Next door is the Lansing Manor, an early nineteenth-century country house, filled with furnishings of the era. Nearby is the 2½-mile Bluebird Trail, named after the state bird and a good place to spot that elusive warbler. With advance reservations, families can venture underground to view giant turbine generators that, by recycling the water between the Blenheim and Gilboa Reservoirs, generate 1.6 billion kilowatt hours of electricity a year.

### Mine Kill State Park (all ages)

161 Mine Kill State Park; (518) 827-6111; www.nysparks.state.ny.us. Open year-round, dawn to dusk; summer parking fee $.

Overlooking the reservoir of the Power Project, this popular 650-acre park offers a nature trail, 8 miles of hiking and biking trails, three swimming pools, ball fields and courts, boating, fishing, picnic areas, and a scenic overlook of Mine Kill Falls. Swimming lessons are offered in summer, and soccer camp and local leagues take the regulation sized pitch in season.

### Gilboa Museum (ages 5 and up)

122 Stryker Rd., Gilboa; (607) 588-6894; www.gilboahome.com. **Free.**

Eons ago a fern forest grew here, along the shores of an ancient Devonian Sea. Discovered in the 1920s, these are the fossilized remains of the oldest trees in the world. About fifty of the ancient tree stumps were found, and although many were shipped to the State Museum, Gilboa still has nine of them, as well as artifacts of the area's agriculture. Outside, at the Gilboa Dam overlook, imagine what life was like here 380 million years ago, when the Earth began its transition from totally marine towards terrestrial and temperate.

## Where to Eat

**Waterfall House.** 714 NY 990V, Gilboa; (607) 588-9891. Steaks, seafood, chicken, and kid-friendly appetizers. $–$$

## Where to Stay

**Country Roads Campgrounds.** 144 Peaceful Rd., Gilboa; (518) 827-6397; www.countryroadscampground.com. Located on a scenic hilltop, with 118 campsites, RV hookups, cabin rentals, a swimming pool, Jacuzzi, playground, tot lot, ball fields, laundry, game room, satellite TV, free Wi-Fi, and special activities including hayrides, bonfires, and bingo. If you happen to have your horse with you, they have campsites that can accommodate both two- and four-legged guests. $

**Nickerson Park Campground.** 378 Stryker Rd., Gilboa; (607) 588-7327; www.nickersonparkcampground.com. Three hundred and seventy grassy, wooded, or waterfront sites on a hundred acres bordered by the Schoharie Creek, with great fishing, swimming, picnic pavilions, an in-ground pool, a sports area, an arcade, Wi-Fi, wagon rides, and holiday-themed family events, festivals, and ice-cream socials.

## Suggested **Reading**

*Drums Along the Mohawk*, by Walter D. Edmonds

*The Pioneers*, by James Fenimore Cooper

*Saratoga Secret*, by Betsy Sterman

*Guns for General Washington*, by Seymour Reit

*Little Maid of Mohawk Valley*, by Alice Turner Curtis

*The Minute Boys of the Mohawk Valley*, by James Otis

*Marco Paul's Travels on the Erie Canal*, by Jacob Abbott

# Schoharie

Continue north on NY 30.

Known as the "Breadbasket of the American Revolution," the rich farmlands of this area yielded the food that fed the troops of General George Washington.

### **Old Stone Fort**  (all ages)

**145 Fort Rd.; (518) 295-7192; www.oldstonefort.org. Open May through Oct, Tues through Sat, 10 a.m. to 5 p.m., Sun noon to 5 p.m. Closed Mon except in July and Aug. $, free for children under 5.**

A former church built in 1772, the Stone Fort was unsuccessfully attacked by Mohawk chief Joseph Brant during the largest British raid in the area. An interesting collection of more than 50,000 artifacts, automobiles, fossils, and firearms are exhibited, and costumed interpreters guide you through the complex of buildings on the site, from a one-room schoolhouse and a Dutch barn, to a Greek Revival mansion and the William Badgely Museum.

# Howes Cave

Continue north on NY 30 to NY 30A north, then connect with NY 7 west.

One hot summer day in 1842, local farmer Lester Howe became curious as to why his cows were standing in the middle of the pasture instead of under the shade of nearby trees. Upon investigation, he discovered a small crevice in the ground with a cool breeze rushing up from it. Lowering himself by ropes, he explored more than a mile of the subterranean cavern, and a short time later he opened the caves to the public.

# New York **Trivia**

People of the Iroquois Confederacy were matrilineal, with each household headed by the family's oldest woman. In peacetime these women chose the clan chiefs, but during war the men appointed their own leaders.

### Howe Caverns (all ages)

**255 Discovery Dr.; (518) 296-8900; www.howecaverns.com. Open daily Apr through Oct, 9 a.m. to 6 p.m.; Nov through Mar, 9 a.m. to 5 p.m.; closed Thanksgiving Day and Christmas. Adults $$$, children $$.**

Descend 156 feet, via elevator, to the heart of Howe Caverns, central New York's oldest tourist attraction. Formed millions of years ago, the one-and-a-half-hour guided tour takes you past shimmering stalactites and stalagmites and ends with a boat ride on the enchanting underground Lake Venus. Gemstone mining, geode cutting, a gift shop, cafe, and a Sweet Shop with homemade fudge offer above-ground fun.

### Secret Caverns (all ages)

**671 Caverns Rd., between NY 7 and US 20; (518) 296-8558; www.secretcaverns.com. Open daily June through Aug, 9 a.m. to 6 p.m.; May and Sept, 10 a.m. to 4:30 p.m.; balance of the season, 10 a.m. to 4 p.m. Adults $$$, children ages 6 to 15 $$, children 5 and under free.**

Left in a natural state, these caverns retain much of their "wild" character. Guided one-hour tours are offered, gleaming flow stone and stalactites and stalagmites bloom everywhere, and a 100-foot underground waterfall cascades down the wall at the far end.

### Iroquois Indian Museum (all ages)

**324 Caverns Rd.; (518) 296-8949; www.iroquoismuseum.org. Open early Sept through Dec and Apr through June, Tues through Sat 10 a.m. to 5 p.m., Sun noon to 5 p.m.; July through Labor Day weekend, Mon through Sat 10 a.m. to 5 p.m., Sun noon to 5 p.m.; closed Jan through Mar and major holidays. Adults $$, children 5 to 12 $, under 5 free.**

The art and artifacts of the Iroquois people from past to present are displayed in this wonderful longhouse museum. The Children's Museum downstairs offers activities from beading bracelets to making music and programs featuring native dances, stories, crafts, and nature walks.

### Caverns Creek Grist Mill Museum (all ages)

**259 Caverns Rd.; (518) 296-8448; www.cavernscreekgristmill.com. $.**

A National Historic Landmark, this 1816 restored gristmill's 1,400-pound millstone is powered by a twelve-foot waterwheel. Exhibits at the museum explain the operations of this pioneer powerhouse, and after you've done the self-guided tour and taken a stroll along the millstream, you can truthfully say you've been through the mill.

## Where to Eat

**The George Mann Tory Tavern.** 104 Vrooman Cross Rd., Schoharie; (518) 295-7128; www.torytavern.com. Once the meeting place for Tories (people loyal to England) and Indians loyal to the Tories, this restored eighteenth-century tavern is helmed by a Culinary Institute of America–trained chef. The American gourmet menu changes daily and uses locally grown bounty of the county, with half-size portions available for children. $$$

## Where to Stay

**Howe Caverns Motel.** 255 Discovery Dr.; (518) 296-8950; www.howecaverns.com. Twenty-one rooms, each with a mountain view; family suites with four double beds; swimming pool, restaurant, cribs available, microwave and refrigerator in most rooms, satellite TV, and kids stay free in the room with adults; across from Howe Caverns. $–$$$

## For More Information

**Regional Information.** (518) 434-1217 or (800) 732-8259.

**Albany County Convention and Visitor's Bureau.** (518) 434-1217 or (800) 258-3582; www.albany.org.

**Fulton County Chamber of Commerce.** (518) 725-0641 or (800) 676-3858; www.fultoncountyny.org.

**Rensselaer County Tourism.** (518) 272-7232; www.rensco.com.

**Saratoga County Chamber of Commerce.** (518) 584-3255; www.saratoga.org.

**Schenectady County Tourism.** (518) 372-5656 or (800) 962-8007; www.sayschenectady.org.

**Washington County Tourism.** (888) 203-8622; www.washingtoncounty.org.

**Cooperstown Chamber of Commerce.** (607) 547-9983; www.cooperstownchamber.org and www.thisiscooperstown.com.

**Chenango County Chamber of Commerce.** (607) 334-1429 or (877) 243-6264; www.chenangocounty.org and www.chenangony.org.

# Schoharie **County Bounty**

**Barber's Farm Greenhouses.** 3621 NY 30, Middleburgh; (518) 827-5454; www.barbersfarm.com.

**Cooper's Ark Farm.** 145 Ark Lane, Schoharie; (518) 295-7662; www.coopersarkfarm.com.

**Maple Hill Farm.** 107 C Crapser Rd., Cobleskill; (518) 234-4858 and (866) 291-8100; www.maplehillfarms.biz.

**Schoharie Valley Farms.** The Carrot Barn, NY 30, Schoharie; (518) 295-7139; www.schohariefarms.com.

**Borhinger's Fruit Farm.** 3992 NY 30, Middleburgh; (518) 827-5783.

**Terrace Mountain Orchard.** Apple Blossom Lane, Schoharie; (518) 295-7755.

# Other Things to See and Do
## in the Mohawk Valley Region

**Cherry Plain State Park.** 26 State Park Rd., Cherry Plain; (518) 733-5400 or (518) 279-1155; www.nysparks.state.ny.us.

**Flag Acres Zoo.** 2 Rowley Rd., Hoosick Falls; (518) 686-3159; www.flagacres zoo.com.

**Sherman's Park.** NY 10 and NY 29, Caroga Lake; (518) 835-4110; www.shermans park.com.

**Pine Lake Park.** 136 Timberline Lane, Caroga Lake; www.pinelakepark.com.

**Delta Lake State Park.** 8797 NY 46, Rome; (315) 337-4670; www.nysparks .state.ny.

**Eagle Mills Cider Company.** 383 CR 138, Broadalbin; (518) 883-8700; www .eaglemillsfun.com.

**Albany Institute of History & Art.** 125 Washington Ave., Albany; (518) 463-4478; www.albanyinstitute.org.

**Fulton County Historical Society Museum.** 237 Kingsboro Ave., Gloversville; (518) 725-2203; www.fultoncountymuseum.com.

**Dakota Ridge Llama Farm.** 189 East High St., Ballston Spa; (518) 885-0756; www.dakotaridgefarm.com.

**Schoharie Llamas.** 311 Warner Hill Rd., Schoharie; (518) 295-7454.

**Northeast Classic Car Museum.** 24 Rexford St., NY 23, Norwich; (607) 334-AUTO; www.classiccarmuseum.org.

**Roland B. Hill Museum of Indian Archeology.** 361 Main St., Otsego; (607) 988-2229.

**Florence Jones Reineman Wildlife Sanctuary.** 155 Wyman Rd., Dolgeville; (518) 568-7101.

**Greenwood Park.** 153 Greenwood Rd., Lisle; (607) 862-9933; www.gobroome county.com.

**Hawkins Pond & Nature Area.** Scouten Hill Road, Windsor; (607) 693-1389; www.gobroomecounty.com.

**Nathaniel Cole Park.** NY 17, West Windsor; (607) 693-1389; www.gobroome county.com.

**Herkimer Chamber of Commerce.** (315) 866-7820 or (877) 984-4636; www.herkimer countychamber.com.

**Madison County Tourism.** (315)684-7320 or (800) 684-7320; www.madisontourism .com.

**Montgomery County Chamber of Commerce.** (518) 853-1800 or (800) 743-7337; www.montgomerycountyny.com.

**Oneida County Convention and Visitors Bureau.** (315) 724-7221 or (800) 426-3132; www.oneidacountycvb.com.

**Schoharie County Chamber of Commerce.** (518) 295-6550; www.schoharie chamber.com.

# The
# Finger Lakes
## Region

Slender strands of sapphire water sparkle amid pastoral farmlands and craggy gorges, a glacier's good-bye caress during the last couple of ice ages. The Haudenosaunee believed the lakes were formed when the Great Spirit reached down to bless the land, leaving behind two handprints. Whatever version you believe, the Finger Lakes have undoubtedly been graced with the spirit of such great men and women as Samuel Clemens, Harriet Tubman, Tahgahjute, George Eastman, and Susan B. Anthony. This was the heart of the Iroquois Confederacy until 1779, when George Washington ordered the destruction of all Native American settlements in the region. The Industrial Revolution spurred factory growth, and country crossroads blossomed into major industrial hubs with the opening of the Erie Canal. The fertile farmlands fed the nation until the mid-nineteenth century, when the focus shifted to fruit orchards and vineyards.

## DRIVING TIPS

Running south from Syracuse, Interstate 81 forms the eastern edge of this region, hemmed in the south by NY 17, in the west by I-390, and in the north by I-90, with NY 14 and NY 89 cutting through the center, hugging the shores of the two largest Finger Lakes, Seneca and Cayuga.

# Syracuse

Syracuse is easily reached via I-481, I-81, and I-90, and NY 5 and US 11.

Sprinkled with salt springs, this area was home to the Onondaga for thousands of years. With the opening of the Erie Canal, the town transformed into a major transportation and manufacturing hub. Incidentally, Syracuse was named after a Sicilian city that was also built around salt springs. Should you visit the Irish neighborhood of Tipperary Hill,

# THE FINGER LAKES REGION

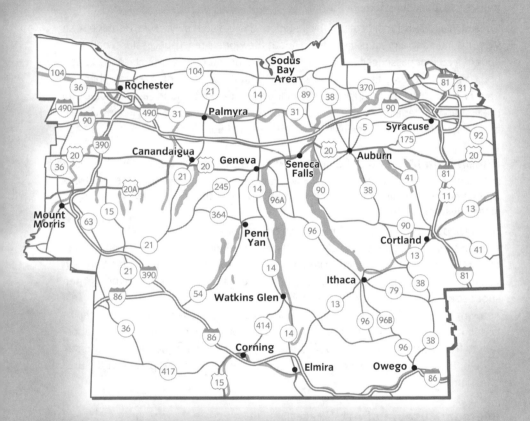

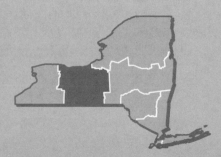

however, you'll want to take note of the "green on top" traffic light, a salute to the Irish immigrants who defied the British, and the only stoplight of its kind in the world.

### Erie Canal Museum  (all ages)

**318 Erie Blvd. East; (315) 471-0593; www.eriecanalmuseum.org. Open Mon through Sat 10 a.m. to 5 p.m., Sun 10 a.m. to 3 p.m. Closed Christmas and New Year's Day. Free, guided tours $2.50. Donations accepted.**

Housed in a former canal boat weighing station, this is also the Syracuse Heritage Area Visitor Center and a great place to learn about the world's most successful canal. Step aboard a 65-foot passenger cargo boat, check out the interactive exhibits in the Education Gallery, and view a film highlighting the adventurous history of Syracuse. Then pick up a **free** walking-tour map and begin your adventure. Renovations are scheduled for the first-floor galleries, due to reopen in 2010, and every Dec an 1800s gingerbread village of more than forty creations rises on the second floor gallery.

### Rubenstein Museum of Science and Technology (MOST)  (all ages)

**500 South Franklin St.; (315) 425-9068; www.most.org. IMAX information (315) 473-IMAX. Open Wed through Sun 10 a.m. to 5 p.m. Extended hours for IMAX movies on Sat evenings. Museum $, IMAX $$.**

Having undergone a recent $6.5 million exhibit revitalization project, this "most" fun science center offers more than 200 new hands-on exhibits in six themed areas. Travel through a huge heart and brain at Life Sciences, then explore the relationship between geology and water inside the realistic Earth Science Discovery Cave. Climb through the super-size Science Playhouse, a five-story multisensory maze of fun, then travel to Technotown, a giant "Rube Goldberg–style" audio-kinetic, interactive sculpture of machines and motion. Star search at the planetarium, or stop by the Telecommunications Laboratory to track a satellite, fly a simulator Cessna or 737, and "phone home" using Morse Code or the Internet. Afterward, you can "feel the reel" at four films playing at the Bristol IMAX Omnitheater.

### Everson Museum of Art  (all ages)

**401 Harrison St.; (315) 474-6064; www.everson.org. Open Sun, Tues, Wed, Thurs, and Fri noon to 5 p.m., Sat 10 a.m. to 5 p.m.; closed Mon. Free.**

Housed in an I. M. Pei masterpiece and with a permanent collection of more than 11,000 objects, including 700 American nineteenth-century and contemporary paintings, photographs, videos, and one of the largest collections of ceramics in the world, this is an amazing place. Artifacts from the Arts and Crafts movement are here, as are over 200 sculptures that grace the grounds and halls. Tours, talks, and classes are offered, but of special interest to families is the Art Zone downstairs, where kids can sculpt clay at the ceramic station, dress up as different people at the portrait gallery, or play with blocks, books, games, videos, and art supplies.

### The Rosamond Gifford Zoo at Burnet Park (all ages)

1 Conservation Place (off South Wilbur Avenue); (315) 435-8511; www.rosamondgiffordzoo
.org. Open year-round, daily 10 a.m. to 4:30 p.m. Closed Thanksgiving, Christmas, and New
Year's Day. Adults $$, children 3 to 15 $, 2 and under free.

From sharks and sheep to snow leopards and Amur tigers, there are nearly a 1000 wild
and domestic animals residing in naturalistic habitats at this forty-three-acre zoo. In sum-
mer, free forty-five-minute tours are offered twice daily, and a new interactive online
game, "Wolfquest," offers visitors the experience of being "part of the pack."

### Onondaga Historical Association Museum (all ages)

321 Montgomery Place; (315) 428-1864; www.cnyhistory.org. Open Wed to Fri 10 a.m. to 4
p.m., Sat and Sun 11 a.m. to 4 p.m. Free, donations appreciated.

Highlighting the history of the county in five theme areas, this interesting museum has
permanent exhibits on the Underground Railroad, Syracuse China, Syracuse Brewing, and
Franklin Automobiles, and ever-changing temporary exhibits on toys, women's suffrage,
and local history through their wonderful art collection.

### Onondaga Lake Park (all ages)

6790 Onondaga Lake Trail, Liverpool; Salt Museum, 106 Lake Drive; Sainte Marie among the
Iroquois, 6680 Onondaga Lake Parkway; (315) 453-6768 and (315) 451-7275; www.onondaga
countyparks.com. Open year-round dawn to dusk. Visitor center, museum, marina, and fort
hours vary. $.

Called "the Central Park of Central New York," this park has it all! Stop at the Joseph A.
Griffin Visitor Center for park and local tourism information and to play baseball, bocce,
or volleyball on the courts outside, or to rent a boat for a mini-voyage. For skaters, skate-
boarders, or BMX bikers, there's a new 16,900-square-foot skate park, and the wonderful
Wegmans Playground has been built for children of all ages and abilities. The nearby Wil-
low Bay area is picnic perfect, with a small playground of its own, and can be accessed
by the Wegman Tram that runs through the park, or by the Shoreline Walking Trail. Along
the shore of the lake is the Salt Museum, a tribute to the city that at one time supplied
the entire country with salt. Also on the lake shore is the site and re-creation of the sev-
enteenth-century French mission Sainte Marie among the Iroquois,
a meeting place for the Haudenosaunee and their fur-trader
friends. Costumed interpreters demonstrate colonial
crafts of carpentry, cooking, candle making, and
blacksmithing. Future plans and hopes include a
family entertainment center reminiscent of the
amusement parks of Long Branch, a historical
trail, and an archeological discovery center. Cel-
ebrate the winter holiday season with the annual
"Lights on the Lake," a 2-mile drive-through
show featuring towering, twinkling fantasy
displays.

### Camillus Erie Canal Park (all ages)

5750 Devoe Rd., Camillus; (315) 488-3409; www.eriecanalcamillus.com. Park is open year-round, museum open Sat 11 a.m. to 3 p.m., and from May through Oct, Wed 10 a.m. to 2 p.m., Thurs noon to 4 p.m. Canal boat tours and museum open May through Oct, Sun 1 to 5 p.m. Museum free, boat tours $.

Tour the towpath of a scenic section of the legendary canal aboard historic vessels or hike along 10 miles of trails, one of which leads to the 1844 Nine Mile Creek Aqueduct. The interesting Sims' Museum explains the Erie Canal experience and houses an authentic canal store and a display of antique steam engines. Step back to the Erie Canal era during the annual Towpath Day, a festival of canal, country, and children's activities from weaving and woodworking to ice-cream making and make-and-take stations.

### Beaver Lake Nature Center (all ages)

8477 East Mud Lake Rd., Baldwinsville; (315) 638-2519; http://onondagacountyparks.com/parks/beaver. Open year-round from 7:30 a.m. to dusk; closed Thanksgiving and Christmas. $.

Eight marked trails wrap around a 200-acre glacial wilderness lake and meander through a variety of habitats, home to at least 200 species of birds and over 800 varieties of plants. The Nature Center has interpretive ecosystem exhibits and offers more than 400 annual programs for families, including guided nature walks, arts and crafts workshops, and canoe and kayak adventures.

### Baltimore Woods Nature Center (all ages)

4007 Bishop Hill Rd., Marcellus; (315) 673-1350; www.baltimorewoods.org. Trails open dawn to dusk; interpretive center open Mon through Fri 9 a.m. to 4 p.m., Sat 10 a.m. to 4 p.m. Closed Sun and major holidays unless event is scheduled. $.

Six miles of trails wind through this 180-acre preserve, and eco–day camps and other environmentally conscious events are offered throughout the year for folks of all ages.

### Green Lakes State Park (all ages)

7900 Green Lakes Rd., Fayetteville; (315) 637-6111; www.nysparks.state.ny. Free.

Two glacial lakes surrounded by a lush upland forest are juxtaposed by a Robert Trent Jones 18-hole golf course that morphs into 10 miles of cross-country ski trails in winter. But what makes these bodies of water so special is that they are meromictic lakes, ecosystems where there is no seasonal mixing of surface and bottom waters, giving the lakes the potential for evidence of ancient plant and animal life. Hmmmm . . . bring your snorkel!

### Highland Forest (all ages)

1254 Highland Park Rd., Fabius; (315) 683-5550 or (315) 683-5550; www.onondagacounty parks.com. Free.

This is the oldest park in the county, with more than 20 miles of year-round trails, rustic cabins, horseback riding, a Pioneer Museum filled with antique farm toys and tools, and the Skyline Lodge, with a cafe serving brunch items, soups, stews, and sandwiches.

### Pratt's Falls (all ages)

7671 Pratt's Falls Rd., Manlius; (315) 682-5934; www.onondagacountyparks.com. Open dawn to dusk spring through early fall; 10 a.m. to 4 p.m. Nov through Mar. $.

Site of the county's first mill operation in 1796, today this geological gift from the glaciers, a scenic 137-foot waterfall, offers opportunities for hikes and picnics. For the Robin Hoods among you, there are also two archery facilities to help you sharpen your skills.

### Otisco Lake Park (all ages)

2525 Otisco Valley Rd., Marietta; (315) 689-9367; www.onondagacountyparks.com. Open daily from dawn to dusk. Free.

The newest three-acre gem in the county park system, a gift from the Hirsch family, is a lovely place to picnic, sit on a bench overlooking the lake, or cast a line into the water.

### Carpenter's Brook Fish Hatchery (all ages)

1644-1893 State Rd. 321, Elbridge; (315) 451-7275; www.onondagacountyparks.com/carpenters. Open Apr through Sept 8 a.m. to 8 p.m.; Oct through Mar 8 a.m. to 4 p.m. Free.

One of four hatcheries in the state, this one has been operating continuously since 1938, producing 70,000 brook, brown, and rainbow trout annually. Hatchery tours for five or more are available by reservation, and special programs for grandchildren with their grandparents, and young anglers of all abilities, are available in summer.

# Also in **the Area**

**Wilcox Octagon House.** 5420 W. Genesee St., Camillus; (315) 488-7800.

**Cedarvale Maple Syrup Co.** 3769 Pleasant Valley Rd., Syracuse; (315) 469-6422; www.cedarvalemaplesyrup.com.

**Mid-Lakes Navigation Company.** 11 Jordan St., Skaneateles; (315) 685-8500 or (800) 545-4318; www.midlakesnav.com.

**Carrier Dome.** 900 Irving Ave., Syracuse; (315) 443-2121, or (888) DOMETIX; www.syr.edu.

**The Museum of Automobile History.** 321 North Clinton St., Syracuse; (315) 478-9552; www.themuseumofautomobilehistory.com.

## Where to Eat

**Dinosaur Bar B Que.** 246 W. Willow St.; (315) 476-4937; www.dinosaurbarbque.com. Fun honky-tonk rib joint serving the best barbecue north of the Mason-Dixon Line, with live music most nights. $–$$

**Pastabilities.** 311 S. Franklin St.; (315) 474-1153; www.pastabilities.com. Wonderful homemade pastas, sauces, soups, salads, pizzas, and desserts, plus fresh-baked bread from their bakery across the street. $$–$$$

## Where to Stay

**DoubleTree Hotel.** 6301 NY 298, East Syracuse; (315) 432-0200; www.syracuse.double tree.com. Two hundred and fifty rooms and suites, high-speed Internet, eighty cable channels, laundry and dry cleaning, health club, indoor and outdoor pools, restaurant, room service, and warm chocolate chip cookies daily. $$$–$$$$

**Residence Inn Syracuse.** 6420 Yorktown Circle; (315) 432-4488; www.marriott.com. One hundred and two suites with full kitchens, free high-speed Internet, and complimentary grocery shopping service. $$$–$$$$

# Cortland

South on I-81.

Cortland is the ski capital of central New York, with three ski centers surrounded by fertile farmland.

## 1890 House Museum (ages 7 and up)

37 Tompkins St.; (607) 756-7551; www.1890house.org. Open year-round, Fri and Sat 1 to 4 p.m.; closed major holidays. $, children under 12 **free.**

Located in the historic district, this restored Victorian château has thirty rooms full of antiques, stained-glass windows, and beautiful hand-carved woodwork.

## Cortland's Country Music Park & Campground (all ages)

1804 Truxton Rd., NY 13; (607) 753-0377; www.cortlandcountrymusicpark.com. Open daily year-round. Campsites and shows $–$$$.

Nicknamed the "Nashville of the East," this is the home of the New York State Country Music Hall of Fame. Kick up your heels to live music or line dance on one of New York's

## New York **Trivia**

The eleven Finger Lakes are Seneca, Cayuga, Canandaigua, Keuka, Hemlock, Honeoye, Owasco, Otisco, Canadice, Coneses, and Skaneateles.

# Snow Fun in **Cortland County**

**Greek Peak.** 2000 NY 392, Cortland; (607) 835-6111 or (800) 955-2754; www .greekpeak.net.

**Labrador Mountain.** 6935 North Rd., NY 91, Truxton; (607) 842-6204 or (800) 446-9559; www.labradormtn.com.

**Song Mountain.** 1 Song Mountain Rd., Tully 13141; (315) 696-5711 or (800) 677-SONG; www.songmountain.com.

**Toggenburg Mountain Winter Sports Center.** Toggenburg Road, off NY 80, Fabius; (315) 683-5842 or (800) 720-8644; www.skitog.com.

**Bear Swamp State Forest Nordic Ski Trail.** 2721 NY 80, Sherburne; (607) 674-4017; www.dec.ny.gov.

largest dance floors. Miniature golf and paddleboats are available when you're too tuckered to two-step.

## Lime Hollow Center For Environment & Culture (all ages)
**338 McLean Rd.; (607)662-4632 ; www.limehollow.org. Visitor center open Tues through Fri 10 a.m. to 5 p.m., Sat and Sun noon to 4 p.m. Closed Mon. $.**

This 375-acre woodland and bog preserve is laced with almost 10 miles of trails and several wildlife viewing stations. The new "green" $1 million visitor center has excellent exhibit space, modular educational displays, and a gift shop, while outside there's a creekside bird sanctuary and a nature trail for people of all abilities. Public programs include a Spring Fishing Festival, Snake Night, Owl Prowls, campfire sing-alongs, and star searches.

## Suggett House Museum (ages 6 and up)
**25 Homer Ave.; (607) 756-6071; www.cortland.org. Open Tues through Sat 1 to 4 p.m. Closed major holidays. $.**

Home of the Cortland County Historical Society, this nineteenth-century Italianate house offers exhibits on the home arts, military history, and a charming children's room complete with antique dolls and toys. During the Doll House Holiday program, from Thanksgiving to Jan, more than thirty different houses and miniature rooms are displayed.

## Where to Eat
**A&W Root Beer Drive-In.** NY 13 and NY 281; (607) 756-2021. The best root beer in the world.

**Doug's Fish Fry.** 3638 West Rd.; (607) 753-9184; www.dougsfishfry.com. Fresh seafood, self-service, outdoor seating, no tipping, and Web page coupons!

## Where to Stay

**Country Inn & Suites by Carlson.** 3707 NY 281; (607) 753-8300 or (800) 456-4000; www.countryinns.com/cortlandny. Eighty-one new rooms and suites, high-speed Internet access, refrigerators and microwaves available, guest laundry facilities, indoor pool, spa, lending library, complimentary hot breakfast, and children under eighteen stay free when accompanied by adult. $$$

**Ramada Hotel & Conference Center.** 2 River St.; (607) 756-4431; www.ramada.com. One hundred and forty-six newly renovated rooms and suites, free high-speed Internet, indoor pool, exercise room, restaurant, and laundry service. $$

# Owego

Take NY 13 south to NY 38 south.

Located on the Susquehanna River, Owego was the home of Belva Lockwood, who, in 1884, became the first woman to run for the presidency of the United States.

### Tioga County Historical Museum (ages 8 and up)

110 Front St.; (607) 687-2460; www.tiogahistory.org. Open year-round Tues through Sat 10 a.m. to 4 p.m. Donation.

Native American artifacts, pioneer crafts and folk art, and local-history exhibits can be found at this county museum and research library. A recent exhibition commemorates the 200th anniversary of Abraham Lincoln's birth, with rare Lincoln pennies and Matthew Brady photographs of the president. At the end of Aug, Civil War reenactors set up camp, complete with cooking, sewing, and historical presentations, then do daily battles on the nearby Rudin Farm, with a nineteenth-century dance party on Sat and a nineteenth-century church service the next morning, to atone for that dance party.

### Tioga Scenic Railroad (all ages)

25 Delphine St.; (607) 687-6786; www.tiogascenicrailroad.com. Operating weekends July through Oct. Also dinner theater, train robbery, and holiday rides. $$–$$$.

Ride the rails aboard a vintage train for an excursion to Newark Valley and the Bement/Billings Farmstead. Costumed guides welcome you at this nineteenth-century living-history museum, offering demonstrations of what life was like more than 150 years ago.

## New York **Trivia**

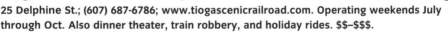

New York has more than 7,600 lakes, including Lake Champlain and Lake George.

# Animal Agritainment in **Tioga County**

**Alpacalachin Farms.** 2571 Chestnut Ridge Rd., Apalachin; (607) 687-6950; www.alpacalachin.com.

**Beeman Apiaries.** 2495 Montrose Turnpike, Owego; (607) 687-2679.

**Forget-Me-Not Farm.** 56 Lathrop Rd., Candor; (607) 659-5630; www.small gracesatforgetmenot.com.

**Foxtail Farms.** 815 Glenmary Dr., Owego; (607) 223-4117; www.foxtailfarm .com.

**Heaven Llama Farm.** 289 Dawson Hill Rd., Spencer; (607) 589-4886.

**Iron Kettle Farm.** 707 Owego Rd., NY 96, Candor; (607) 642-5120; www.iron kettlefarm.com.

**Jackson's Farm.** 6425 NY 17C, Endicott; (607) 754-4819.

**Crocker Creek Buffalo Farm.** 3145 Dutchtown Rd., Endicott; (607) 786-0571; www.angelfire.com/ny3/frontierdays.

**Side Hill Acres Goat Farm.** 70 Spencer Rd., Candor; (607) 659-4121 www.side hillacres.bizland.com.

### Tioga Gardens (all ages)

2217 NY 17C; (607) 687-2940 or (800) 649-0494; www.tiogagardens.com. Open Mon through Wed 8:30 a.m. to 6 p.m., Thurs 8:30 a.m. to 7 p.m., Fri 8:30 a.m. to 6 p.m., Sat 8:30 a.m. to 5 p.m., and Sun 10 a.m. to 5 p.m. $

A two-acre water garden, a solar dome conservatory filled with rare and unusual plants, eight outdoor greenhouses, and a Japanese garden are featured at this lush tropical oasis.

### Waterman Conservation Education Center (all ages)

403 Hilton Rd., Apalachin; (607) 625-2221; www.watermancenter.org. Open daily Mon to Fri 9 a.m. to 4 p.m., Sat 10 a.m. to 4 p.m.; closed Sun. Free.

This nature museum offers interesting hands-on exhibits on the ecosystems of four wildlife refuges along the Susquehanna River and trail information for some fauna-filled nature hikes, plus a great gift shop. The center also manages three other interesting sites. About 2 miles away is Hiawatha Island, a beautiful place any time of the year but especially magical during the program "A Walk Through Time." In midsummer, journey across the river and back in time to Hiawatha Island aboard the *Susquehanna Queen,* and experience life in the "olden days." Attend a Native American powwow and watch costumed

## Also in **the Area**

**Bement-Billings Farmstead.** NY 38, Newark Valley; (607) 642-9516; www
.nvhistory.org.

**The Newark Valley Depot Museum.** Depot Street, Newark Valley; (607) 642-
9516; www.nvhistory.org/depotmuseum.

**Frisbie Homestead Museum.** 1670 Halsey Valley Rd., Spencer; (607) 589-4492.

**Susquehanna River Archeological Center of Native Indian Studies.** 345
Broad St., Waverly; (607) 565-7960; www.sracenter.org.

**The Pines Miniature Golf.** NY 96, Owego; (607) 687-2668.

**Owego Bowl.** 1404 Taylor Rd., Owego; (607) 687-5631; www.owegobowl.com.

craftspeople carve flint, make soap, and fire by friction. Visit the local mountain man or
look inside an Eastern Woodland Iroquois longhouse, then dance to fiddle music and
indulge in Indian tacos and buffalo burgers. Nearby, off NY 17C, is the thirty-acre wetlands
preserve Brick Pond, with a pontoon bridge encircling the pond and a very visible beaver
colony. Along NY 17 is the Apalachin Marsh, considered one of the best bird-watching
sites in the state, and a bit further away, on Robinson Hill Road, is the Glen, a 200-acre forest of majestic trees, sparkling waterfalls, and abundant wildlife.

## Where to Eat

**Awakenings Coffeehouse.** 208 Front St.;
(607) 687-1336. Good brunch, lunch, desserts, and cappuccino. $

**Mario's Pizza.** 51 Fox St.; (607) 687-5121.
Great pizza, pasta, and people. $

**River Rose.** 180 Front St.; (607) 687-6643.
Creative soups, sandwiches, salads, and
vegetarian choices, with outdoor deck dining
overlooking the river in summer. $

## Where to Stay

**Hampton Inn Owego.** 1030 NY 17C; (607)
687-4600; www.hamptoninn.com. Sixty-six
rooms and suites, indoor pool and exercise
room, laundry service, cribs, and complimen-
tary breakfast. $$

**Owego Treadway Inn and Conference
Center.** 1100 NY 17C; (607) 687-4500; www
.owegotreadway.com. Located by the river,
with an indoor pool and fitness center, cable
TV, high-speed Internet, laundry and dry
cleaning, cribs on request, and restaurant.
$–$$

# Ithaca

Head north on NY 96 to intersect with NY 96B.

Once the site of a thriving Cayuga community, Ithaca is situated at the southern shore of Cayuga Lake and surrounded by steep slopes and sparkling waterfalls. Stroll through the Commons, a lovely pedestrian mall where State and Tioga Streets meet, then walk north up Cayuga Street to see the cascades of Ithaca Falls, located off Falls Street. In 1892 the ice-cream sundae was invented here, by a friendly pharmacist, supposedly to cool down an over-heated minister after a sizzling Sunday sermon.

## The Sciencenter (all ages)

601 1st St.; (607) 272-0600; www.sciencenter.org. Open year-round Tues through Sat 10 a.m. to 5 p.m.; Sun noon to 5 p.m.; holiday Mondays, and Mondays in July and Aug, 10 a.m. to 5 p.m. Galaxy Golf open until 8 p.m. in July and Aug. Closed New Year's Day, Thanksgiving, and Christmas. Adults $$, seniors and children 3 to 17 $, children under 3 free.

This nationally acclaimed museum, which grew from a science program run by volunteer teachers, has more than a hundred hands-on interactive exhibits, from puzzles and pendulums to magnets and meteorites. At the Reinvention Station, kids can craft creations from recycled materials, and the Discovery Space offers kits and games for fingerprinting, magnification, memory, and more. For children four and under, the Curiosity Corner encourages exploration with blocks, a water table, and art activities, and a new exhibit, "Connect to the Ocean," explores marine environments with touch tanks of tide pool animals. More creatures reside in the Saltonstall Animal Room, from frogs and snakes to hissing cockroaches and giant millipedes. Outside, at the Emerson Science Park, kids can blow giant bubbles or stand inside one, build bridges, sandcastles, or dams, make music on steel drums or washboards, and climb a geometric rope jungle gym. Galaxy Golf, possibly the most scientific mini-golf game ever designed, challenges players to be on par with principles of math and science at every curve of the course. Special events and programs include "Chemagine!," where families work together solving real-life chemical challenges, or the summer Weekly Wonders adventures in slime concoction or rocket blasting.

## Buttermilk Falls State Park (all ages)

Located 6 miles south of town off NY 13 South; (607) 273-5761 or (607) 273-3440; www.nys parks.state.ny. Park open year-round; seven cabins and forty-six campsites open mid-May through Oct. $$. Call ahead to confirm changes to hours, activities available, and possible closures due to pending state budget cuts.

Cascading more than 500 feet down a series of ten waterfalls into a natural swimming pool at its base, this is a great place to cool off on a hot summer day. The upper section of the park has hiking trails that wind through woodlands, and a gorge rim trail that leads to Pinnacle Rock and Lake Treman, The lower section has picnic pavilions, a playground, and ball fields, and behind the ball fields is the lush Larch Meadows, a wetlands wildlife

# Performing **Arts of Ithaca**

The arts are alive in Ithaca, as evidenced by the vast array of venues for live self-expression. Below is a partial list of places to amuse the muse in your child. Call for performance schedules or stop by the Ticket Center in the **Center Ithaca building** at 171 E. State St., The Commons; (607) 273-4497 or (800) 284-8422; www.ithacaevents.com for one-stop ticket shopping.

**Hangar Theatre.** 801 Taughannock Blvd.; (607) 273-8588 or (800) 284-8422; www.hangartheatre.org.

**Kitchen Theatre Company.** 116 N. Cayuga St. (607) 272-0403, (607) 273-4497, or (800) 284-8422; www.kitchentheatre.org.

**Ithaca College Theatre.** (607) 274-3920; www.ithaca.edu/theatre.

**Ithaca Ballet.** 504-506 N. Plain St.; (607) 277-1967; www.ithacaballet.org.

**The Schwartz Center for Performing Arts.** 430 College Ave.; (607) 254-2700; www.theatrefilmdance.cornell.edu.

**Cayuga Chamber Orchestra.** 116 North Cayuga St.; (607) 273-8981; www.cayugachamberorchestra.org.

**State Theatre of Ithaca.** 107 W. State St.; (607) 273-6633; www.statetheatre ofithaca.com.

wilderness with a nature trail. Park naturalist events include guided gorge treks and flora and fauna walks from July 4 through Labor Day.

## Robert H. Treman State Park (all ages)

105 Enfield Falls Rd.; (607) 273-3440; www.nysparks.state.ny. Park open year-round; campground open mid-May through Nov; all Gorge trails close early Nov. $.

Traverse the trails and craggy gorges of the Devil's Kitchen and Lucifer Falls, then revel in the rustic beauty of scenic Enfield Glen. This 1,070-acre former film "back lot" offers twelve waterfalls to "wow" at along a 3-mile hike (hold little hands!). Before the "iffy" Ithaca weather prompted the country's budding movie industry to move to sunny California, many of the early westerns were shot here. Cabins, campsites, and RV hookups are available, and ranger-led eco-walks and owl prowls are offered in summer.

## The History Center (ages 7 and up)

401 East State St.; (607) 273-8284; www.thehistorycenter.net. Open year-round Tues, Thurs, and Sat 11 a.m. to 5 p.m. Donation.

This excellent museum highlights the history of Tompkins County. Drawing on a collection of thousands of artifacts, from family albums to books, maps, memorabilia, and over 100,000 photographs, the exhibits focus on Ithaca's fascinating film heritage, industrial achievements, and regional arts. The largest object in their collection, bought for $10 in 1953, is the nineteenth-century Eight Square Schoolhouse, located on Upper Hanshaw Road. An eight-sided classroom was an efficient Quaker concept, partly because octagonal shapes provide more interior space than a square or rectangle, and partly because it made the teacher the center of attention. Historical walking-tour—takers will encounter time-travel vignettes and reenactments along the way, and family festivals feature scavenger hunts, live music, and **free** ice-cream sundaes.

### Cayuga Nature Center  (all ages)

**1420 Taughannock Blvd. (NY 89); (607) 273-6260; www.cayuganaturecenter.org. Trails open year-round daily dawn to dusk. Main lodge open June through Aug daily 9 a.m. to 5 p.m. Fall, winter, and spring hours subject to change. $.**

Overlooking Cayuga Lake, this lovely preserve has 5 miles of easy to medium marked nature trails winding through 120 miles of forests, fields, gorges, and waterfalls. The main lodge has live animals and ecology exhibits, and an activity room for kids. Outside are more animals, a seasonal butterfly house, and TreeTops, a six-story kid-scale tree house to explore.

# Cornell **University**

The 745-acre dramatically beautiful campus of Cornell, an internationally acclaimed teaching and research university in Ithaca, includes more than 250 major buildings and a variety of natural areas, some open to the public. Below are several interesting places to explore **free** of charge, a real bargain in these days of tuition increases.

**Cornell Plantations.** 1 Plantation Rd.; (607) 255-2400; www.plantations.cornell .edu.

**Sapsucker Woods Bird Sanctuary.** 159 Sapsucker Woods Rd.; (607) 254-2473 or (800) 843-2473; www.birds.cornell.edu.

**Wilder Brain Collection.** Uris Hall, second floor, at East Avenue and Tower Road; (607) 255-6074 or (607) 254-INFO; www.news.cornell.edu.

**Herbert F. Johnson Museum of Art.** Central and University Avenues; (607) 255-6464; www.museum.cornell.edu.

# Interesting Ithaca Entertainment

**Cayuga Lake Cruises.** 708 Buffalo St., Ithaca; (607) 256-0898; www.cayuga lakecatering.com.

**Bowl O Drome.** 401 3rd St., Ithaca; (607) 256-2695.

**The Rink.** 1767 E. Shore Dr., Ithaca; (607) 277-RINK; www.therink.org.

**Cass Park Rink and Pool.** 701 Taughannock Blvd., Ithaca; (607) 273-9211; www.cityofithaca.org.

**Ithaca Clock Museum.** 136 W. State St., Ithaca; (607) 227-2303; www.ithaca clockmuseum.com.

## Museum of the Earth (all ages)

1259 Trumansburg Rd.; (607) 273-6623; www.museumoftheearth.org. **Open Memorial Day through Labor Day, Mon through Sat 10 a.m. to 5 p.m., Sun 11 a.m. to 5 p.m.; and Labor Day through Memorial Day, Mon and Thurs through Sat 10 a.m. to 5 p.m., Sun 11 a.m. to 5 p.m. Closed Thanksgiving, Christmas, and New Year's Day. Adults $$, children $, under 3** **free.**

Founded in 1932, the Paleontological Research Institute cares for more than three million fossils, one of the largest collections in the country, and publishes the oldest paleontological journal in the Western Hemisphere. In 2003 the institute opened the Museum of the Earth, an 18,000-square-foot facility focusing on the history of Earth and its life, especially this part of the planet. Marvel at a massive mastodon or a 500-foot mural chronicling 540 million years of time, touch history at the Fossil and Dino Labs, study the life and death

# Sagan Planet Walk

Billions and billions of stars twinkle over Ithaca every evening, but to get a closer view of the planets, you'll have to take a walk. Stretching 1,200 meters from the Ithaca Commons to the Sciencenter is the **Sagan Planet Walk,** named for astronomer Carl Sagan. On a scale of one to five billion, the sun and nine planets are accurately sized and spaced and marked by monuments displaying fascinating facts and photos. Pick up a "Passport to the Solar System" at the Sciencenter or various other locations for $4 and get it stamped with the Greek symbols that correspond to the Sun and each planet, and you'll receive a souvenir button and one **free** admission to the Sciencenter. (607) 272-0600; www.sciencenter.org/saganpw.

# Nature Areas **Near Ithaca**

**Finger Lakes National Forest.** 5218 NY 414, Hector; (607) 546-4470; www.fs .fed.us.

**Sweedler Preserve at Lick Brook.** Town Line Road, Danby; (607) 275-9487; www.fllt.org.

**Lindsay-Parsons Biodiversity Preserve.** NY 34/NY 96, West Danby; (607) 275-9487; www.fllt.org.

of an endangered species, as Right Whale No. 2030's 44-foot skeleton hovers above your head, or discover our origins through four short state-of-the-art audiovisual presentations. On display are phenomenal fossils, including a 4-foot Tyrannosaurus rex skull and the world's largest sea scorpion fossil. If you feel inspired to start a collection of your own, family-friendly fossil field trips are scheduled in summer.

## Taughannock Falls State Park  (all ages)

2221 Taughannock Rd., Trumansburg; (607) 387-6739; www.nysparks.state.ny. Park open year-round; campground open late Apr through mid-Oct. Rim Trail closes in winter. $.

Possibly one of the prettiest falls in the state and 30 feet higher than Niagara, the Taughannock Creek plunges 215 feet down, past a dramatic steep stone amphitheater. The 783-acre park offers campsites, cabins, hiking trails, swimming, fishing, rowboat rentals, a picnic and playground area, recreation programs, a summer concert series, and ice-skating, cross-country skiing, and sledding in winter.

## Where to Eat

**The Boat Yard Grill.** 525 Taughannock Blvd.; (607) 256-9585; www.boatyardgrill .com. On the waterfront, serving two-handed sandwiches, three-mustard salmon, five-onion soup, ribs, chicken, steaks, pasta, and small plates of shrimp, scallops, crab cakes, and ribs, using local breads, cheeses, and produce. $–$$$

**Moosewood Restaurant.** 215 N. Cayuga St., Dewitt Building; (607) 273-9610; www .moosewoodrestaurant.com. Serving creative vegetarian cuisine for over three decades, and having published eleven cookbooks, this legendary landmark was named one of the most influential restaurants of the twentieth century. An ever-changing menu of seasonal organic ethnic, eclectic, and American regional cuisine is offered, with fresh fish, seafood, and terrific homemade desserts. $$

## Where to Stay

**Clarion Hotel University Hotel & Conference Center.** 1 Sheraton Dr.; (607) 257-2000; www.clarionhotel.com. One hundred and six rooms and suites, with indoor pool, sauna, fitness center, restaurant, and complimentary hot breakfast. Kids under eighteen stay free with an adult. $$$$

## Outside **Ithaca Area Activities**

**Cayuga Lakeside Stables.** 9186 Booth Rd., Trumansburg; (607) 387-9050.

**T-Burg Mini Golf.** 1966 Trumansburg Rd., Trumansburg; (607) 387-7888; www.tburgminigolf.com.

**Wind Rider Balloon Company.** 44 Deer Run Rd., Newfield; (607) 564-1009.

**Ringwood Raceway.** 1975 Dryden Rd., Freeville; (607) 247-4198.

**Patchwork Therapeutic Riding Center.** 90 Old Peruville Rd., Groton; (607) 898-3808; www.patchworkridingcenter.org.

**Inn on Columbia.** 228 Columbia St.; (607) 272-0204; www.columbiabb.com. Family-friendly bed and breakfast, vegan and special diets welcome, with wireless Internet, TV, gardens, and multiple night discounts. $$–$$$

**Turtle Dreams Bed & Breakfast.** 481 Lafayette Rd., Groton; (607) 838-3492; www.dreamingturtles.com. Kid-friendly, fun place with six turtle-titled rooms and four 27-foot tall tepee tents (bring your own gear), farm animals, woodland paths along a creek, blackberry picking in summer, a summer-time family camp, and often didjeridoo storytelling, campfire drumming, and marshmallow roasting. A portable playpen, stroller, child mattress, sound machine, baby monitors, and baby backpack are available on request, and child care can be provided at additional cost with advance notice.

# Auburn

Head north on NY 34B to NY 34 north.

Located north of Lake Owasco, this is the birthplace of Abner Doubleday, the inventor of baseball; Tahgahjute (Logan), the great Cayuga orator; Millard Fillmore, U.S. president; and T. E. Case, the inventor of sound movies.

## Emerson Park  (all ages)

6879 East Lake Rd., NY 38A; (315) 253-5611; www.co.cayuga.ny.us/parks/emerson. Park open dawn to dusk. Merry-Go-Round Playhouse (315) 255-1785, (315) 255-1305, or (800) 457-8897; www.merry-go-round.com. Agricultural Museum (315) 252-7644; www.cayuganet.org/agmuseum. Museum open mid-May to mid-Sept, 11 a.m. to 4 p.m. Parking fee $; donation.

## Other Parks in the Area

**Fillmore Glen State Park.** 1686 NY 38, Moravia; (315) 497-0130; www.nys parks.state.ny.us.

**Long Point State Park.** 2063 Lake Rd., Aurora; (315) 497-0130; www.nysparks .state.ny.us.

Located on the northern shore of Owasco Lake, Emerson Park has something for everyone in the family. Swimming, fishing, and boat rentals are available for lake lovers, plus there are places for picnics, a disc golf course, a huge playground area with classic swings, slides, and a roller coaster, a carousel, and other kiddie rides. The newly renovated Merry-Go-Round Playhouse stages five professional musicals every summer, as well as ten youth theater productions throughout the year. The Ward W. O'Hara Agricultural Museum features farm tools and tractors, a 1900 farm kitchen, creamery, blacksmithery, woodshop, vet's office, general store, and herb garden, and hosts special events, from Draft Horse & Hay Day to a Victorian Doll House Day.

## Harriet Tubman Home (ages 5 and up)

**180 South St.; (315) 252-2081; www.nyhistory.com/harriettubman. Open Feb through Oct, Tues through Fri 11 a.m. to 4 p.m., Sat by appointment. $.**

Born a slave in 1821, Harriet Tubman escaped to freedom in the North in 1849. Known as the "Moses of her People," she made nineteen dangerous trips south in eleven years, risking her life to deliver more than 300 slaves to freedom via the Underground Railroad. She also served as a nurse, scout, and spy for the Union Army.

## Auburn **Amusements**

**Reese's Dairy Bar & Miniature Golf.** NY 5 and US 20; (315) 252-7323.

**Arnold Palmer Miniature Golf.** Gates Road, off NY 5 and US 20; (315) 253-8072.

**Finger Lakes Drive-In.** NY 5 and US 20; (315) 252-3969; www.drive-ins.com.

**Reva Rollerdrome.** 357 West Genesee St.; (315) 252-8225.

**Casey Park.** 150 N. Division St.; (315) 253-4247; www.ci.auburn.ny.us.

**Starlight Lanes.** 1663 Clark Street Rd., NY 5 and US 20; (315) 253-8489.

## Seward House (ages 5 and up)

**33 South St.; (315) 252-1283; www.sewardhouse.org. Open Feb through June and mid-Oct through Dec, Tues through Sat 1 to 4 p.m.; July through mid-Oct, Tues through Sat 10 a.m. to 4 p.m., Sun 1 to 4 p.m. Closed major holidays. Adults $$, students and seniors $, children under 10 free.**

Home for more than fifty years to William Henry Seward, who was governor of New York, a U.S. senator, secretary of state to Abraham Lincoln (and almost assassinated the same night as the president), and promoter of the $7.2 million purchase of that Russian property, Alaska, known as Seward's Folly. After retiring from the State Department, he traveled the world, and when he died, with his family around him, his last words were "Love one another." Take a guided tour of his family's seventeen-room Federal-style house,

# The Underground **Railroad**

Between 1450 and 1850, more than 12 million Africans were unwillingly transported across the Atlantic and sold into lives of slavery. After the Revolutionary War, some Americans freed their slaves, but the U.S. Constitution and the Fugitive Slave Act of 1793 extended slaveholders' rights over their "property," even into free states and territories.

An abolitionist movement to assist fugitive slaves probably started in the late eighteenth century. By 1831 the antislavery sentiment was picking up steam, as was the Underground Railroad, a network of people and places connecting freedom seekers with "conductors" who guided them to safety in the Promised Land of Canada. Passengers were hidden by "stationmasters" at safe houses by day, then directed to "follow the drinking gourd," or Big Dipper, north on moonless nights. "Stockholders" provided the "cargo" with food, clothes, and money for the perilous journey.

New York was a major hub for the Underground Railroad, partly because it was a free state with access to Canada, and also because it had more antislavery groups than any other state, powered by persistent abolitionists including Frederick Douglass, John Brown, Sojourner Truth, and Harriet Tubman. No one knows for certain how many rode the Underground Railroad to freedom, but estimates run roughly between 30,000 to 100,000 passengers.

To retrace the rails of the Underground Railroad, and to obtain a list of known stations and other places of interest, check out these sites:

**National Parks Service:** www.nps.gov/history/ugrr

**National Underground Railroad Freedom Center:** www.freedomcenter.org

# Roadster Rooters, **Rejoice!**

Weedsport is the speed-sport capital of Cayuga County. Around this town wheels rule, so rally the crew and race over to the Cayuga County Fairgrounds (2919 NY 31), the home of **DIRT Motorsports Hall of Fame and Classic Car Museum** and the **Weedsport Speedway**. For more information and a schedule of events, contact them at (315) 834-6606; www.cayugacounty fairspeedway.com. For slot car speedsters, steer over to **Weedsport Raceway Slot Cars,** 2645 Erie Dr.; (315) 834-8736.

once a stop on the Underground Railroad, and you will see an amazing collection of rare and unusual souvenirs from Seward's travels and career.

### Cayuga Museum and Case Research Lab  (ages 7 and up)

**203 W. Genesee St.; (315) 253-8051; www.cayuganet.org/cayugamuseum. Museum open Tues through Fri noon to 5 p.m. Case Research Lab open noon to 4:30 p.m. Closed Mon, all major holidays, and in Jan. Suggested donation $.**

Permanent and changing exhibits highlighting the history of Cayuga County can be found in this Greek Revival mansion, from Native American culture to Civil War relics. In a building behind the Willard Case Mansion is the research laboratory of Theodore W. Case, where, in 1923, the "talkies" were born.

### Auburn Doubledays  (all ages)

**Leo Pinckney Field at Falcon Park, 130 North Division St.; (315) 255-2489; www.auburn doubledays.com. Season runs June through Sept. $.**

Named for baseball founder Abner Doubleday, this single A farm team for the Houston Astros has been playing in the New York–Penn League for more than forty years. Take everyone out to the ball game some summer night for half the cost of a movie—and twice as many memories.

## Where to Eat

**Lasca's.** 252 Grant Ave.; (315) 253-4885; www.lascas.com. Steak, chicken, pastas, salads, and homemade desserts, plus a carry-out menu perfect for picnics. $$$

**The Restaurant at Elderberry Pond.** 3228 Center Street Rd.; (315) 252-6025; www .elderberrypond.com. Located in the center of a hundred-acre organic farm, serving freshly harvested homegrown seasonal vegetables, fruits, and herbs grown on-site, plus pasture-raised meats, free-range poultry, fresh fish, and biodynamic organic wines, with meals prepared by Culinary Institute of America–trained chefs. On summer Sundays, free farm tours are offered.

## Cayuga County Agritainment

The bounty of the county is a beauty to behold, and the furry fauna is fun, too. Visit these friendly farms for up-close and personal agrarian adventures.

**Buffalo Farm Tours.** 2500 NY 41A, Sempronius; (315) 496-2925; www.pdhbuffalo farm.com.

**Rice Alpaca Farm.** www.ricealpacafarm.com.

**Owen Orchards.** 8174 NY 5, Weedsport; (315) 252-4097; www.owenorchards .com.

**Ontario Orchards.** 15273 Sterling Center Rd., Sterling; (315) 343-6328; www .ontarioorchards.com.

**Long Point Orchard.** 2007 NY 90, Aurora; (315) 364-5889.

**Bibbens Farms.** 3282 East Brutus Rd. (NY 31B), Weedsport; (315) 834-6500.

**Pine Hill Berry Patch.** 2333 Turnpike Rd., Auburn; (315) 252-9086.

**Hillcrest Dairy.** 66 W. Cayuga St., Moravia; (315) 497-0659.

**Grisamore Farms.** 749 Cowan Rd., Locke; (315) 497-1347; www.grisamore farms.com.

**Joyful Acres.** 1020 Howell Rd., Port Byron; (315) 776-8569.

## Where to Stay

**Holiday Inn Auburn.** 75 North St.; (315) 253-4531; www.hiauburn.com. One hundred and sixty-three rooms, two jet-tub suites, high-speed Internet in room, wireless in the Courtyard, cable TV, indoor pool, exercise room, laundry room and same-day laundry and dry-cleaning service, game room, restaurant, and Irish pub. $$

**Inn at Finger Lakes.** 12 Seminary Ave.; (315) 253-5000; www.innatthefingerlakes .com. Deluxe complimentary continental breakfast, fitness center, free Wi-Fi, free newspaper, coin laundry center, plus spa, wine, golf, fishing, chocolate, and shopping activity packages available. $$

# Seneca Falls

From Auburn, take NY 5 and US 20 west to Seneca Falls.

"We hold these truths to be self-evident; that all men and women are created equal." So began the Declaration of Sentiments, written in 1848 in Seneca Falls, the birthplace of the women's rights movement in America.

### Seneca Falls Heritage Area Visitor Center (ages 10 and up)

115 Fall St.; (315) 568-2703; www.senecafalls.com/history-heritage.php. Open year-round Mon through Fri 9 a.m. to 4 p.m., Sat 10 a.m. to 4 p.m. Closed Sun and all major holidays. **Free.**

This interpretive center explores the area's history of industry and transportation, its heritage of social reform, and Native American culture. **Free** tours of the center are offered for folks over the age of five, scavenger hunt items are fun to find, and maps and brochures of the area are available.

### Seneca Falls Historical Society (all ages)

55 Cayuga St.; (315) 568-8412; www.sfhistoricalsociety.org. Open year-round Mon through Fri 9 a.m. to 4 p.m. $.

A variety of permanent and changing exhibits can be found in this lovely twenty-three-room 1880 Queen Anne mansion. Along with beautiful Victorian furnishings, there's a colorful collection of costumes and circus toys in the playroom, and take note of the checkerboard pattern on the stairs, once used by the family children to play checkers on all six landings.

### National Women's Hall of Fame (ages 6 and up)

76 Fall St.; (315) 568-8060; www.greatwomen.org. Open May through Sept, Mon through Sat 10 a.m. to 5 p.m., Sun noon to 5 p.m.; Oct through Apr, Wed through Sat 11 a.m. to 5 p.m. Closed major holidays and in Jan. $, members and children under 5 **free.**

This museum and education center offers exhibits and displays honoring the achievements of, at last count, 226 distinguished American women. In 2009 plans were announced to move the Hall of Fame to the historic Seneca Knitting Mill, but until renovations there are complete, the current location will remain open.

### Women's Rights National Historical Park (ages 6 and up)

136 Fall St.; (315) 568-0024; www.nps.gov/wori. Dial and Discover audio tour (315) 257-9370. Grounds open sunrise to sunset; center open daily year-round 9 a.m. to 5 p.m. Closed major holidays except Memorial Day, July 4, and Labor Day. Adults $, under 16 **free.**

Located across the street from the ruins of the Wesleyan Chapel and site of the first Women's Rights Convention, this center offers an orientation film, "Dreams of Equality," interactive videos, and exhibits on political issues ranging from women's employment and sports to fashion and marriage. Come face-to-face with the life-size bronze statues of the sisters who started the suffragist movement in America, then walk outside to Declaration Park, where the text of their document demanding feminist emancipation is etched on a bluestone water wall. Take a ranger-conducted tour or bring your cell phone for Dial

## Also in **the Area**

**Scythe Tree.** 841 Waterloo-Geneva Rd., NY 5 and US 20, 2 miles west of Waterloo; (800) 732-1848; www.fingerlakescentral.com.

**Lively Run Goat Dairy.** 8978 CR 142, Interlaken; (607) 532-4647; www.lively run.com.

and Discover, a self-guided audio tour. Kids can become a National Parks Service Junior Ranger by completing a fun booklet filled with questions, puzzles, and coloring pages about the women's rights movement, and for folks collecting stamps for their NPS passport, this site offers three for **free!**

### Elizabeth Cady Stanton House  (ages 6 and up)
**32 Washington St.; (315) 568-2991; www.nps.gov/wori. Open daily 9 a.m. to 5 p.m.; tours offered in spring, summer, and fall. $.**

In the mid-nineteenth century, women in America were not allowed to own property or money, be legal guardians of their own children, or vote. Exhibits highlight Stanton's life and times in the restored Greek Revival home where she raised her seven children and the nation's consciousness.

### Seneca Museum of Waterways and Industry  (all ages)
**89 Fall St.; (315) 568-1510; www.senecamuseum.com. Open year-round Tues through Sat 10 a.m. to 5 p.m.; summer Sundays 1 to 5 p.m. $.**

Interactive exhibits, dioramas, and artifacts explain how harnessing the power of the Seneca River turned the town into an industrial hub. At the Children's Center, play with pulleys, inclined planes, gears, and water pumps at interactive stations, and watch weaving demonstrations on an antique loom or operate a very old printing press.

### Cayuga Lake State Park  (all ages)
**2678 Lower Lake Rd.; (315) 568-5163; www.nysparks.state.ny. Park open year-round; campground opens last weekend in Apr and closes the last weekend in Oct. Beach opens mid-June. $**

Once part of a Cayuga reservation, this park has several hundred campsites and cabins, a sandy beach for swimming, a playground, playing fields, picnic pavilions, a nature trail, and great fishing for bass, bullheads, carp, lake trout, and landlocked salmon.

### Montezuma National Wildlife Refuge  (all ages)
**3395 US 20 East; (315) 568-5987; www.fws.gov/r5mnwr. Refuge open year-round dawn to dusk, Visitor center open Apr 1 to Dec 1, Mon through Fri 10 a.m. to 3 p.m., Sat and Sun 10 a.m. to 4 p.m. Free.**

This 7,068-acre haven is a terrific place to observe more than 242 species of a million migrating birds, as it's located in the middle of the one of the busiest flight lanes in the Atlantic Flyway. More than forty-two species of mammals and at least thirty species of reptiles and amphibians live here, too, at least for part of the year. In spring and summer, you can view osprey nesting via Osprey Cam, and in winter more than 100,000 Canadian geese gather. A 3-mile auto tour takes you past the Refuge's Main Pool, the best place to see the biggest variety of wildlife, and several easy, short trails wind through the woods and wetlands. In summer, special adventures for kids include nature hikes, wildlife photography and birding expeditions, T-shirt painting projects, and bonfires at dusk.

### Sampson State Park  (all ages)

6096 NY 96A, Romulus; (315) 585-6392. Museum (315) 585-6203; www.nysparks.com/parks. Park open daily year-round; campground open late Apr through mid-Nov. Museum open Memorial Day weekend through Labor Day, Wed through Sun 10 a.m. to 4 p.m.; early Sept through Columbus Day, weekends only. Free, vehicle fee $$.

On the shores of Seneca Lake, this 1,852-acre park is the home of the Sampson Memorial Naval Museum. The park offers 245 electric campsites and 64 nonelectric ones, hiking and nature trails, ball fields and courts, a playground and picnic area, swimming with a sand beach, a marina, lake fishing, bicycling, a recreation program, wildlife watches and great terrain for winter sledding, cross-country skiing, and snowshoeing.

## Where to Eat

**Abigail's Restaurant.** 1978 NY 5 and US 20, between Seneca Falls and Waterloo; (315) 539-9300. All-you-can-eat luncheon deli bar buffet, steaks, seafood, stir-fry tofu, chicken, and pasta specials for dinner, on a deck overlooking Seneca-Cayuga Canal. $–$$

**Mac's Drive-In.** 1166 Waterloo-Geneva Rd. (NY 5 and US 20), Waterloo; (315) 539-3064. The area's largest drive-in, open for the past fifty years, features carhop service and offers burgers, baskets of fried chicken or shrimp with fresh-cut french fries, pizza, hot dogs, ice-cream sundaes, and root beer in frosted mugs. $

**ZuZu Cafe.** 107 Fall St.; (315) 568-2230; www.zuzuscafe.com. Inspired by the character in Capra's movie *It's A Wonderful Life,* this charming cafe serves fresh pastries, salads, sandwiches, quiche, and fruit smoothies. $

## Where to Stay

**Holiday Inn Waterloo-Seneca Falls.** 268 Mound Rd., Waterloo; (315) 539-5011; www .hiwaterloo.com. One hundred and forty-eight rooms and suites, heated outdoor pool, tennis court, free high-speed Internet, microwave and refrigerator on request if available, fitness center, room service, laundry facilities,

a lounge with billiards and a big-screen TV, a restaurant where children under twelve eat free when accompanied by parent, and Seneca White Deer tours and Back-to-School shopping packages. $$

**Seneca Falls Microtel Inn.** 1966 NY 5 and US 20; (315) 539-8438; www.microtelinn

.com. Sixty-nine rooms and twenty-one suites, microwave and refrigerator in suites, unique window seat in every room, fitness room, plus all of these for free: Wi-Fi, phone calls, parking, cribs, and continental breakfast. The Cayuga-Seneca Canal is right outside. Children under sixteen stay free in same room as an adult. $

# Geneva

Take NY 5 and US 20 west.

Known as Kanadesaga by the Seneca who lived here until the eighteenth century, Geneva is also where Elizabeth Blackwell became the first woman in America to earn her medical diploma.

### Prouty-Chew House (ages 6 and up)
**543 S. Main St.; (315) 789-5151; www.genevahistoricalsociety.com. Open year-round Tues through Fri 9:30 a.m. to 4:30 p.m., Sat 1:30 to 4:30 p.m., plus Sun 1:30 to 4:30 p.m. in July and Aug. Closed holidays. Free.**

This nineteenth-century Federal-style mansion is the home of the Geneva Historical Society, and houses several interesting exhibits on the area's history and culture, plus two nineteenth-century furnished period rooms. Of special interest to kids is the Charles Bauder Children's Discovery Room, an exhibit designed for six- to ten-year-old explorers, with hands-on activities like lock loading, Seneca basket making and beading, and "rebuilding" downtown Geneva. Maps for self-guided walking and driving tours of the town are also available.

### Rose Hill Mansion (ages 8 and up)
**East Lake Road, NY 96A; (315) 789-3848. Open May through Oct, Tues through Sat 10 a.m. to 4 p.m., Sun 1 to 5 p.m. Closed Mon. $, children under 10 free.**

Overlooking Seneca Lake, this beautiful 1838 Greek Revival estate is a National Historic Landmark with twenty-one period rooms filled with elegant Empire-style furniture. In summer a history camp is offered for young children.

### Seneca Lake State Park (all ages)
**1 Lakefront Dr., NY 5 and US 20; (315) 789-2331; www.nysparks.state.ny.us. Park open year-round daily sunrise to sunset. Vehicle fee $. Call ahead to confirm changes to hours, activities available, and possible closures due to pending state budget cuts.**

The deepest of the Finger Lakes, this is a favorite place for swimming and fishing for trout. There are two excellent marinas, playing fields, picnic pavilions, a playground, and a spontaneously spouting Sprayground, with a hundred jets of splash-happy fun.

### Finger Lakes Scenic Railway (all ages)

Geneva Station, 68 Border City Rd.; (315) 374-1570 or (315) 209-1029; www.fingerlakesscenic
railway.com. $$$.

Ride the rails along 132 miles of track on themed train rides throughout the Finger Lakes.
Excursions include Blues-n-Brews, nineteenth-century women's rights reenactors, music
and fall foliage rides, Halloween and Christmas trips, and my personal favorite, "Throw
Mama ON the Train."

## Where to Eat

**Emile's.** 369 Waterloo-Geneva Rd. (NY 5 and
US 20); (315) 789-2775; www.emilesrestaurant
.net. Casual continental cuisine, featuring
prime rib, baby back ribs, seafood, salad bar,
and a big children's menu. $–$$$

**Torrey Park Grill.** 89 Avenue E; (315) 789-
1629; www.torreypark.com. Located in the
area of Geneva's Little Italy of the late nineteenth century, serving Italian-American specialties, plus burgers, pizza, bar food, a Friday
fish fry, a $5 kids' menu, Finger Lakes wines,
and a large HDTV, tuned to sports, above the
fireplace.

## Where to Stay

**Belhurst Castle.** 4069 NY 14 South; (315)
781-0201; www.belhurst.com. Listed on
the National Register of Historic Places, this
fabulous nineteenth-century Romanesque
stone castle overlooks Seneca Lake, and has
fourteen unique antique decorated rooms,
two terrific restaurants, Edgar's and Stonecutters, and wine from their own vineyards.
Two other properties, White Springs Manor
and the Vinifera Inn, are also managed by Belhurst and have a variety of interesting rooms
and suites. $$$

**Geneva-on-the-Lake.** 1001 Lochland Rd.,
NY 14 South; (315) 789-7190 or (800) 343-
6382; www.genevaonthelake.com. A historic
landmark on ten lavishly landscaped acres,
this Italianate villa has a private lakefront,
twenty-three suites, six studios, ten with
two bedrooms, lawn games, swimming in
a 70-foot outdoor pool, pontoon boat lake
cruises, bicycling, tennis, golf privileges, and
a great gourmet restaurant. $$$$

**Ramada Geneva Lakefront.** 41 Lakefront
Dr.; (315) 789-0400 or (800) 990-0907; www
.genevaramada.com. Located on the lake,
with 148 rooms, nine suites, Wi-Fi, walking
trail, laundry/valet, free parking, restaurant,
lounge, and patio dining. $$$

# Lake **Drums**

For centuries local folks have spoken of unusual rumbling sounds coming
from the middle of Seneca Lake. Native Americans thought the eerie noises
were the drums of their gods or ancestors, but scientists today believe the
booms may be the result of methane gas bubbling up from cracks in the lake
bed. Some still summer night, sit by Seneca Lake and see if you can spot
some of the pure-white deer said to wander the eastern shore, and listen care-
fully for the music of the "lake drums."

# Penn Yan

Take NY 14 south to NY 54 south.

Located on the northern tip of slingshot-shaped Keuka Lake, this peaceful village was named for the Pennsylvanians and Yankees who settled here in the early nineteenth century.

## The Keuka Outlet Trail  (all ages)

**Nine access points between Penn Yann and Dresden; (315) 536-4111, (315) 536-8895, or (800) 868-9283; www.keukaoutlettrail.net. For complete trail assistance, stop at the visitor center at 2375 NY 14A, south of the village. Free.**

This 7-mile linear trail follows an abandoned railroad bed along the Keuka Outlet, which links Keuka and Seneca Lakes. Although the trail descends nearly 300 feet, it's an easy and scenic hike past woods, wildlife, waterfalls, and old abandoned mill towns. There are nine access points along the trail, and maps are available at the visitor center and local shops in town. If you choose to bike it, wheels can be rented at the nearby Carey's Rentals, and there's a Mr. Twistee's Ice Cream stand to reward you at the end of the road in Dresden.

## Keuka Lake State Park  (all ages)

**3370 Pepper Rd., Bluff Point; (315) 536-3666; www.nysparks.state.ny.us; Park open year-round; campground open May through mid-Oct. Vehicle fee $.**

Located 6 miles southwest of Penn Yan, this 621-acre park along the shores of Keuka Lake offers vineyard views, swimming at a gravel beach, good fishing, docks and a boat launch, a playground, picnic area, hiking trails, and 150 campsites.

## Other Parks **in the Area**

**Red Jacket Park.** 303 Lake St., NY 54, Penn Yan; (315) 536-3015; www.village ofpennyan.com.

**Indian Pines Park.** NY 54A, Penn Yan; (315) 536-3015; www.villageofpennyan .com.

**High Tor Wildlife Area.** NY 245, at Canandaigua Lake, Naples; (585) 226-2466; www.dec.ny.gov.

**Cumming Nature Center.** 6472 Gulick Rd., Naples; (585) 374-6160; www.rmsc .org/cummingnaturecenter.

## Cruising on **Keuka Lake**

*Viking Spirit.* NY 54, 680 E. Lake Rd., Penn Yan; (315) 536-7061; www.viking resort.com.

*Keuka Maid.* NY 54, Champlain Beach, Hammondsport; (888) 372-2628.

*The Esperanza Rose.* 3537 NY 54A, Bluff Point; (315) 595-6618; www.esperanza rose.com.

### Glenn H. Curtiss Museum  (ages 5 and up)

8419 NY 54, Hammondsport; (607) 569-2160; www.glennhcurtissmuseum.org. Open May through Oct, Mon through Sat 9 a.m. to 5 p.m., Sun 10 a.m. to 5 p.m.; Nov through Apr, Mon through Sat 10 a.m. to 4 p.m., Sun 10 a.m. to 4 p.m. Adults $$, children 7 to 18 $, children 6 and under **free.**

A motorcycle, airplane, and dirigible daredevil, Curtiss made the world's first preannounced airplane flight, developed the world's first amphibious plane, opened the first flight school in this country, and was awarded the first U.S. pilot's license. In 1907 he attained a speed of 136 mph on his V-8 powered motorcycle and became the "fastest man on earth." Known today as the Father of Naval Aviation and the founder of the aircraft industry in America, he also developed the cities of Hialeah, Miami Springs, and Opa-locka in Florida. Historical aircraft, vintage boats, bicycles, and motorcycles make up the majority of the collection, and there's always a project to observe in the Restoration Shop (currently a 1910 Albany Flyer is being repaired). There are also early-American artifacts from the Civil War and World Wars I and II, including antique dolls and their houses, toys, clothing, fire engines, farm implements, and quilts. The Children's Interactive Center explores inventions, speed, and flight with hands-on activities, and an indoor tot lot provides planes, blocks, and books for the younger pilots present.

### C. E. K. Mees Observatory  (ages 6 and up)

6604 E. Gannett Hill Rd., Naples; (585) 275-4385 or (585) 230-9548; www.mees.rochester astronomy.org. Tours by reservation available selective Fri and Sat nights June through Aug.

Star search on a summer night through a terrific 24-inch telescope, controlled by computers and guided by University of Rochester astronomy students. **Free,** donations appreciated.

## Also in the Area

**Keuka Karts Go-Karts.** 2245 NY 54A, Penn Yan; (315) 536-4833.

**Doug Kent's Lakeside Lanes.** NY 14A, Penn Yan; (315) 536-9595.

**Sugar Shack Blueberry Farm.** 824 East Swamp Rd., Penn Yan; (585) 526-5442.

**Apple Barrel Orchards.** 2673 Sand Hill Rd., Penn Yan; (315) 536-2744.

**The Windmill Farm & Craft Market.** 3900 NY 14A, Penn Yan; (315) 536-3032; www.thewindmill.com.

**Black Rock Speedway.** NY 14A South, Dundee; (607) 243-8686; www.black rockspeedway.net.

**Dundee Family Fun Center.** Water Street, Dundee; (607) 243-5940.

## Where to Eat

**Essenhaus Restaurant.** 1300 NY 14A; (315) 531-9500; www.essenhaus-restaurant.com. German-American hearty cuisine, serving homemade soups, salads, steak, stroganoff, sauerbraten, pasta, burgers, wraps, and coconut cream pie. $–$$

**Keuka Restaurant.** 12 Main St.; (315) 536-5852; www.keuka-restaurant.com. Great appetizers, from apricot baked brie to bourbon chicken wings, fresh seafood, steaks, pasta, burgers, wraps, salads, and all-you-can-eat crab legs on Wed. $$–$$$

## Where to Stay

**Best Western Vineyard Inn & Suites.** 142 Lake St.; (800) 823-0612; www.vineyard innandsuites.com. Forty-three rooms and suites, indoor heated pool, fitness center, microwave, refrigerator, cable TV, complimentary deluxe hot breakfast, free Wi-Fi, children under twelve free with adult. $$

**Viking Resort.** 680 E. Lake Rd., NY 54; (315) 536-7061; www.vikingresort.com. Thirty-nine knotty-pine-style rooms, suites, and efficiencies, plus two cottages, with 1,000 feet of private lakeshore, an outdoor pool and hot tub, free rowboats for fishing, plus rental power and pontoon watercraft, late-afternoon cruises on Keuka Lake aboard *The Viking Spirit,* and bonfires at dusk. $–$$$

# Watkins Glen

Take NY 54 east to NY 14 south.

Situated on the southern shore of Seneca Lake, this is the home of American road racing and the site of some seriously spectacular waterfalls.

# New York **Trivia**

The Iroquois Confederacy's Great Law of Peace proposed the rights of free-dom of speech, equal representation, and impeachment and served as a framework for the U.S. Constitution.

## Watkins Glen State Park  (all ages)

**North Franklin Street, junction of NY 14 and 414; (607) 535-4511; www.nysparks.state.ny .us. Park is open daily year-round; campground open early May to mid-Oct; Gorge Trail closed early Nov to mid-May. Timespell (607) 535-8888 or (800) 853-SPELL. $$.**

Running through the heart of this park is a dramatic gorge bejeweled by nineteen water-falls and creek-carved crags. Hike the 1.5-mile Gorge Trail, nature's version of the Stair-master, up 832 stone steps through tunnels and over bridges to the top, where you can hop a shuttle bus or walk back to the entrance. The park also offers an Olympic-size swim-ming pool, ball fields, a playground and picnic area, recreation programs, 305 campsites, and the popular Finger Lakes Hiking Trail and the North Country National Scenic Trail. When darkness descends, Timespell takes visitors on a sound, light, and laser journey through the creation of this 450-million-year-old gift from the glaciers.

## Farm Sanctuary  (all ages)

**3100 Aikens Rd., off CR 22, next door to Sugar Hill State Forest, 8 miles west of town; (607) 583-2225; www.farmsanctuary.org. Guided tours on the hour 11 a.m. to 3 p.m. Wed through Sun from June through Aug; weekends in May, Sept, and Oct. $.**

Haven to hundreds of rescued farm animals, this 175-acre refuge aims to educate and enlighten everyone about compassionate care for all living things, through tours of their

# Speedsters and **Sailors**

**Watkins Glen International Raceway.** 2790 NY 16; (607) 535-2486; www.the glen.com.

**The International Motor Racing Research Center at Watkins Glen.** 610 S. Decatur St.; (607) 535-9044; www.racingarchives.org.

**Captain Bill's Seneca Lake Cruises.** 1 N. Franklin St.; (607) 535-4541.

**Seneca Sailing Adventures.** Village Marina; (607) 724-5100; www.senecasailing adventures.com.

*Malabar X* **Seneca Daysails.** Public Fishing Pier; (607) 535-5253; www.seneca daysails.com.

barns and opportunities to meet the residents. Every animal here has a story, and many of them are told at the People Barn, with exhibits, videos, and literature, and there's a special Kids' Korner and gift shop with books, posters, and vegetarian snacks. If you'd like to stay longer, and perhaps pitch in with the farm chores, several cabins overlooking the sanctuary are available to rent, and come with a vegan continental breakfast. $.

**Skyland Farm**  (all ages)

**4966 NY 414, Hector; (607) 546-5050; www.skylandfarm.net. Open late June to Sept, Wed through Sun 11 a.m. to 5 p.m.; early Sept through mid-Dec, Fri through Sun 11 a.m. to 5 p.m.; Dec 19 through 23, daily 11 a.m. to 5 p.m. $.**

Overlooking Seneca Lake, this friendly farm features the crafts and creations of over 300 local, New York, and American artists, as well as a barnyard of goats, sheep, and chickens, a cut-your-own flower garden, a labyrinth, and a cafe built around a two-story oak tree with terrific treetop views.

## Where to Eat

**Savard's Family Restaurant.** 601 N. Franklin St.; (607) 535-4538; www.savards familyrestaurant.com. Great breakfasts, soups, sandwiches, salads, burgers, steak, scampi, chicken, and pasta, with half-size portions available, plus a kids' menu. Everything from bread to dessert is homemade. $

**Seneca Harbor Station.** 1 N. Franklin St.; (607) 535-6101; www.senecaharborstation .com. Dockside dining inside or out, at a restored 1876 train station overlooking Seneca Lake, with salads, sandwiches, burgers, steaks, seafood, pasta, a children's menu, and homemade raspberry bongo or cinnamon bread pudding for dessert. $$–$$$$

## More Parks around **Watkins Glen**

**Havana Glen Gorge.** 135 Havana Glen Rd., Montour Falls; (607) 535-4300; www.nyfalls.com/havanaglen.

**Catherine Valley Trail.** Off NY 14, Montour Falls; (607) 535-4511; www.nys parks.state.ny.us.

## Where to Stay

**Longhouse Lodge Motel.** 3625 NY 14; (607) 535-2565; www.longhouselodge.com. Just outside of Watkins Glen, this friendly motel has an outdoor heated pool and free continental breakfast and movies. Children stay free. $

**Seneca Lodge.** NY 329, off NY 14, at south entrance to Watkins Glen State Park; (607) 535-2014. Eighty units in the motel, cabins, and A-frames, with a restaurant, tavern, pool, tennis courts, and hiking trails leading to Watkins Glen State Park. $$

# Elmira

Continue south on NY 14.

Known as the Soaring Capital of America and Mark Twain's town, Elmira also has the largest concentration of Victorian-era architecture in the state and more than twenty town parks. To tour Elmira by foot, follow either the red or blue footprints painted on the sidewalks, each a 1-mile loop of the downtown area. For more information call (607) 737-5510.

### Eldridge Park  (all ages)

**Entrances off Grand Central Avenue, Westside Avenue, Woodlawn Avenue, and the new South entrance; (607) 737-5679; www.eldridgepark.us. Park open year-round; carousel, boat rides, ice-cream shop, snack bar, and gift shop generally open weekends from Memorial Day to Labor Day. $**

One of the largest and most popular parks in town, Eldridge offers a scenic walking trail along the lake, ball fields, picnic pavilions, a roller-sports park, a game arcade, and an ice-cream shop and snack bar. The jewel of the place, however, is the recently restored fifty-six-animal Eldridge Park Carousel, considered to be the fastest in the world, spinning at almost 18 miles per hour. If you can grab the brass ring on this majestic merry-go-round, you rock! There's a dragon out in the lake by the name of Jasper II, and he gives a great ride. If you'd like to drive your own dragon, Jasper's hatchlings, brightly colored paddleboats, are also available. A future addition in the works is the installation of a three-quarter-scale steam train and over a mile of track to transport people around the park.

### First Arena  (all ages)

**155 N. Main St.; (607) 734-7825 or (607) 722-3711; www.firstarena.com. $–$$.**

Home of the professional hockey team, the Elmira Jackals, this state-of-the-art multipurpose facility features two NHL regulation-size ice rinks and a full schedule of live entertainment throughout the year. Events range from wrestling exhibitions and monster-truck shows, to family fare such as Dora the Explorer, the Harlem Globetrotters, and the Lipizzaner Stallions, along with high-quality concerts, circuses, and ice shows. There's a restaurant on-site, as well as a snack bar and video-game arcade, and year-round ice-skating and hockey lessons are available at the recreation rink.

### Clemens Center  (all ages)

207 Clemens Center Parkway; (607) 734-8191; www.clemenscenter.com. $$–$$$.

This terrific performing arts center has two stages, the intimate Mandeville Hall and the spectacular, recently renovated, 1925 vaudeville-era, 1,618-seat Powers Theater. Five professional Broadway shows are presented each season, as well as music, dance, and comedy productions for all ages.

### Mark Twain's Study  (ages 6 and up)

1 Park Place; Elmira College Campus, off NY 14; (607) 735-1941; www.elmira.edu. Open June through Labor Day, Mon through Sat 9 a.m. to 5 p.m. Free.

Relocated to the Elmira College campus from the nearby Quarry Farm, this octagonal cottage was the birthplace of Tom Sawyer and Huckleberry Finn. Samuel Langhorne Clemens, better known as Mark Twain, spent many years here, typing on a Remington Rand from early morning to late afternoon. Nearby, in Hamilton Hall, is the Mark Twain Exhibit, with photographs, furniture, clothing, and memorabilia about the man. The bronze Mark Twain statue outside stands 12 feet tall, which is equal to 2 fathoms, or in river pilot speak, "mark twain."

### Chemung Valley History Museum  (ages 7 and up)

415 E. Water St.; (607) 734-4167; www.chemungvalleymuseum.org. Open year-round Tues through Sat 10 a.m. to 5 p.m.; closed holidays. $.

Dedicated to the preservation of the area's history, this regional museum houses more than 18,000 artifacts, 16,000 photographs, and thousands of books, manuscripts, and maps. Three galleries offer temporary exhibits on a wide variety of topics, from Native American history to Mark Twain, and special activities and events for kids include old fashioned games, nineteenth-century chores, and a Ghost Walk. Historical themed bus tours are scheduled throughout the year, and a free Revolutionary War driving guide is available at the desk, with a self-guided, one-hour loop tour past points of interest, particularly the Newtown Battlefield.

### National Soaring Museum  (all ages)

51 Soaring Hill Drive, Harris Hill, Elmira; (607) 734-3128; www.soaringmuseum.org. Harris Hill Soaring Center (607) 734-0641; www.harrishillsoaring.org. Open daily year-round 10 a.m. to 5 p.m. Closed some major holidays. Adults $$, children $, 4 and under free; sailplane rides $$$$; amusement park free admission, pay as you go for attractions $.

More than a dozen vintage sailplanes are hangared here, the largest collection of its kind in the world. Scale models of gliders, from 1833 to today, will appeal to professional and pretend pilots alike, and during regattas and festivals the sailplanes take to the skies like flocks of silent pterodactyls. At the Harris Hill Soaring Center, overlooking the museum, glider rides are offered daily, weather permitting, and the view from the blue is spectacular. For a more earthly entertainment, the Harris Hill Amusement Park next door provides pint-size thrills with motorized kiddie rides, arcade games, a micro-racetrack, horseshoe pits, mini-golf, batting cages, a driving range, heated pool, and an ice-cream shop.

### Wings of Eagles Discovery Center (all ages)

17 Aviation Dr., Elmira-Corning Regional Airport, Horseheads; (607) 739-8200; www.wings ofeagles.com. Open Wed through Sat 10 a.m. to 4 p.m., Sun noon to 4 p.m. $–$$$.

Aircraft of World War II and the Korean War, many still airworthy, are assembled at this volunteer-run aviation museum. Dozens of warbirds, from Avengers to Tomcats, are parked in the hangars or on the tarmac outside, and exhibits highlight historic planes such as the B-17 Flying Fortress, and the advent of the Atomic Age. Seven operational flight simulators are available to try, there's always an aircraft restoration to watch, and the air show in Aug is awesome.

### Tanglewood Nature Center and Museum (all ages)

443 Coleman Ave.; (607) 732-6060; www.tanglewoodnaturecenter.com. Trails open sunrise to sunset, museum open Tues through Sat 9 a.m. to 5 p.m. $–$$.

United by a web of trails, the unique ecosystems of Frenchman's Bluff and Gleason Meadows offer opportunities to spot the abundant wildlife wandering through the wildflowers. Black bears, foxes, deer, rabbits, coyotes, porcupines, snakes, frogs, and turtles live here, along with a variety of birds. Inside the museum are eco-exhibits and more animals, such as Bernice, an African spurred tortoise, and Iggy, an iguana. Annual events for families include Winterfest, Eggstravaganza, and Haunted Happenings, and reptile raps and owl prowls are offered in summer.

### Newtown Battlefield State Park (all ages)

451 Oneida Rd.; (607) 732-6067; www.nysparks.state.ny.us and www.chemungvalley.org. Open mid-May to mid-Oct, dawn to dusk. Call ahead to confirm changes to hours, activities available, and possible closures due to pending state budget cuts.

The site of Gen. John Sullivan's victory over the Iroquois during the Revolutionary War is now a 330-acre state park, with a rustic lodge, sixteen campsites, five cabins, six picnic pavilions, nature trails, playgrounds, ball fields, and an outdoor deck overlooking the battlefield.

### Arnot Museum (all ages)

235 Lake St.; (607) 734-3697; www.arnotartmuseum.org. Open Tues through Sat 10 a.m. to 5 p.m., Sun 1 to 5 p.m. $.

This museum in a mansion has a wonderful permanent collection of seventeenth- to nineteenth-century European paintings and a growing collection of nineteenth- to twentieth-century American art, including new contemporary works.

## Where to Eat

**Hill Top Inn.** 171 Jerusalem Hill; (607) 732-6728; www.hill-top-inn.com. Chemung County's oldest licensed restaurant, with panoramic views, serving surf and turf, lamb, chicken, pasta, ribs, and homemade desserts. $$$

**Maple Lawn Dairy and Restaurant.** 3162 Lower Maple Ave.; (607) 733-0519. Delicious hearty home-style cuisine for breakfast, lunch, and dinner, and famous for their home-made ice cream. $

**Moretti's Restaurant.** 800 Hatch St.; (607) 734-1535; www.morettisrestaurant.net. Italian-American cuisine, offering steaks, chops, chicken, pasta, seafood, and pizza, plus full menu available for takeout. $$

## Where to Stay

**Holiday Inn Elmira-Riverview.** 760 E. Water St.; (877) 863-4780; www.holidayinn .com. One hundred and forty-nine rooms and suites, indoor and outdoor pools, fitness center and sauna, laundry facilities, same-day dry cleaning, high-speed Internet, lounge, room service, live entertainment, restaurant, and kids eat free. $–$$

**Linenwald Haus.** 1526 Grand Central Ave.; (607) 733-8753 or (800) 440-4287; www.lin denwaldhaus.com. Eighteen unique rooms and suites in an elegant nineteenth-century mansion on five acres, two full porches, an elevator, air-conditioning, a full hot breakfast, Wi-Fi throughout the house and grounds, and children welcome. $–$$

# Corning

Take NY 17 west.

Take a walk down the Crystal City's Market Street, a restored nineteenth-century historic district with boutiques, museums, and glass studios all along the brick-paved sidewalks and tree-lined streets.

### Corning Museum of Glass (all ages)

1 Museum Way; (607) 974-2000, (607) 937-5371, or (800) 732-6845; www.cmog.org. Open daily year-round 9 a.m. to 5 p.m.; to 8 p.m. in July and Aug. Closed major holidays. $$, children and teens 19 and under free.

Gaze at 3,500 years of glittering glass, gleaned from the museum's collection of more than 35,000 priceless objects displayed in the Art and History and the Sculpture Galleries. Glass you can touch, bend, and play with can be found at the **Glass Innovation Center,** with a variety of interesting interactive tech and manufacturing exhibits. The amazing **Hot Glass Show,** where artisans craft crystalline creations, is not to be missed! Finally, tour the **Steuben Factory,** the only place in the world to see Steuben glass being melted, molded, cut, polished, and engraved. Family-friendly audio tours explain the collections, and there are opportunities for kids to create one-of-a kind masterpieces at the Make Your Own Glass exhibit. In summer special programs are offered, such as Little Gather, a storytelling adventure for kids ages three to ten, and Vitreous Adventures, a sleuthing exploration of glass for kids ages eight to ten. The GlassMarket, one of the largest museum gift shops in the country, displays the creations of more than two hundred glass artisans, with a selection of over 15,000 items available for purchase.

### Rockwell Museum of Western Art  (all ages)

**111 Cedar St.; (607) 937-5386; www.rockwellmuseum.org. Open daily 9 a.m. to 5 p.m.; Memorial Day through Labor Day, 9 a.m. to 8 p.m. Closed major holidays. Adults $$, seniors and students $, children 19 and under free. Combination tickets with Corning Museum of Glass available $$$.**

Housed in the historic Old City Hall, this is considered to be the most comprehensive collection of art of the American West in the East. Upstairs are more than 2,000 objects of Steuben glass designed by Frederick Carder. Special activities for children include free *Explore the West* booklets, ArtPack backpacks filled with puzzles and games, an art scavenger hunt, and a Kids' West Play area, complete with costumes, tepee, and trading post.

### Patterson Inn Museum Complex  (all ages)

**59 West Pulteney St.; (607) 937-5281; www.pattersoninnmuseum.org. Open June through Aug, Mon through Fri 10 a.m. to 4 p.m., Sat 10 a.m. to 2 p.m.; Sept through May by appointment. Closed major holidays. Free, donations accepted.**

Costumed guides bring nineteenth-century America to life at this complex of historic buildings that include a settler's cabin, schoolhouse, tavern, blacksmith shop, and agricultural exhibits.

# Also in the Area

**The Fun Park.** 11233 E. Corning Rd., Corning; (607) 936-1888.

**Nasser Civic Center Ice Rink.** 8 Civic Center Plaza, Corning; (607) 936-3764; www.rinktime.com.

**Birdseye Hollow Park and State Forest.** 7291 Coon Rd., Bath; (607) 776-2165; www.dec.ny.gov.

**Mossy Bank Park and Nature Center.** Mossy Bank Park Road, Bath; (607) 776-3811; www.trails.com.

**Pinnacle State Park and Golf Course.** 1904 Pinnacle Rd., Addison; (607) 359-2767; www.nysparks.state.ny.us.

**Vitrix Hot Glass Studio.** 77 W. Market St., Corning; (607) 936-8707; www.vitrix hotglass.com.

**Hands-on Glass.** 124 Crystal Lane, Corning; (607) 962-3044 or (866) 962-3044; www.handsonglass.com.

### Spencer Crest Nature Center (all ages)

2424 Spencer Hill Rd.; (607) 962-9012; www.spencercrest.org. Trails open daily dawn to dusk year-round. Nature center open Mon through Sat 9 a.m. to 3 p.m. Free, $ for programs.

Wander 7 miles of nature trails winding through 250 acres of woods and past two ponds, and participate in a variety of adventures, such as family fishing derbies, pumpkin hunts in the woods, and Sept star treks.

### New York State Fish Hatchery (all ages)

7169 Fish Hatchery Rd., Bath; (607) 776-7087 or (518) 402-8043; www.dec.ny.gov. Open daily 8 a.m. to 3:45 p.m. Call for weekend hours. Free.

One of twelve hatcheries in the state, this one specializes in lake, brown, and rainbow trout, producing about 86,000 pounds per year.

## Where to Eat

**Market Street Brewing Co. and Restaurant.** 63 W. Market St.; (607) 936-BEER; www.936-beer.com. Corning's first brewpub, brewing six beers right on the premises, and a terrific eclectic menu including coconut shrimp, sushi nachos, homemade soups, chicken potpie, glazed salmon, and sirloin steak, plus a $5 kids menu. $$–$$$

**Three Birds Restaurant.** 73 E. Market St.; (607) 936-8862; www.threebirdsrestaurant .com. Creative gourmet cuisine, using organic herbs and produce, serving salads, sandwiches, Kobe burgers, hanger steaks, rack of lamb, stuffed chicken, pasta, salmon, shrimp, crab cakes, rainbow trout, and nineteen kinds of martinis. $$–$$$$

## Where to Stay

**Radisson Hotel Corning.** 125 Denison Parkway East; (607) 962-5000 or (800) 395-7046; www.radisson.com/corningny. Convenient to the downtown area, with 177 rooms and suites, free high-speed Internet, microwave, refrigerator, rollaway bed and crib available upon request, room service, laundry service and facilities, heated indoor pool, fitness center, a big Jacuzzi, a restaurant and lounge on-site. $$–$$$

**Staybridge Suites Corning.** 201 Townley Ave.; (607) 936-7800; www.staybridge.com. Studios, one and two bedroom suites with full kitchens, twenty-four-hour convenience store, free high-speed Internet, free laundry facilities, an indoor pool, fitness center, a recreation and sports court, free breakfast, and kids eat free. $$–$$$

# Mount Morris

Take NY 17 west to I-390.

The largest dam east of the Mississippi is here, causing folks to say this is the "Best Town by a Damsite."

## Letchworth State Park (all ages)

Off NY 36 (exit 7 off I-390), 6 miles south of Mount Morris, and 1 Letchworth State Park, Castile; (585) 493-3600 or (800) 456-2267; www.nysparks.state.ny.us. Park open year-round; 270 campsites and 82 cabins open mid-May through mid-Oct; winterized cabins open year-round. South Pool is closed indefinitely. Vehicle fee $ mid-May through mid-Oct. Balloons over Letchworth (585) 493-3340; www.balloonsoverletchworth.com. Adventure Calls Outfitters (585) 343-4710; www.adventure-calls.com. $–$$.

Stretching for 14,350 acres along the Genesee River, this vast park has a variety of activities for families. Perhaps one of the prettiest sights in the state is the 17-mile scenic Letchworth Gorge, the river's work in progress for thousands of years, nicknamed the "Grand Canyon of the East." The three waterfalls that glisten through the gorge were saved from hydroelectric power plant destruction by William P. Letchworth, who deeded much of this area to the people of New York in 1910. Sixty-six miles of trails lace the place, fun for hiking, biking, and horseback riding, and there's a pool, a playground, picnic pavilions, and playing fields. Nature, history, and performing arts programs are offered, as well as guided walks and tours. Winter activities include cross-country skiing, snow tubing, ice-skating, snowmobiling, and horse-drawn sleigh rides. For a bird's-eye perspective, take a breathtaking hot-air balloon ride over the gorge, or for a fish's-eye perspective, go white-water rafting down the river (Class I and II rapids).

## William Pryor Letchworth Museum (all ages)

1 Letchworth State Park, Castile; (585) 493-2760 or (585) 493-3600; www.letchworthpark history.com. Open daily mid-May through Oct, 10 a.m. to 5 p.m., Nov and Dec weekends only, 10 a.m. to 3 p.m. Donation.

Located within the park near Middle Falls, the recently renovated Letchworth Museum houses a collection of Seneca and settler artifacts, along with regional, natural history, and archaeological displays. Of particular interest to children is the exhibit on Mary Jemison, known as the "White Woman of the Genesee," an Irish immigrant girl captured by a Shawnee war party in 1758 when she was 15 years old and adopted by the Seneca. Given

## The Finger Lakes Trail

Stretching 875 miles across the state, this linear and loop trail system is part of the official North Country National Scenic Trail. When completed, it will extend 4,600 miles from eastern New York to central North Dakota. Mountain bikes, motorized vehicles, and horses are prohibited along this ribbon of wilderness, and the scenery is spectacular. If biking is your preference, pedal along Bike Route 17 (follow small green oval road signs with a bicycle), a 435-mile path from the Hudson River to the Erie Canal. For more information: www.fingerlakestrail.org or (585) 658-9320.

the name Dehgewanus, she remained with the Seneca for the rest of her life, raised seven children, and became a respected leader. Her grave is near the museum.

## Mount Morris Dam (ages 7 and up)

**1 Mount Morris Dam, off NY 408; (585) 658-4790 or (585) 658-4790; Visitor center open daily in May and early Sept through mid-Nov from 8 a.m. to 4 p.m.; Memorial Day through Labor Day to 5 p.m. Call for winter hours. Guided dam tours Tues, Wed, and Thurs at 2 p.m.; Fri, Sat, and Sun at 11 a.m. and 2 p.m. Free.**

Stop by the William B. Hoyt II Visitor Center for a tour given by the U.S. Army Corps of Engineers of the largest dam east of the Mississippi. The newly remodeled museum has a short film with construction and catastrophe footage, and an interactive, activity-filled Kids Corner for emerging engineers.

## Stony Brook State Park (all ages)

**10820 NY 36 South, Dansville; (585) 335-8111; www.nysparks.state.ny.us. Park open year-round, campground open mid-May through mid-Oct. $. Call ahead to confirm changes to hours, activities available, and possible closures due to pending state budget cuts.**

Swim in two stream-fed gorge pools, hike the Gorge Trail, enjoy the picnic area, playground, baseball fields, and tennis courts, and camp out at one of the 125 sites on 577 wooded acres.

# Also in **the Area**

**Mount Morris Lanes.** 9 Erie St., Mount Morris; (585) 658-2540 or (585) 658-2540.

**Nor-Mar Ostrich Farm.** 2804 DeNoon Rd., Caledonia; (585) 624-4882.

**Cal Bowl.** 3156 State St., Caledonia; (585) 538-6530; www.calbowl.com.

**Livingston Lanes.** 4260 Lakeville Rd. (US 20A), Geneseo; (585) 243-1760.

**Minnehan's Family Entertainment Center.** 5601 Big Tree Rd., Lakeville; (585) 346-6167.

**Genesee Valley Kart Club.** 2123 NY 15, Avon; (585) 226-2940; www.gvkc.org.

**East Avon Vintage Drive-In.** 1520 NY 15, Avon; (585) 226-9290; www.vintage drivein.com.

**Hemlock Hills Alpaca Farm.** 4151 Clay St., Livonia; (585) 367-2518; www .hemlockhillsalpacas.com.

**Wolcott Farms.** 3820 Hermitage Rd., Warsaw; (585) 786-3504; www.wolcott farms.com.

## Where to Eat

**Brian's USA Diner.** 5524 NY 36; (585) 658-9380; www.briansusadiner.com. Great diner, everything homemade, with fourteen kinds of burgers and the best "dam" chicken sandwich in town. $–$$

**Charcoal Corral.** 7037 Chapman Ave., Perry; (585) 237-5270; www.charcoalcorral.com. Char-grilled hot dogs, burgers, roast chicken, pizza, ice cream, barbecued ribs, a Wednesday all-you-can-eat pasta buffet, plus a great mini-golf course, an arcade, giant inflatables to climb, and the only outdoor movie theater in the county, the fabulous Silver Lake Drive-In. $$

## Where to Stay

**Country Inn & Suites.** 130 N. Main St.; (585) 658-4080; www.countryinns.com. Located near the entrance to Letchworth State Park, with sixty rooms and suites, free phone calls, free high-speed Internet, free newspaper, cable TV, heated indoor pool, fitness center, and free deluxe continental breakfast. $$–$$$

**Glen Iris Inn.** Inside Letchworth State Park, Castile; (585) 493-2622; www.glenirisinn.com. Once the country estate of William P. Letchworth and converted into an inn in 1914, the inn offers a variety of rooms, suites, efficiencies, and cottages, and a wonderful gourmet restaurant with a children's menu and picnics packed to go. $–$$$$

# Canandaigua

Take I-390 north to NY 5 and US 20.

The name is derived from the Seneca word *Kanadarque,* meaning "The Chosen Spot."

## Sonnenberg Gardens and Mansion State Historic Park (all ages)

151 Charlotte St.; (585) 396-7433; www.sonnenberg.org. Open daily May, Sept, and Oct, 9:30 a.m. to 4 p.m.; open to 5:30 p.m. Memorial Day through Labor Day. Adults $$, children $, under 12 **free.**

Perhaps the finest Victorian gardens in America are here, spread over fifty lush acres and landscaped in a variety of themes. Nine different styles of horticultural artistry can be explored on a self-guided tour of the Japanese, Italian, Colonial, Rose, and Rock Gardens. There's also a thirteen-room conservatory, Butterfly House, a very long greenhouse to stroll through, and the ornately furnished 1887 stone mansion. Kids can take the Trail Adventure, collecting clues and stamps hidden along a garden path, culminating in a prize at the end. The High Noon Café serves soups, salads, and sandwiches, and provides boxed lunches for perfect picnics. Come for a midsummer Moonlight Stroll on a Fri night, when the gardens are artistically lit and live music, from bluegrass to Big Band, fills the fragrant air.

### Granger Homestead and Carriage Museum (all ages)

**295 North Main St.; (585) 394-1472; www.grangerhomestead.org. Open late May through mid-Oct, Tues and Wed 1 to 5 p.m., Thurs and Fri 11 a.m. to 5 p.m.; Sat and Sun, June through Oct, 1 to 5 p.m. $, preschoolers free.**

Once the home of Gideon Granger, postmaster general under President Thomas Jefferson, this early-nineteenth-century, Federal-style mansion is filled with four generations of original furnishings, and the Carriage Museum out back houses a collection of more than seventy horse-drawn vehicles, all restored to their gleaming glory. Period Tea Parties, for tea-totalers ages six to eleven, come with costumes, cut-out sandwiches, Victorian craft activities, and a photo. Costumed drivers offer historical carriage rides through Canandaigua's historic district, and in Oct, Civil War reenactors set up camp. A Christkindl arts and crafts fair is held in Dec.

### Ontario County Historical Museum (all ages)

**55 North Main St.; (585) 394-4975; www.ochs.org. Open year-round Tues through Sat 10 a.m. to 4:30 p.m., Wed evenings until 9 p.m. Closed Mon and major holidays. Adults $, children free when accompanied by adult.**

In 1794 the Senecas and the pioneer settlers signed the Pickering Treaty, granting the latter the right to settle the Great Lakes Basin. An original copy of this important treaty can be seen here, along with a life mask of Abraham Lincoln, local-history displays, and a discovery room with hands-on activities for children.

### Ontario County Courthouse (ages 7 and up)

**27 N. Main St.; (585) 396-4239. Open year-round Mon through Fri 8:30 a.m. to 5 p.m. Free.**

Legend has it that when Susan B. Anthony was brought here to be tried for the heinous crime of attempting to vote in the national election in Rochester, the arm of Lady Justice, perched atop the courthouse, fell to the ground when the suffragette was fined $100.

### Kershaw Park (all ages)

**19 Lakeshore Dr.; (585) 396-5080. Open daily Memorial Day through Labor Day, 9 a.m. to 9 p.m. $.**

Eight acres along the north shore of Canandaigua Lake offer opportunities for swimming, sailboarding, volleyball, picnicking, and photo ops at a picturesque gazebo.

### Onanda Park (all ages)

**4965 CR 16; (585) 396-2752; www.townofcanandaigua.org; (585) 394-1120 or (585) 396-2518. Open year-round dawn to dusk. $.**

Enjoy fishing, swimming, and hiking along more than 2 miles of scenic interpretive trails at this eighty-acre park, with picnic areas, a playground, children's programs, and cabin and lodge rentals available.

# Cruising **Canandaigua Lake**

**Captain Gray's Boat Tours.** 115 Howell St.; (585) 394-5270.

**The Canandaigua Lady.** 205 Lakeshore Dr.; (585) 396-7350; www.steamboat landingonline.com.

**Sutter's Canandaigua Marina.** 808 S. Main St., City Pier; (585) 394-0918; www.suttersmarina.com.

## Ganondagan State Historic Site (all ages)

1488 NY 444, Victor; (585) 742-1690; www.ganondagan.org. Trails open year-round, visitor center open mid-May through Oct, Tues through Sun 9 a.m. to 5 p.m. Closed Nov through Apr. $.

This was once the site of a thriving Seneca settlement of more than 4,500 people. Destroyed by the French in 1687 to cut down on the competition for the fur industry, today this Village of Peace is the only national landmark east of the Mississippi dedicated to Native Americans. Interpretive trails wind through 500 acres, and exhibits are presented on the history and culture of the Senecas, the native plants they prized, and the brutal destruction of their village.

## Roseland Water Park (all ages)

250 Eastern Blvd.; (585) 396-2000; www.roselandwaterpark.com. Water park open mid-June through Labor Day, 11 a.m. to 6 p.m., with longer midsummer hours; $$$, kids 2 and under **free.**

Get set to get wet at this fun family splash spot, as you twirl down The Twister, plunge off The Cliff, and experience extreme tube rides together. Face painting, sidewalk art, a bounce house, animal shows, and boat rentals provide drier options.

## Bristol Mountain Resort (all ages)

5662 NY 64; (585) 374-6000; www.bristolmountain.com. Open daily 9 a.m. to 5 p.m.; extended nighttime hours from early Dec through mid-Mar. $$$$.

With thirty-three trails, six lifts, and two terrain parks, this is a fun place to play in the snow, and in autumn the chairlifts offer scenic foliage flights.

# Where to Eat

**Doc's Lakeside Seafood Restaurant.** 726 S. Main St.; (585) 394-3460; www.docssea food.com. Helmed by a Culinary Institute of America graduate nicknamed "Chef Gilligan," serving fresh seafood, steaks, pasta, Maine lobster flown in daily, and a special kids' menu. $$$

**Max on the Lake.** 770 S. Main St.; (585) 394-7800; www.theinnonthelake.com/dining.

## Also in **the Area**

**Valentown Museum.** 7370 Valentown Sq., Victor; (585) 924-4170; www.valen town.org.

**Wizard of Clay Pottery.** 7851 US 20A, Bloomfield; (585) 229-2980; www.wizard ofclay.com.

**Copper Creek Farm.** 5041 Shortsville Rd., Shortsville; (585) 289-4441.

**Willow Pond Aqua Farm.** 3581 Swamp Rd., Canandaigua; (888) 854-8945; www.willowpondaquafarms.com.

Elegant and friendly restaurant with lovely lake views, serving omelets, salads, steak, seafood, poultry, and pasta, with an extensive Finger Lakes wine list. The nearby seasonal Sand Bar offers a Caribbean casual outdoor deck dining experience. $–$$$$

## Where to Stay

**Finger Lakes Inn.** 4343 NY 5 and US 20; (585) 394-2800 or (800) 727-2775; www .fingerlakesinn.com. The largest inn in the Finger Lakes, with 124 rooms, located on ten landscaped acres, has a family activity center, a heated Olympic-size outdoor pool, sundeck, basketball and volleyball courts, picnic area, gas grills, complimentary continental breakfast; and more than twenty-five restaurants nearby. $

**The Inn on the Lake.** 770 S. Main St.; (585) 394-7800 or (800) 228-2801; www.theinnon thelake.com. Rooms with mini fridges and kitchenette suites, indoor and outdoor pool, whirlpool, fitness center, cable TV, free high-speed Internet, restaurants, located on the lake. $$$$

# Palmyra

Take NY 21 north.

The Erie Canal brought prosperity to Palmyra, making the town an important agricultural and industrial distribution center. Ancient earthen mounds from the Adena Culture, a prehistory tribe of very tall people, were found in the area, and the Iroquois considered this to be a sacred space. Later it became the birthplace of the Latter Day Saints movement, better known as the Mormon Church.

## Palmyra Historical Museum  (ages 6 and up)

132 Market St.; (315) 597-6981; www.historicpalmyrany.com. Open late spring to fall, 11 a.m. to 4 p.m., Tues to Sat; and fall to spring, 10 a.m. to 5 p.m. $. Family Trail Ticket ($$)

includes admission to all four historic Palmyra museums for a family of four, plus a gift from the Alling Coverlet Museum gift shop.

The town's history is highlighted here in twenty-three themed rooms filled with elegant furniture, household articles, local memorabilia, and a collection of antique toys. An unusual tour, not for the fainthearted, is a real nighttime Ghost Hunt through the museum and the Phelps General Store next door. During the Palmyra Pirates Weekend, the museum offers buccaneer tales and treasure hunts, and you won't want to miss the Pillage 'n The Village Bed Race Regatta.

### William Phelps General Store Museum  (ages 6 and up)
140 Market St.; (315) 597-6981; www.historicalpalmyrany.com. Open late spring to fall, Tues through Sat 11 a.m. to 4 p.m.; and fall to spring, Tues through Thurs 10 a.m. to 5 p.m. $.

As if frozen in time, this nineteenth-century store contains much of its original merchandise, and the upstairs residence has been left as if the owners just stepped out—or never left at all, if you believe the ghost hunters.

### Print Shop Museum  (ages 8 and up)
140 Market St.; (315) 597-6981; www.historicpalmyra.com. Open late spring to fall, Tues through Sat 11 a.m. to 4 p.m.; and fall to spring, Tues through Thurs 10 a.m. to 5 p.m. $.

The newest addition to the historic Palmyra collection, this small museum has an assortment of printing presses, cutters, type trays, and typewriters.

### Alling Coverlet Museum  (ages 8 and up)
122 William St.; (315) 597-6737 or (315) 597-6981; www.historicpalmyrany.com. Open June to mid-Sept, 1 to 4 p.m. daily; closed July 4.

The largest collection of coverlets in the country are housed in a 1901 newspaper printing office, along with looms, spinning wheels, and weaver's tools. Because there are so many quilts and covers, it takes more than six years to rotate these unique American tapestries through public display.

### Long Acre Farms  (all age )
1342 Eddy Rd., Macedon; (315) 986-4202; www.longacrefarms.com. Open May through Oct, 10 a.m. to 6 p.m. Adults $$, children $, 4 and under free.

Home of the Amazing Maize Maze, this is a field of dreams you could get lost in . . . literally. But since that's the general idea, your family will have some seriously un-cornditional fun. Maze masters are around to give "Kernels of Knowledge" to the hopelessly lost, and special events include evening Moonlight Maze runs and a Fall Family Fun Fest. The Back 40 Activity Area has a giant jumping pillow, slides, mini-mazes, a Trike Track, a Straw Jump, a climbing wall, and a huge sandbox, The ABC Preschool Club teaches the alphabet of agriculture with games, stories, and crafts, and bags of fossil or ruby rich ore can be bought and mined at the Gemstone Panning sluice. Since this is a real farm, stop by the market and pick up some produce, homemade fudge, and ice cream.

## Also in **the Area**

**County Line Raceway.** 311 Pittsford-Palmyra Rd., Macedon; (315) 986-5876; www.countylinegocarts.com.

**Sportworks Family Fun Park.** 180 NY 31, Macedon; (315) 986-4245; www.golf bigswing.com.

**Doug Kent's Rose Bowl Lanes.** 725 W. Miller St., Newark; (315) 331-2007.

**Tiki Putt.** 228 Van Buren St., Newark; (315) 331-7888.

**Spencer Speedway.** 3020 NY 104, Williamson; (315) 589-3018; www.spencer speedway.org.

**Hoffman Clock Museum.** Newark Public Library, 121 High St., Newark; (315) 331-4370.

**Museum of Wayne County History.** 21 Butternut St., Lyons; (315) 946-4943; www.waynehistory.org.

**Joseph Smith Farm.** 830 Stafford Rd., Palmyra; (315) 597-5851; www.hill cumorah.org.

## Where to Eat

**Muddy Waters Cafe.** 100 Division St.; (315) 597-4197; Soups, salads, sandwiches, wraps, smoothies, and ice cream. $

**Yellow Mills Diner.** 2534 NY 31; (315) 597-4613. Delicious diner delights. $

## Where to Stay

**Palmyra Inn.** 955 Canandaigua Rd.; (800) 426-9900; www.palmyrainn.com. Rooms and family-friendly suites, kitchenettes in every room, high-speed Internet, big Jacuzzi spa, fitness center, free shuttle to local sites, and free deluxe continental breakfast. $$$

# Sodus Bay Area

Take NY 21 north, then turn east onto NY 104.

### Sodus Bay Lighthouse Museum (all ages)

7606 N. Ontario St., Sodus Point; (315) 483-4936; www.soduspointlighthouse.org. Open May and Oct, Tues through Sun 10 a.m. to 5 p.m. $.

Built in 1870, this lighthouse is now a maritime museum with ship models, dioramas, and other memorabilia reminiscent of life on Lake Ontario. Climb the stairs to the Lens Room for a view of the Sodus Point Piers and the shoreline bluffs. In summer, **free** concerts are presented at the Lighthouse Gazebo, and the four acres of mowed grounds are perfect for a picnic overlooking the lake.

### Fair Haven Beach State Park (all ages)

**14985 State Park Rd., Fair Haven; (315) 947-5205; www.nysparks.state.ny.us. Park open year-round, campground open Apr through Oct. $$.**

The steep bluffs and white-sand beaches of this 862-acre park are beautiful, and the nearby marshlands are home to a wide variety of birds. Hiking and nature trails wind through the wetlands, and there's good swimming at two sandy beaches, fishing in the pond, bay, or lake, small boat rentals, a playground and picnic area, a ball field, recreation programs, three campgrounds, and a cabin colony.

### Chimney Bluffs State Park (all ages)

**7700 Garner Rd., Wolcott; (315) 947-5205; www.nysparks.state.ny.us. Open year-round dawn to dusk. Summer vehicle fee $$. Call ahead to confirm changes to hours, activities available, and possible closures due to pending state budget cuts.**

If you haven't booked a ticket to the moon or Mars lately, this place is the next best thing. Ice Age glaciers deposited drumlins along the shore of Lake Ontario, and the eroded result is an eerie and surreal landscape of chimney-shaped rocks, ridges, and spires. Towering over the lake, with names like Dragon's Back and Castle Spire, this place is New York's version of the Badlands. Be extra careful on the trails in this undeveloped park, however, for they do skirt steep edges of the cliffs.

# More Sodus Bay **Area Activities**

**Phillips Park.** 542 Main St., Fair Haven; (315) 947-5112; www.co.cayuga.ny.us/fairhaven.

**West Barrier Bar Park.** West side of Fair Haven Bay, Fair Haven; (315) 253-5611; www.tourcayuga.com.

**Blue Cut Nature Center.** 7210 NY 31W, Lyons; (315) 946-5830; www.dec.ny.gov.

**Sterling Lake Shore Park and Nature Center.** 15730 Jensvold Rd., off 104A, Sterling; (315) 947-6143; www.cayuganet.org/sterlingpark.

**Huckleberry Swamp.** Catchpole Road, North Rose; (585) 338-1820; www.ofofinc.org.

**Montezuma Audubon Center.** NY 89, Savannah; (315) 365-3580; www.ny.audubon.org/montezuma.

**My-T-Putt Fun Center.** 7902 Lake Rd., Sodus Point; (315) 483-7223.

## Alasa Farms (all ages)

**6450 Shaker Rd., Alton; (315) 483-6321; www.crackerboxpalace.org. Open June through Oct. $.**

Once the site of a nineteenth-century Shaker community, this friendly 700-acre agritainment complex offers seasonal apple picking, tours of the farm, tractor-drawn hayrides, birds of prey demonstrations, scavenger hunts, sheep shearing, and nature walks to a creek scattered with fossils that you can collect and take home. It's also the home of Cracker Box Palace, a haven for neglected and abused animals. More than 140 rescued animals, including horses, geese, ducks, chickens, rabbits, goats, sheep, and pigs live in peace here, cared for by volunteers and local veterinarians as they await adoption or sponsorship. Workshops for children are offered in summer, and a Family Camping Weekend, complete with a chuck-wagon dinner and karaoke around the campfire, is held in late Sept.

## Where to Eat

**Abe's Waterfront Boat House Bar & Grill.** 8527 Greig St., Sodus Point; (315) 483-4444; www.abeswaterfront.com. The newest and largest waterfront restaurant in town, serving steamers, battered veggies, create-your-own pasta, steaks, and seafood, plus a kids' menu and a crab and clam bar on an upper deck overlooking the lake and bay. $$–$$$

**Hot's Point.** 8482 Greig St., Sodus Point; (315) 483-9301; www.hotspoint.com. Hot dogs, white hot dogs, chili dogs, cheese dogs, chili-cheese dogs, garbage plates, twenty-five flavors of ice cream, breakfast, and a kids' menu. $

## Where to Stay

**Bonnie Castle Farm Bed & Breakfast.** 6603 Bonnie Castle Rd., Wolcott; (315) 587-2273 or (800) 587-4006; www.bnbfinder.com. Lovely turn-of-the-twentieth-century waterfront B&B, with eight rooms and full breakfast; children are welcome. $$–$$$

**The Cliffs at Sodus Point.** 7961 Lake Rd., Sodus Point; (315) 483-4309; www.thecliffsat soduspoint.com. Upscale B&B on five acres overlooking Lake Ontario, with four large guest rooms and one cabana, each with private bath, plus full breakfast. $$$

# Rochester

Head west on NY 104.

Known as the Lilac City because of its gorgeous gardens, Rochester is also the place that gave us cameras, contact lenses, and copiers.

## The Center at High Falls Heritage Center (all ages)

**60 Brown's Race; (585) 325-2030; www.centerathighfalls.org. Open year-round; call for hours. Extended hours during laser season. Laser shows Fri and Sat nights. Free.**

Before roaming Rochester, stop here for walking-tour maps and current information about area events. The center has an interesting "Power of the People" interactive exhibit highlighting the contributions of famous Rochesterians, a gallery of regional artwork, as well as the Triphammer Forge excavation, the Pont de Rennes pedestrian bridge to High Falls, and **free** nighttime summer laser light shows presented on the gorge walls.

## ARTWalk  (all ages)

**179 Atlantic Ave.; (585) 473-5787; www.rochesterartwalk.org. Office open Mon and Fri 9 a.m. to 5 p.m. Free.**

Running along University Avenue, from the Memorial Art Gallery to the George Eastman House, this permanent urban art trail connects art centers and public places within the Neighborhood of the Arts. Pick up a Neighborhood of the Arts *Walking Guide,* and get art smart.

## Strong Museum of Play  (all ages)

**1 Manhattan Square; (585) 263-2700; www.museumofplay.org. Open Mon through Thurs and Sat 10 a.m. to 5 p.m., Fri 10 a.m. to 8 p.m., and Sun noon to 5 p.m. Adults $$, children $.**

Margaret Strong was an avid collector. From early childhood she collected anything and everything that interested her, and she had eclectic taste. From toys to tea sets, paperweights to parasols, Margaret accumulated more than 300,000 objects all by herself by 1969. Three decades later the collection has grown to half a million items, and the doll collection, numbering nearly 30,000, is the largest in the world.

In 2006 renovations doubled the size of the museum, and the focus changed to the study of play. This is now the second largest children's museum in the country, so plan to spend some time here. Whirling in the lobby is the 1918 Elaine Wilson Carousel, with the Strong Express Train skirting the perimeter. A 1,700-gallon coral reef aquarium looms large behind the admissions desk. Do you know the way to Sesame Street? If not, ask for directions, because all your furry friends are waiting for you there. Sit on the famous 123 Sesame St. stoop, or play with interactive exhibits teaching letter and number concepts, then see yourself on TV with the Muppets. The Berenstein Bears have moved into the neighborhood, too, along with their tree house, restaurant, woodworking shop, quilt shop, dentist office, barn, clubhouses, and art classes, complete with costumes, supplies, and props. Feel like shopping? Stop by the Super Kids Market and cruise the aisles with a kid-size cart, bar-scan your faux food at checkout, then produce your own cooking show at the WKID-TV station. Field of Play is a hands-on laboratory, divided into the six major elements of play (Anticipation, Surprise, Pleasure, Understanding, Strength, and Poise).

My favorite exhibit is Reading Adventureland, a giant playscape of five different literary landscapes. Follow the Yellow Brick Road into Mystery Mansion, the Upside-Down Nonsense House, Adventure Island, the Wizard's Workshop, and the Fairy Tale Forest. Books about those subjects can be read there or checked out from the mini-branch of the Rochester Library on-site. The TimeLab teaches American History, and Kid to Kid helps create communication. Upstairs are 500 Barbie dolls, and 800 butterflies flitting inside the Dancing Wings Garden.

# Cruising around **Rochester**

A variety of tour boats ply the waters around town, with mini-voyages on the Erie Canal, the Genesee River, or Lake Ontario. Call for current sailing schedules.

**Corn Hill Navigation.** *Sam Patch* (departs from Pittsford) and *Mary Jemison* (departs from downtown Rochester); (585) 262-5661; www.samandmary.org.

*Colonial Belle.* 400 Packett's Landing, Fairport; (585) 223-9470; www.colonial belle.com.

*Harbor Town Belle.* Port of Rochester, Charlotte; (585-342-1810; www.harbor townbelle.com.

This is also the new home of the National Toy Hall of Fame, highlighting the forty-four toys (so far) that have inspired creative play for generations. For gamers, more than a hundred arcade games have been set up at Videotopia, and by 2012 this will also be the home of the National Center for the History of Electronic Games, with public access to over 10,000 video-game consoles and titles.

### Rochester Museum and Science Center & Strasenburgh Planetarium  (ages 7 and up)

**657 East Ave.; (585) 271-4320 or (585) 271-1880; www.rmsc.org. Open Mon through Sat 9 a.m. to 5 p.m., Sun noon to 5 p.m. Closed Thanksgiving and Christmas. $–$$.**

Originally designed in 1912 to house historical Rochester relics, the collection has grown to more than a million objects and includes the finest and largest assortment of Haude-nosaunee artifacts in the world. Three floors of hands-on interactive exhibits in history, technology, archaeology, and anthropology are here. The science section has lots of rocks and fossils, a couple of Mastodons, and one of the largest flock-stuffed flocks of the extinct passenger pigeons in the country. Among the 60,000 documents are a weathered "certificate of freedom" belonging to a former enslaved woman and an autographed speech by Frederick Douglass. The 70,000-piece clothing collection includes two quilts made by Susan B. Anthony, and there are 94,000 nineteenth-century household objects, toys, and technology items from the area, as well. The Flight to Freedom: Rochester's Underground Railroad exhibit explores the experiences of some of the famous freedom seekers and also offers a child's perspective in Songs of Freedom. In summer, Family Fridays offer opportunities to explore a different science subject each week together.

At the Strasenburgh Planetarium next door, you can watch nature films on a giant screen, rock to a laser light show, star search into virtual deep space, see the sky for real through a 12.5-inch-diameter reflector scope, and experience a high tech, hands-on simulation of a space mission at the Challenger Learning Center.

### The Susan B. Anthony House  (ages 7 and up)

17 Madison St.; (585) 235-6124; www.susanbanthonyhouse.org. Open Tues through Sun 11 a.m. to 5 p.m. $.

Writing the *History of Women's Suffrage* in her third-floor attic, Susan B. Anthony led the revolution for women's rights from her residence here from 1866 to 1906. Police arrested her here for the crime of voting, and her home became a hotbed of social reform as she met with Frederick Douglass, Elizabeth Cady Stanton, and other revolutionaries of her day.

### George Eastman House International Museum of Photography and Film  (all ages)

900 East Ave.; (585) 271-3361; www.eastmanhouse.org. Open year-round Tues through Sat 10 a.m. to 5 p.m. (to 8 p.m. Thurs), Sun 1 to 5 p.m. Closed major holidays. Adults $$, children $, under 4 free.

Dropping out of school at age thirteen to work and support his mother, George was gifted with an insatiable curiosity. At age twenty-three he bought a camera and experimented with ways to simplify film development. Working in his mother's kitchen, he invented a dry-plate machine, and several years later he created a camera with rolled film. He became a multimillionaire, sharing his wealth with Rochester and the world. Of all his beneficent acts, my favorite is the time he gave a free Kodak camera to every 13-year-old child in America.

Tours, either led by a docent or self-guided, are available of his fifty-room mansion and the gardens gracing the ten-and-a-half-acre estate. Free audio tours in English or Spanish are also available at the admissions desk. The world's largest and finest collection of cameras, photographs, and historic films is housed here. The museum contains

## Suggested **Reading**

*The Story of Harriet Tubman,* by Kate McMullan

*Sweet Clara and the Freedom Quilt,* by Deborah Hopkinson

*The First Woman Doctor,* by Rachel Baker

*A Brilliant Streak: The Making of Mark Twain,* by Kathryn Lasky

*Follow the Drinking Gourd,* by Jeanette Winter

*Indian Captive: The Story of Mary Jemison,* by Lois Lenski

*Magic by the Lake,* by Edward Eager

*Waiting for Deliverance,* by Betsy Urban

*Gaia Girls Enter the Earth,* by Lee Welles

more than 400,000 photographs shot by over 14,000 photographers, plus 25,000 movies, and three million artifacts of film and its history. The recently renovated Dryden Theatre screens current and rare films, and the galleries display revolving exhibitions of emerging photographers and memory-making machines. On the second floor of the house is the Discovery Room, a hands-on activity center where kids can make sun prints and animation strips, and photography workshops are offered in summer. The museum cafe, which has Wi-Fi, serves soups, sandwiches, and baked goods, and the gift shop stocks great photography books, DVDs and T-shirts.

## Memorial Art Gallery  (all ages)

**500 University Ave.; (585) 276-8900; www.mag.rochester.edu. Open Wed through Sun 11 a.m. to 5 p.m., Thurs 11 a.m. to 9 p.m. Closed Mon, Tues, and major holidays. Adults $$, children $, ages 5 and under free.**

Journey through 5,000 years of art history at this excellent teaching museum. The permanent collection contains over 12,000 works of art, considered to be the best balanced in the state, outside New York City. Paintings by Monet and Winslow Homer, along with a Rembrandt portrait, are some of the treasures exhibited, and new art arrives all the time. The Dorothy McBride Gill Discovery Center provides a place for families to explore different facets of art together. Currently, there's an installation of an Egyptian mummy exhibit, complete with kid-friendly Egyptologist activities. In the Fountain Court is a 600-pipe, full-size Italian baroque organ, the only one of its kind in North America. Sunday concerts featuring the organ, as well as mini-recitals from local student musicians, and annual family cultural celebrations are some of the many activities offered year-round.

## Seneca Park Zoo  (all ages)

**2222 Saint Paul St.; (585) 336-7200; www.senecaparkzoo.org. Open daily year-round, Jan through Mar, 10 a.m. to 4 p.m.; Apr through Oct, 10 a.m. to 5 p.m.; and Nov through Dec, 10 a.m. to 4 p.m. Closed first Sat in June for Zoobilation, as well as Thanksgiving, Christmas, and New Year's Day. Admission booth closes one hour prior to zoo closing. $.**

Nestled on fifteen acres of historic Seneca Park, this conservation-minded zoo cares for orangutans, ocelots, wallabies, white rhinos, African elephants, and Amur tigers (the correct name for Siberian tigers). Special events for kids range from Genesee Trail Day, where Seneca clan stations are scattered around the zoo for discovery, to a "Bunk with the Beasts!" family sleepover. The "Go Green!" recycle rallies occur three times a year, and last year recycled almost 30,000 pounds of stuff while saving wildlife. A new program for parents is the Parents Night Out, where you can drop off your kids, age five and older, and have a few hours of time to yourself, while they play games, make crafts, have a snack, get a visit from an animal, and watch a movie.

## Seabreeze Amusement Park  (all ages)

**4600 Culver Rd.; (585) 323-1900 or (800) 395-2500; www.seabreeze.com. Open mid-May through mid-Sept, 11 a.m. to 10 p.m. most days, but call for specific dates. Adults $$$$, children $$$, special Websaver coupons and Night Rider passes available.**

# Rochester **Recreation**

**Humane Society at Lollypop Farm.** 99 Victor Rd., off NY 31 East, Fairport; (585) 223-6500 ; www.lollypop.org.

**New York State Fish Hatchery.** NY 36, 16 North St., Caledonia; (585) 538-6300; www.dec.ny.gov.

**Rochester and Genesee Valley Railroad Museum.** 6393 E. River Rd., West Henrietta; (585) 533-1431; www.rgvrrm.org.

**Stone-Tolan House Museum.** 2370 East Ave., Rochester; (585) 546-7029; www.landmarksociety.org.

**Charlotte-Genesee Lighthouse.** 70 Lighthouse St., Rochester; (585) 621-6179; www.geneseelighthouse.org.

Opened in 1879, this is the fourth-oldest amusement park in America. Seventy-five rides are offered, including four roller coasters; an assortment of boat, barnstormer, and T-Bird kiddie rides; circus shows; an arcade; midway games; and a carousel and its museum. The Raging Waters water park has tube slides, body flumes, a giant wave pool, a lazy river, and a Looney Lagoon for the little ones. Food stands feature the famous Zweigle's hot dogs, plus pizza, french fries, sugar waffles, and Slush Puppies.

## Ontario Beach Park  (all ages)

1 Beach Ave.; (585) 256-4950. Park open daily year-round 7 a.m. to 11 p.m.; swimming allowed 11 a.m. to 7 p.m. during summer; carousel operates Memorial Day through Labor Day, noon to 9 p.m., and weekends only through Columbus Day. $.

One of the oldest carousels in the country, circa 1905, still spins at this lakeside beach, a half-mile ribbon of sand, with a picturesque boardwalk to stroll, seven picnic pavilions, a playground, sports courts and fields, a concession stand, and **free** concerts of Big Band, jazz, rock 'n' roll, and country in summer.

## Genesee Country Village & Museum  (all ages)

1410 Flint Hill Rd., Mumford; (585) 538-6822; www.gcv.org; open mid-May through mid-Oct, Tues through Fri 10 a.m. to 4 p.m., Sat and Sun 10 a.m. to 5 p.m.; adults $$$, children $$, 3 and under **free.**

Visit a village of sixty-eight nineteenth-century buildings, the largest collection of its kind in the Northeast, from a blacksmith shop and schoolhouse to the largest collection of out-houses in the country (thirty, so far). Costumed interpreters demonstrate colonial crafts, from weaving and hearth cooking to barrel making and butter churning. There are also five short, themed nature trails winding through this 175-acre area, and the Nature Center has hands-on exhibits and several small live animals to observe. To feel firsthand what frontier life was like, sign up online for "Live like a Pioneer," a program designed for families; after being trained and dressed in colonial couture, you will spend a time-travel weekend of cooking over an open hearth, feeding farm animals, and sleeping on straw-filled beds. Nineteenth-century baseball games are held most weekends in season, the War of 1812 is reenacted in June, and by mid-July the Civil War happens all over again.

## Hamlin Beach State Park (all ages)

**1 Camp Rd., Hamlin; (585) 946-2462; www.nysparks.state.ny.us. Open year-round, daily, 6 a.m. to 10 p.m.; campsites available early May through Columbus Day. $. Call ahead to confirm changes to hours, activities available, and possible closures due to pending state budget cuts.**

Set along the south shore of sparkling Lake Ontario, this popular beach offers 264 tent and trailer campsites, hot showers, a coin-operated laundry, shaded picnic tables, a convenience store, two snack bars, and a recreation hall. To escape some of the summer crowds, and to spot some wildlife, head for the easternmost end of the beach for a mile-long walk along the Yanty Creek Nature Trail. Special events include Civil War reenactments, demonstrations of chainsaw art, and a Hamlin Hoe Down in late summer.

## Where to Eat

**Dinosaur Bar B Que.** 99 Court St.; (585) 325-7090; www.dinosaurbarbque.com. Racks of ribs, fried green tomatoes, catfish strips, shrimp, chili, and live blues every night. $–$$

## Where to Stay

**Hyatt Regency Rochester.** 125 E. Main St.; (585) 546-1234; www.rochester.hyatt .com. Three hundred and thirty-eight newly renovated rooms and suites, Wi-Fi, free newspaper, a twenty-four-hour gym and whirlpool, indoor heated pool, cribs and roll-away beds on request, room service, restaurant, and lounge. The hotel also offers a shopping service for families, "Babies Travel Lite," where you can shop online in advance for over a 1,000 baby products and have them delivered to your hotel room upon arrival. Awesome. $$–$$$

**Strahallan Hotel.** 550 East Ave.; (585) 461-5010; www.strathallan.com. In addition to its standard rooms, the hotel offers suites with a refrigerator and microwave, cable TV, video games, cribs and high chairs on request, fully equipped kitchens subject to availability, and

room service. The hotel also features a full-service AAA four-diamond restaurant and has special museum combo packages. $$–$$$

## For More Information

**Finger Lakes Association.** (800) 548-4386; www.fingerlakes.org.

**Binghamton Convention and Visitors Bureau.** (607) 772-8860 or (800) 836-6740; www.visitbinghamton.org.

**Cayuga County Office of Tourism.** (315) 255-1658 or (800) 499-9615; www.tour cayuga.com.

**Chemung County Chamber of Commerce.** (607) 734-5137 or (800) MARK TWAIN; www.marktwaincountry.com.

**Cortland County Convention & Visitors Bureau.** (800) 859-2227; www.cortlandtour ism.com.

**Livingston County Tourism.** (585) 243-2222 or (800) 538-7365; www.fingerlakeswest .com.

**Ontario County Tourism.** (877) 386-4669; www.visitfingerlakes.com.

# Other Things to See and Do
## in the Finger Lakes Region

**Tired Iron Tractor Museum.** US 20A, Cuylerville (Leicester); (585) 382-9736; www.antiquetractormuseum.com.

**International Speedway.** 3011 NY 104, Williamson; (315) 589-3018; www .spencerspeedway.org.

**Victorian Doll Museum.** 4332 Buffalo Rd., North Chili; (585) 247-0130; www .chilidollhospital.com

**Big Flats Historical Museum.** 258 Hibbard Rd., Big Flats; (607) 562-7460; www.bigflatsny.gov.

**Genoa Historical Association's Rural Life Museum.** 920 NY 34B, King Ferry; (315) 364-8202.

**Little Red Schoolhouse Museum.** 1290 NY 104A, Sterling; (315) 564-6189.

**Hammond Hill State Forest.** Hammond Hill Road, Dryden; (607) 753-3095; www.dryden.ny.us.

**1941 Historical Aircraft Group Museum.** Geneseo Airport, 3489 Big Tree Lane, Geneseo; (585) 243-2100; www.1941hag.org.

**Moses Mountain Horseback Riding.** 1504 Lick St., Moravia; (315) 497-3412.

**Greater Rochester Visitors Association.** (800) 677-7282; www.visitrochester.com.

**Schuyler County Chamber of Commerce.** (800) 607-4552; www.watkinsglen chamber.com.

**Seneca County Tourism.** (315) 568-2906 or (800) 732-1848; www.senecachamber.org.

**Steuben County Convention and Visitors Bureau.** (607) 936-6544 or (866) 946-3386; www.corningfingerlakes.com.

**Syracuse/Onondaga County Convention and Visitors Bureau.** (315) 470-1800 or (800) 234-4797; www.visitsyracuse.org.

**Tioga County Chamber of Commerce.** (800) 671-7772; www.visittioga.com.

**Ithaca-Tompkins County Convention and Visitors Bureau.** (800) 284-8422; www .visitithaca.com.

**Wayne County Office of Tourism.** (800) 527-6510; www.waynecountytourism.com.

**Yates County Chamber of Commerce.** (800) 868-9283; www.yatesny.com.

# The North Country

ost folks agree the North Country begins at the Canadian border and runs all the way to the Mohawk River, embraced in the east by Lake Champlain and in the west by the Saint Lawrence River. Within that region is the largest wilderness area in the lower forty-eight states, the six million acres of Adirondack Park. This vast expanse is larger than all our continental national parks put together, dotted with several thousand glistening lakes and ponds; more than 30,000 miles of pristine brooks, streams, and rivers; more than forty mountains topping 4,000 feet; and more than 2,000 miles of scenic hiking trails. There are more trees here than people, and the breathtaking primeval forests beckon exploration. But there are plenty of other attractions for families, too. From a multitude of miniature golf courses and amusement parks to historical reenactments, cool runs on a bobsled, or cruising a crystal clear lake in an antique boat, the activities are endless. Whatever you choose to do, you will discover that the haunting call of the loon, the dazzling glow of the Northern Lights, and the pristine beauty of the wilderness will stay with your family for generations.

## DRIVING TIPS

There are more miles of hiking trails in the Adirondacks than there are roads, which means for drivers it's pretty hard to get lost, but sometimes it can be difficult or time-consuming to get where you want to go. Still, the scenery is spectacular, so just take your time, and watch out for the wildlife. In general, the section of I-87 (also known as the Adirondack Northway) that runs from Queensbury to Ausable Chasm is particularly scenic, and it parallels NY 9N, which hugs the western shore of Lake George. NY 30 bisects the mountains down the center, from the Canadian border in the north to the Mohawk River in the south. Going east to west, NY 8 cuts through the southern Adirondacks, scenic NY 28 snakes through the central region, and dramatic NY 3 winds from Plattsburgh, on the shores of Lake Champlain, across the northern peaks, all the way to Lake Ontario. The Seaway Trail, comprised of several roads, follows the coastline of Lake Ontario, and the Saint Lawrence River and is one of the most beautiful byways in the country.

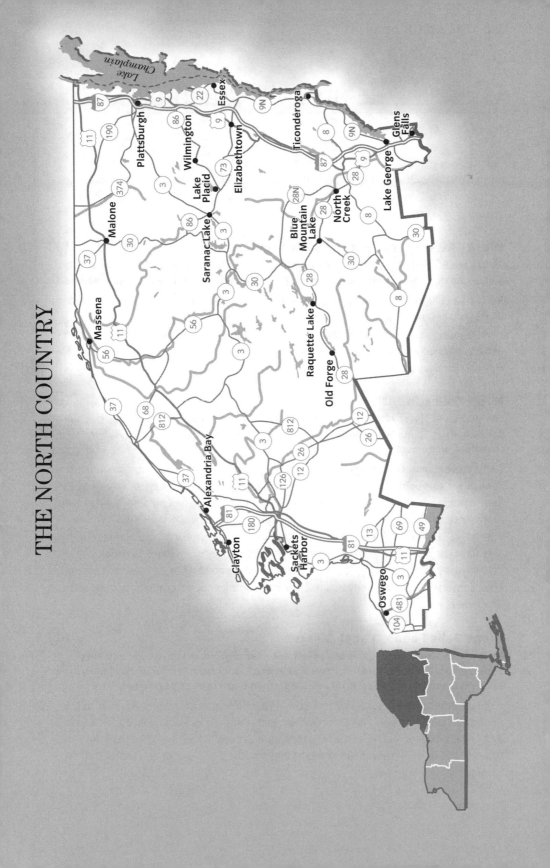

THE NORTH COUNTRY

# Glens Falls and Queensbury

Take exit 18 or 19 off I-87.

Glens Falls was called Chepontuc by the Iroquois and Wing's Falls in 1763 by sawmill entrepreneur Abraham Wing. Apparently a high roller, Wing gambled the town away to Col. Johannes Glen in a card game, and the town's name changed again to honor the victor.

### World Awareness Children's Museum  (all ages)

**79 Warren St.; (518) 793-2773; www.worldchildrensmuseum.org. Open Mon through Fri, 10 a.m. to 2 p.m. Permanent home, located at 89 Warren St., is currently under renovation. $.**

Become a culture vulture at this interactive home for international children's art. Exhibits range from self portraits of kids around the world and their art inspired by dance, to folktale telling and celebrations of light. When the new 12,000-square-foot space is completed, galleries will offer opportunities to explore music, marketplaces, currencies, and cultures from around the globe.

### Hyde Collection  (all ages)

**161 Warren St.; (518) 792-1761; www.hydecollection.org. Open year-round Tues through Sat 10 a.m. to 5 p.m., Sun noon to 5 p.m. Closed Mon and all national holidays. Free, donations welcomed.**

This excellent museum houses an important collection of western art from the fourth century B.C. through the twentieth century, displayed in the Italian Renaissance villa of the original collector. Rembrandt, Rubens, Degas, van Gogh, Picasso, and other masters are represented here, along with a variety of changing exhibits. The Artist's Studio is a new interactive family space, with art activities, books, and costume play opportunities. Conversation Kits, filled with "looking tools," questions, and assorted items to encourage art talk may be borrowed during your visit, and special programs include Tuesday Tours for Tots, seasonal events featuring a famous artist, monthly scavenger hunts, and vacation art classes.

### Glens Falls Feeder Canal  (all ages)

**21 Thomson Ave. Numerous access points, listed at www.feedercanal.com; two easy access points are on Richardson Street and at the Feeder Dam, located in Haviland's Cove Park, off Shermantown Road; (518) 792-5363. Open dawn to dusk year-round. Free.**

A nineteenth-century engineering feat designed to deliver water from Glens Falls to the Champlain Canal through a series of thirteen locks, this feeder canal was also an important link for loggers. Added to the list of National Historic Places in 1985, today the 7-mile towpath is a favorite trail for hiking and biking, and the canal is open to canoes and kayaks.

# Also in **the Area**

**Cooper's Cave Overlook.** US 9, between Glens Falls and South Glens Falls; (518) 761-3864 or (518) 793-1455.

**Chapman Historical Museum.** 348 Glen St., Glens Falls; (518) 793-2826; www .chapmanmuseum.org.

**Crandall Public Library & Folklife Center.** 251 Glen St., Glens Falls; (518) 792-6508; www.crandallibrary.org.

**The Lower Adirondack Regional Arts Council (LARAC).** 7 Laph Place, Glens Falls; (518) 798-1144; www.ARC.org.

**Trolley Rides.** Glens Falls; (518) 792-1085; www.cityofglensfalls.com.

**Upstate Model Railroaders.** 190 Glen St. (basement of Aime's), Glens Falls; (518) 423-7519; www.upstatemodelrailroaders.com.

**Moreau Lake State Park.** 605 Old Saratoga Rd., Gansevoort; (518)793-0511; www.nysparks.state.ny.us.

**Moreau Sandbar Beach.** Hudson River, South Glens Falls; (518) 792-9387.

## Crandall Park (all ages)

US 9; (518) 761-3813. Open daily dawn to dusk year-round. **Free.**

Easy nature trails lace through here, and there's good fishing from a stocked pond; ball fields and courts; a playground; and picnic and barbecue pavilions.

## Pack Demonstration Forest (all ages)

276 Pack Forest Rd., Warrensburg; (518) 582-4551 or 402-8014; www.dec.ny.gov.

This 2,600-acre environmental demonstration forest, an outdoor campus of SUNY's Forestry College, has 10.5 miles of looped, mostly level paths, as well as opportunities for fishing, biking, and canoeing. The easy 1-mile Grandmother's Tree Nature Trail is one of the few paths in the Adirondacks accessible to all hikers of abilities and features a 315-year-old white pine tree, listed on the state's historic tree registry. Many years ago, landowner John Woodward planned to cut the tree down so he could sell the wood to buy his wife, Margaret, a set of dishes for their anniversary. Margaret protested, saying she would rather have the tree than dishes, and the tree has been protected ever since.

# Family Fun Centers in
# Glens Falls and Queensbury

**The Fun Spot.** 1035 US 9, Queensbury; (518) 792-8989; www.lakegeorgefun
.com.

**Adventure Racing Family Fun Center.** 1079 US 9, Queensbury; (518) 798-
7860; www.gocartslakegeorge.com.

**Adirondack Billiards and Video Games.** 197 Glen St., Glens Falls; (518) 798-
5406.

**Pine Lanes.** 166 Saratoga Ave., South Glens Falls; (518) 793-9606; www.grand
standers.org/pinelanes.

**Tilt Family Entertainment Center.** Aviation Mall, 578 Aviation Rd., Queensbury; (518) 792-2180; www.tilt.com.

**RockSport Indoor Climbing and Outdoor Guiding Center.** 138 Quaker Rd.,
Queensbury; (518) 793-4626; www.rocksportny.com.

**Halfpipe Thrills.** 25 Fairview St., South Glens Falls; (518) 743-9200; www.half
pipethrills.com.

**Exit 17 Golf.** Exit 17N of I-87, US 9, South Glens Falls; (518) 745-8415.

**Glen Drive-In Theater.** Lake George Rd., Glens Falls; (518) 792-0023.

**Pirate's Cove Adventure Golf.** 1089 US 9, Queensbury; (518) 75-1887; www
.piratescove.net.

**TreePaad Family Entertainment Center.** 217 Dix Ave., Glens Falls; (518) 832-
7958; www.treepaad.com.

**Explore!** 103 Warren St., Glens Falls; (518 793-7803; www.exploreingglensfalls
.com.

**Dog Ate My Homework.** 206 Glen St.; (518) 792-0133; www.dogatemy
homework.net.

**Hillbilly Fun Park.** Corner of
Hadlock Pond Road and NY 149,
West Fort Ann; (518) 792-5239;
www.lakegeorge.com.

### Hovey Pond (all ages)

Lafayette Street, Queensbury; (518) 761-8216; www.queensbury.net. Open year-round dawn to dusk. Free.

Fish from a stocked trout pond, cycle along the Warren County Bikeway that runs through here, or go ice-skating in winter. Volunteers recently built a wide wooden walkway and viewing platform over the marsh, perfect for wildlife watching.

### West Mountain (all ages)

59 W. Mountain Rd., Queensbury; (518) 793-6606; www.skiwestmountain.com. Snow conditions determine season opening; Mon through Fri 10 a.m. to 10 p.m., Sat and Sun 8:30 a.m. to 6 p.m. $$$–$$$$.

This family ski scene has twenty-seven trails for all skiing levels, a ski school, night skiing, a snowboard park, and a snow-tubing park. In summer, mountain biking offers downhill dry runs.

### Empire East Aviation (all ages)

Floyd Bennett Memorial Airport, 443 Queensbury Ave., Queensbury; (518) 798-3091; www .flyeea.com. Call for appointment. Daily year-round. Half hour $125, one hour $225 for up to three people.

For a bird's-eye view, slip the surly bonds of Earth and soar on silver wings in a scenic area airplane ride.

### The Great Escape and Splashwater Kingdom (all ages)

1172 US 9, Queensbury; (518) 792-3500; www.sixflags.com/greatescape. Open daily Memorial Day through Labor Day, 10 a.m. to 7 p.m.; water park open 11 a.m. to 6 p.m. Adults $$$$, children under 48 inches $$$.

This is New York's largest theme park, with one admission price for over 125 wet and dry rides. While there are five rocking roller coasters, thirty of the rides are designed for younger folks. Live entertainment includes Bugs Bunny and friends, the Wiggles, fairy tales told at Story town, and stunt-diving shows. Kids can climb through Tweety's Tweehouse, ride Cinderella's Coach, raft around Capt'n Hook's Adventure River, and swim and splash in Noah's Sprayground, There are dozens of food choices, including the new Skillet Market and the Bavarian-style Alpine Fest Haus, along with the theme park cuisine of cotton candy, ice cream, and Dutch funnel cakes. A new seasonal celebration is Holiday in the Park, from late Nov to New Year's Eve, complete with sledding, carolers strolling the streets, twinkling lights, hot chocolate, and a visit with Santa.

## Where to Eat

**Aimie's Dinner & Movie.** 190-194 Glen St.; (518) 792-8181; www.aimiesdinnerandmovie .com. Dinner and a movie—what a great concept! First-run movies screened as you feast on Chaplin's Chicken Fingers, A Fish Called Wanda, and Lord of the Onion Rings. $$$

**Boston Candy Kitchen.** 21 Elm St.; (518) 792-1069. Serving breakfast and lunch since 1902, this restaurant also features an old-fashioned soda fountain and homemade candy. $

**Cooper's Cave Ale Company.** 2 Sagamore St.; (518) 792-0007; www.cooperscave ale.com. Eleven flavors of homemade sodas, including sarsaparilla, orange cream, and Gracie's grape; fifteen flavors of homemade ice cream; fabulous sundaes, shakes, flurries and floats; six unfiltered homemade ales; and burgers and wraps. $

## Where to Stay

**Country Inn & Suites Queensbury.** 1130 US 9; (518) 745-0180 or (800) 596-2375; www .countryinns.com/queensburyny. Eighty-three rooms and suites, heated indoor pool, outdoor seasonal pool, exercise room, **free** Wi-Fi, **free** continental breakfast, **free** newspaper, free parking, picnic area, and cable TV. $$$

**The Queensbury Hotel.** 88 Ridge St.; (800) 554-4526; www.queensburyhotel.com. Recently renovated, with 125 rooms and suites, free Wi-Fi, indoor pool, exercise room, restaurant, seasonal outdoor cafe, and on-site massage therapist. $$

# Lake George

Take US 9 north.

An interesting dichotomy of spectacular natural beauty and kitschy amusements, Lake George offers families a wide variety of activities from which to choose.

## Fort William Henry (all ages)

**Canada Street; (518) 668-5471; www.fwhmuseum.com. Open May through Oct, daily 9 a.m. to 6 p.m. Adults $$$, children $$, under 3 free.**

For fans of James Fenimore Cooper's classic *The Last of the Mohicans,* this is the fort featured in his story, based (a bit inaccurately) on an incident that occurred in 1757 during the French and Indian War. Completely restored, this colonial fortress offers a window to eighteenth-century frontier life, with living-history demonstrations of musket and cannon

## Retro **Rides**

**Lake George Village Trolley Rides.** 495 Queensbury Ave., Queensbury; (518) 792-1085; www.lakegeorge-vacations.com.

**Lake George Carriage Rides.** Beach Road, Lake George; (518) 321-3595; www.lakegeorge.com/carriage.

# Swimming, Picnicking, and "Flying" around **Lake George**

**Million Dollar State Beach.** Beach Road, Lake George; (518) 668-3352; www.lakegeorge.com.

**Diamond Point Beach.** Lake Road, Diamond Point; (518) 668-5722; www.town.lakegeorge.ny.us.

**Usher Park.** NY 9L, Lake George; (518) 668-5722; www.lakegeorge.com.

**Shepard Park.** Canada Street, Lake George; (518) 668-5771; www.lakegeorgevillage.com.

**Echo Lake.** Hudson Street, Warrensburg; (518) 623-2161; www.warrensburg.chamber.com.

**Rogers Memorial Park Beach.** US 9 (Main Street), Bolton Landing; (518) 644-3831; www.boltonchamber.com.

**Veteran's Park.** US 9 (Main Street), Bolton Landing; (518) 644-3831; www.boltonchamber.com.

**Para-sailing Adventures.** At Shoreline Cruises, 2 Kurosaka Lane, Lake George; (518) 668-4644; www.lakegeorgeshoreline.com.

**Sun Sports Para-Sail Rides.** Chic's Marina, NY 9N, Bolton Landing; (518) 644-3470; www.chicsmarina.com.

**National Water Sports.** 7 Christie Lane, Lake George; (518) 668-4013; www.parasailjoes.com.

**Lake George Boat Rentals & Parasail Rides.** Lower Amherst Street, Lake George; (518) 668-4828; www.shorelineboatsales.com

firing by costumed guides, audiovisual displays, and artifacts uncovered on-site. Children are invited to join the King's Army and given a uniform, a musket to "fire," a certificate of enlistment, and a coin for payment. Native American crafts are demonstrated in the courtyard, beading tables are available for kids to make their own souvenirs, and family-friendly ghost tours are offered on Fri and Sat nights.

## Lake George Historical Museum (ages 5 and up)

290 Canada St.; (518) 668-5044; www.lakegeorgehistorical.org. Open mid-May through June, Sat and Sun 11 a.m. to 4 p.m.; July through Aug, Tues, Fri, and Sat 11 a.m. to 4 p.m.,

## Launches of **Lake George**

**Lake George Steamboat Company.** 57 Beach Rd., Lake George; (518) 668-5777 or (800) 553-2628; www.lakegeorgesteamboat.com.

**Lake George Shoreline Cruises.** 2 Kurosaka Lane, Lake George; (518) 668-2875 or (518) 668-4644 ; www.lakegeorgeshoreline.com.

**Indian Pipes Passage Co.** At the Sagamore Resort, 110 Sagamore Rd., Bolton Landing; (518) 644-2979 or (518) 644-9400, ext. 6030; www.lakegeorgenew york.com/indianpipes.

**The Morgan.** At the Sagamore Resort, 110 Sagamore Rd., Bolton Landing; (800) 358-3585 and (518) 644-9400; www.thesagamore.com.

**Pontoon Boat Tours of Lake George.** (877) 547-6686; www.adventurevacation .com.

**Wed through Thurs 3 to 8 p.m., closed Sun and Mon; Sept, open Fri, Sat, and Sun 11 a.m. to 4 p.m.; Oct to mid-month, Sat and Sun 11 a.m. to 4 p.m. $.**

Located in the Old County Courthouse, this local museum has interesting artifacts, historical maps, and prints recalling the history of the area, including a new exhibit about the women of Lake George, "Herstory." But the nineteenth-century jail cells will really fascinate the kids as they imagine what sort of desperados were detained here more than a hundred years ago.

## Lake George **Land Conservancy**

For over two decades this nonprofit conservation organization has worked to protect the water quality and the rare plants and animals in the watershed of Lake George. To date, more than 48,500 feet of shoreline and over 12,500 acres have been preserved for future generations at four unique ecosystems. Cook Mountain (Ticonderoga), Cat and Thomas Mountain (Bolton), and Pilot Knob Ridge (Fort Ann) offer moderate hiking trails past ponds and waterfalls, with panoramic vistas, and the Gull Bay Preserve (Putnam) has a rare great blue heron rookery. For more information contact the Conservancy at 4905 Lake Shore Dr., Bolton Landing (518-644-9673), and visit their Web site, www .lglc.org, to view trail guides.

### Prospect Mountain Veteran's Memorial Highway (all ages)

**US 9, south of Lake George Village; (518) 668-5198; www.dec.ny.gov/outdoor/9176.html. Open daily Memorial Day weekend to mid-Oct, 9 a.m. to 5 p.m. Vehicle fee $.**

Drive this 5.5-mile road to the parking area for panoramic 100-mile views of Vermont's Green Mountains, New Hampshire's White Mountains, the Adirondack high peaks region, and the Laurentian Mountains of Canada. Then take the "viewmobile" van to the 2,030-foot summit for even more spectacular views.

### Up Yonda Farm (all ages)

**5239 Lake Shore Dr., Bolton Landing; (518) 644-9767; www.upyondafarm.com. Open year-round Mon through Sat 8 a.m. to 4 p.m., closed Sun, and July 4th and Labor Day. $.**

This seventy-three-acre environmental education center features a variety of year-round nature programs, tours of the farm, nature trails to explore, bird and bat houses dotting the woods, a butterfly garden, special activities for children, and scenic views overlooking Lake George.

## More Family Fun Centers around Lake George

**Magic Forest.** 1916 US 9; (518) 668-2448; www.magicforestpark.com.

**Water Slide World.** 2136 US 9, Lake George; (518) 668-4407; www.lake george-vacations.com.

**Spare Time.** 2211 Canada St.; (518) 668-5741; www.sparetimelakegeorge.com.

**Fun World Arcade.** 129 Canada St.; (518) 668-2708.

**Playland Arcade North.** 227 Canada St.; (518) 668-5255.

**Wild West Ranch and Western Town.** Bloody Pond Road, off US 9, Lake George; (518) 668-2121; www.wildwestranch.com.

**Alien Encounter.** 255 Canada St., Lake George; (518) 668-5910; www.scary faces.com.

**House of Frankenstein Wax Museum.** 213 Canada St.; (518) 668-3377; www .frankensteinwaxmuseum.com.

**Dr. Morbid's Haunted House.** 115 Canada St., Lake George; (518) 668-3077.

**Adirondack Extreme Adventure Course.** 35 Westwood Forest Lane, Bolton Landing; (518) 494-7200; www.adirondackextreme.com.

### Lake George Wild Forest  (all ages)

NY 86, Ray Brook; (518) 897-1310; www.dec.ny.gov. Open daily year-round. **Free.**

Encompassing 71,133 acres and eleven towns in the southeastern Adirondacks, this huge area has numerous hiking trails for all abilities. Within the forest is the Hudson River Recreation Area, where you can take trails along the water, such as the Ferguson Brook Trail, or a trek to Buttermilk Falls by way of the Bear Slide Trail.

### Warren County Fish Hatchery  (all ages)

145 Echo Lake Rd., Warrensburg; (518) 623-2877; www.warrencounty dpw.com. Open daily 8 a.m. to 4 p.m. year-round. **Free.**

This hatchery is home to the yearling brown, rainbow, and tiger trout that stock the rivers and lakes of the area. Families can stop by the visitor center, watch a fish film, learn some fish facts, then tour the trout tanks.

### Warren County Nature Trail System  (all ages)

Located off Hudson Avenue, north of town beyond the golf course, Warrensburg; (518) 623-5576; www.warrencountydpw.com. Open daily year-round. **Free.**

Adjacent to the Hudson River, this area has several easy to moderate trails leading to a nice vista and features unusual rock formations at the water's edge, perfect in any season. Pick up a brochure at the trailhead parking area.

## Miniature Golf at **Lake George**

**Around the World Miniature Golf.** Beach Road; (518) 668-2531; www .aroundtheworldgolf.com.

**Gooney Golf.** Corner of US 9/NY 9N; (518) 668-2589; www.gooneygolf.com.

**Magic Castle Indoor Golf.** 273 Canada St.; (518) 668-3777.

**Lumberjack Pass Mini Golf.** 1511 US 9; (518) 793-7141; www.lumberjack minigolf.com.

**Putts N Prizes.** 8 Beach Rd., Lake George; (518) 668-9500.

**Pirate's Cove Adventure Golf.** 2115 US 9, Lake George; (518) 668-0493; www .piratescove.net.

# Up, Up **and Away**

**SunKiss Ballooning.** 78 Knight St., Glens Falls; (518) 798-0373; www.sunkiss ballooning.com.

**Ballooning Adventures.** 17 Kimberly Lane, Queensbury; (518) 798-4143; www .ballooningadventures.net.

**Majestic Balloon Flights.** 18 River St., Queensbury; (518) 761-2694; www .majesticballoonflights.com.

**A Beautiful Balloon.** 47 Assembly Point Rd., Lake George; (518) 656-9328; www.balloon-rides.com.

**Adirondack Balloon Flights.** Aviation Road, Glens Falls; (518) 793-6342; www.adkballoonflights.com.

## Hickory Ski Center (ages 4 and up)

**43 Hickory Hill Rd., off NY 418, Warrensburg; (518) 523-5754; www.hickoryskicenter.com. Season depends on snowfall; open weekends and holidays 9 a.m. to 4 p.m. Adults $$$$, children $$$.**

This alpine spot offers a 1,200-foot vertical drop, a ski school, and eighteen trails for all levels of skill.

## Where to Eat

**The Barnsider Smoke House Restaurant.** US 9 South; (518) 668-5268; www.barn sider.com. Great barbecue, outdoor deck, very family friendly. $$

**Log Jam Restaurant.** 1484 US 9, at NY 149; (518) 798-1155; www.logjamrestaurant .com. Wonderful Adirondack decor, salad bar, steak, chicken, seafood, and a children's menu. $$–$$$

## Where to Stay

**The Lodges at Cresthaven Resort.** 3210 Lakeshore Dr.; (518) 688-3332 or (800) 853-1632; www.cresthavenlodges.com. Upscale two-bedroom townhouses with full kitchens, entertainment systems including three TVs, washer/dryer, indoor/outdoor pool facility, kiddie pool, recreation center, fitness center, playground, Internet access, grocery delivery service, picnic area, ball courts, putting green, and a restaurant. Weekly rentals only. $$$$

**Marine Village Resort.** 370 Canada St.; (518) 668-5478; www.marinevillage.com. Located on the shores of Lake George, with rooms and suites, microwave, refrigerator, cable, Wi-Fi, heated pool, small boats available for rent, snack bar, and a new playground. Kids always eat free at the Morgan restaurant. $$–$$$$

**Six Flags Great Escape Lodge & Indoor Waterpark.** 89 Six Flags Dr., Queensbury; (518) 792-3500 or (888) 708-2684; www.six flagsgreatescapelodge.com. Located across from the Great Escape, this is New York's first

## Horsing around **Warren County**

**Saddle Up Stables.** 3513 Lake Shore Dr., Lake George; (518) 668-4801; www .ridingstables.com.

**Bennett's Riding Stables.** NY 9N, Lake Luzerne; (518) 696-4444; www.lake georgenewyork.com/horses.

**Bailey's Horses.** 2151 Lake Ave., Lake Luzerne; (518) 696-4541.

**Bit 'n Bridle Ranch.** 184 W. Tucker Rd., Stony Creek; (518) 696-2776.

**Circle B Ranch.** Friends Lake, 771 Potterbrook Rd., Chestertown; (518) 494-4888; www.circlebranch.net.

**1000 Acres Ranch Resort.** 465 Warrensburg Rd., Stony Creek; (518) 696-2444 or (800) 458-7311; www.1000acres.com.

**Loon Lake Riding Stables.** 5408 NY 8, Loon Lake, Chestertown; (518) 494-5168; www.loonlaketrailrides.com.

**Ruggiero's Horseback Riding.** 1571 Lake Ave., Lake Luzerne; (518) 696-2905; www.mtkenyon.com.

**Wolf Pond Stables.** 473 Wolf Pond Rd., Stony Creek; (518) 696-7200; www .wolfpondstables.com.

indoor water park. Open year-round, and only to lodge guests, it's especially welcoming in winter. With more than 38,000 square feet of aquatic action, from surfing lessons to tackling the Tall Timbers Treehouse, and with 160 interactive water features, there are tube slides and raft rides to please everyone. For landlubbers, there's a forty-five-game arcade, two gift shops, and lots of activities with the resident Looney Tunes characters. $$$$

# Ticonderoga

Head north on NY 9N.

Strategically located between Lake Champlain and Lake George, Ticonderoga is steeped in the military history of three countries and two wars. Today Ticonderoga is also known for its popular fishing derbies, scenic boat tours, and the birthplace of the first commercial pencil and school supply essential, the No. 2 Ticonderoga. Farther north, near Crown Point, is the reported lair of Lake Champlain's Champ, a prehistoric sea monster known to the Iroquois for hundreds of years. There have been more than 300 sightings of Champ since the seventeenth century, mostly in the area around Bulwagga Bay, a favorite local beach. To the west is scenic Schroon Lake, as well as more than seventy other sparkling lakes and ponds. For a picturesque drive, follow Boreas Road (NY 2) as it winds from North Hudson past many spectacular natural wonders, including the lovely Blue Ridge Falls.

## Fort Ticonderoga  (all ages)

Fort Road, off NY 74; (518) 585-2821; www.fort-ticonderoga.org. Open daily mid-May through mid-Oct, 9:30 a.m. to 5 p.m. Adults $$$, youth 7 to 12 $$, children under 7 free.

This restored colonial fort, erected by the French in 1755 to protect their southern frontier, was called the "Key to the Continent." Captured by the British in 1759 during the French and Indian War, the fort was captured sixteen years later by Ethan Allen and his Green Mountain Boys during the Revolutionary War. Costumed interpreters offer half-hour tours, the military museum houses some interesting artifacts, including a lock of George Washington's hair, musket firings are demonstrated daily, and a restaurant offers refreshments. In Sept, Revolutionary War reenactors set up camp and battle the British in a déjà vu encounter.

## Ticonderoga Heritage Museum  (ages 5 and up)

East end of village on Montcalm Street at Bicentennial Park; (518) 585-2696; www.ticonderoga heritagemuseum.com. Open Memorial Day through June and Labor Day through Columbus Day, weekends only, 10 a.m. to 4 p.m., and July to Sept, daily 10 a.m. to 4 p.m. Donation.

Everything you ever wanted to know about mills, be they of the saw, grist, graphite, iron, cotton, wool, or paper variety, can be gleaned here, along with other historical and regional lore. Special summer workshops for children include learning seventeenth-century skills such as beadwork, clay pot crafting, weaving, songwriting, toy making, and Native American cooking.

# Animals of the **Adirondacks**

The Adirondacks are alive with animals! Aside from the numerous wildlife parks, petting zoos, ranches, and farms that dot the area, the North Country is the habitat for 53 species of mammals, 220 species of birds, 66 species of fish, and 35 species of reptiles and amphibians. White-tailed deer, black bear, lynx, red foxes, porcupines, beavers, and moose live here, as well as bald eagles, peregrine falcons, osprey, and wild turkeys.

# U-Drive **Boat Rentals**

For the more adventurous, there are numerous marinas dotting the lake offering families the chance to be captains of their own destiny, or at least captains of a variety of watercraft ranging from rowboats and canoes to motorboats and sailboats. Here's a partial list:

**Lake George Boat Rentals.** 204 Canada St., Lake George; (518) 685-5331; www.lgboatrental.com.

**Lake George Recreation U-Drive Boat Rentals.** 2 Kurosaka Lane, Lake George; (518) 668-4644; www.lakegeorgerecreation.com.

**Yankee Boating Center.** 3910 US 9, Diamond Point; (518) 668-2862; www .yankeeboat.com.

**Fischer's Marina.** Kattskill Bay; (518) 656-9981

**Dunham's Bay Marina.** NY 9L, 10 Dunham's Bay Rd., Lake George; (518) 744-2627 or (518) 656-9244; www.dunhamsbaymarina.com.

**F.R. Smith & Sons Marina.** 36 Sagamore Rd., Bolton Landing; (518) 644-5181.

**Waters Edge Marina.** Sagamore Road, Bolton Landing; (518) 644-2511; www .watersedgemarina.net.

**Chic's Marina.** NY 9N, Lakeshore Drive, Bolton Landing; (518) 644-2170.

**Gilchrist Marina.** 3686 Lakeshore Dr., Bolton Landing; (518) 668-2028 or (518) 668-5848

**Dockside Landing Marina.** 9130 Lakeshore Dr., Hague; (518) 543-8888 or (518) 668-4300; lakegeorgeboats.com.

**Halls Marina.** 9 Front St., Lake George; (518) 668-5437; www.hallsboat.com.

**Snug Harbor South.** NY 9N, Lake Shore Drive, Silver Bay; (518) 543-8866; www.snugharborsouth.com.

## Ticonderoga Cartoon Museum  (all ages)

**Ticonderoga Community Building, Lower Montcalm Street; (518) 585-7015; www.ticonderoga cartoonmuseum.com. Open Mon, Wed, and Fri 2 to 4 p.m. $.**

Dedicated to the appreciation of political and comic cartoons, this small museum houses more than 600 framed, original, classic cartoons, from Disney to Doonesbury. In summer, cartoon and sketching classes are offered for all ages by resident curator and cartoonist Stan Burdick.

### Natural Stone Bridge and Caves (all ages)

535 Stone Bridge Rd., off US 9, Pottersville; (518) 494-2283; www.stonebridgeandcaves
.com. Open daily Memorial Day to Labor Day, 9 a.m. to 7 p.m.; early Sept to Columbus Day
and late May through June, 10 a.m. to 5 p.m. Adults $$$, children 5 through 12 $$.

Take a self-guided tour of the caves, grottos, gorge, underground river, and waterfall
of this unique geological formation or fish in the trout-laden pools, hike the easy nature
trails, pan for pretty rocks in an enriched sluiceway, or gaze at the gems and geodes
inside the rock shop and museum.

### Crown Point State Historic Site (all ages)

739 Bridge Rd., Crown Point; (518) 597-4666/3666; www.nysparks.state.ny.us. Park open
9 a.m. to dusk; museum open May to Oct, Wed through Mon 9 a.m. to 5 p.m. Grounds
free, museum $, vehicle fee $.

Fort Saint Frederic was built in 1734 by the French in an effort to control the narrows of
Lake Champlain. In 1759 the British wrested control and built Fort Crown Point. Today
you can walk among the windswept ruins of two lost empires and imagine life on the front
lines of the frontier.

### Essex County Fish Hatchery (all ages)

Creek Road (CR 2), Crown Point; (518) 597-3844. Open daily year-round 7 a.m. to 4 p.m. $.

At this indoor and outdoor hatchery for three types of trout, coin-operated feeding stations are part of the circle of life, from fry fish to fish fry.

### Penfield Homestead Museum (ages 8 and up)

703 Creek Rd., Crown Point; (518) 597-3804; www.penfieldmuseum.org. Open early June
through early Oct, Thurs through Sun 11 a.m. to 4 p.m. $.

This local museum features exhibits on nineteenth-century inventor and industrialist Allen
Penfield, as well as the area's iron industry and Civil War history.

## Where to Eat

**Carillon Restaurant.** 872 NY 9N; (518) 585-
7657; www.carillonrestaurant.com. Serving
steaks, seafood, pasta, roast duckling, and
homemade bread. $$$

**Hot Biscuit Diner.** 14 Montcalm St.; (518)
585-3483; www.hotbiscuitdiner.com. Com-
fort food, from homemade meat loaf and pot
roast to freshly baked biscuits and desserts. $

## New York **Trivia**

The record low temperature in the state is –52 degrees F, which was recorded
in Old Forge on Feb 18, 1979. The record high temperature in the state is 108
degrees, recorded in Troy on July 22, 1926.

## Where to Stay

**Best Western Ticonderoga Inn & Suites.** 260 Burgoyne Rd.; (518) 585-2378; www.bestwesternnewyork.com/ticonderoga. Rooms and suites, indoor heated pool, spa, fitness center, cable TV, laundry service, room service, microwave available, refrigerator, **free** Wi-Fi, **free** newspaper, **free** continental breakfast, restaurant, and children under eighteen free with adult. $$

**Elk Lake Lodge.** Elk Lake Road, off Blue Ridge Rd., north of North Hudson; (518) 532-7616 or (518) 942-0028; www.elklakelodge.com. Breathtaking, peaceful retreat located on private lake, inside a 12,000-acre preserve laced with hiking trails. $$–$$$

# Elizabethtown, Essex, and Plattsburgh

Take NY 9N/NY 22 north along Lake Champlain to Westport, then turn left onto NY 9N to Elizabethtown, or continue north toward Essex on NY 22 into Plattsburgh.

Stroll the shore of the Saranac, through Plattsburgh's historic area, along RiverWalk Park. The Heritage Trail, a self-guided walking tour, originates here as well and winds past many of the town's architectural gems. The nearby villages of Elizabethtown and Essex also have a wealth of beautifully preserved historic districts, and both are surrounded by lush scenery. In Elizabethtown walk around the Hand-Hale neighborhood or plan a picnic at Lincoln Pond. Essex boasts 160 structures built between the 1790s and 1860s, and the whole town is listed on the National Register of Historic Places.

### Clinton County Historical Museum  (all ages)

**98 Ohio Ave., Plattsburgh; (518) 561-0340. Open year-round Tues through Fri 9 a.m. to 2 p.m. Closed holidays. $.**

This interesting museum, with artifacts from 1600 to the present, has textiles, cannons, rifles from after the War of 1812, and the Redford Glass exhibit, as well as many archaeological artifacts discovered beneath the lake's surface.

### Point au Roche State Park  (all ages)

**19 Camp Red Cloud Rd., Plattsburgh; (518) 563-0369; www.nysparks.state.ny.us. $. Call ahead to confirm changes to hours, activities available, and possible closures due to pending state budget cuts.**

Formerly farmland near the northwestern shore of Lake Champlain, this park offers a nature center, swimming at a sandy beach, a playground, picnic areas, playing fields, and hiking trails through diverse habitats.

## Cumberland Bay State Park (all ages)

152 Cumberland Head Rd., Plattsburgh; (518) 563-5240; www.nysparks.state.ny.us. Open daily early May through early Columbus Day, 8 a.m. to 8 p.m. $.

Encompassing 319 acres on the western shore of Lake Champlain, this park and campground has a long sand beach, a playground, basketball and volleyball courts, a recreation room, camp store, biking and hiking trails, fishing, and 152 campsites.

## Ausable Chasm (all ages)

2144 US 9; Ausable Chasm; (518) 834-7454 or (800) 537-1211; www.ausablechasm.com. Open mid-May through late June and early Sept through late Oct, 9 a.m. to 4 p.m.; late June through early Sept, 9 a.m. to 5 p.m. Adults $$$, children 5 to 12 $$, under 5 free; raft rides and tube rentals additional charge.

One of the oldest tourist attractions in the country and the only natural water park in the East, this dramatic gorge is the Ausable River's 500-million-year-old work in progress. Walk past unusual rock formations named Jacob's Ladder, the Punch Bowl, and the Elephant's Head, then explore the new Rim Trail that runs the entire length of the Chasm. For a closer look, take a guided rubber raft trip or hop onto a tube and ride the gentle rapids through the canyon. Horseback riding and gemstone mining are drier options, and the spooky nighttime Lantern Tour is very cool.

## Adirondack Center Museum (all ages)

7590 Court St., Elizabethtown; (518) 873-6466; www.adkhistorycenter.org. Open Memorial Day through Columbus Day, Mon through Sun 10 a.m. to 5 p.m. $, under 6 free.

Eleven exhibit areas, housed in a former schoolhouse, examine pioneer life, wilderness exploration, mining, lumbering, transportation, and the area's Native American heritage. A Champlain Valley sound-and-light show offers a multimedia presentation of the French and Indian War, and there's also an extensive doll collection, a colonial garden, and a 58-foot fire observation tower to explore.

# Where to Eat

**Cobble Hill Inn.** 7432 US 9, Elizabethtown; (518) 873-6809; www.cobblehillinn.com. American cuisine, with soups, salads, burgers, wraps, pizzas, chicken fingers, and homemade desserts. $–$$

**The Deer's Head Inn.** 7552 Court St., Elizabethtown; (518) 873-9903; www.deershead inn.com. Excellent steaks, seafood, pasta, chicken, plus pub food, and kids eat free with an adult on Tues. Served in oldest inn in the Adirondack Park. $$–$$$$

# Where to Stay

**Marine Village Cottages.** 82 Dickson Point Rd., Plattsburgh; (518) 563-5698; www .marinevillagecottages.com. Twenty-five three-bedroom cottages, fully equipped kitchens, fireplace, TV, plus beach, playground, and boat docks. $–$$

**Rip Van Winkle Motel.** 15 Commodore Thomas MacDonough Highway, Plattsburgh; www.ripvanwinklemotel.com. Rooms, cabins, and efficiencies, high-speed Internet access, cable TV, refrigerator, microwave, coin laundry, and free local calls. $–$$

# Lake Placid and Wilmington

Take I-87 south to NY 9N west, to NY 86 southwest.

Centered in the heart of the High Peaks region, Lake Placid has always possessed spectacular scenery. But after hosting the 1980 Olympics, it captured the heart of American winter sports as well. Nearby Wilmington sits snugly at the feet of the fifth-highest peak in New York, majestic Whiteface Mountain. Iroquois legend tells the tale of the Great White Stag, whose death by magic arrows transformed the mountain's surface to white.

### The Olympic Center  (all ages)

**2634 Main St., Lake Placid; (518) 523-1655; www.orda.org. Open daily year-round. Museum open daily 10 a.m. to 5 p.m., closed Thanksgiving and Christmas; self-guided audio tour $. Public skate hours during the evening; dates and times vary weekly. Center free, except for special events, museum, and skating $.**

With four ice rinks, this is where the pros practice, and the U.S. Hockey Team and figure-skating champions train year-round. A small museum houses exhibits from the Lake Placid Olympics of 1932 and 1980, and for a brief period on summer nights, families can skate the site of our hockey team's 1980 "Miracle on Ice."

### Olympic Ski Jump Complex  (all ages)

**NY 73, Lake Placid, 7 miles southeast of town; (518) 523-2202; www.whiteface.com. Open daily year-round 9 a.m. to 5 p.m. Closed Thanksgiving and Christmas. $$.**

Take a ride on the chairlift elevator to the 120-meter ski jump tower used in Olympic and World Cup events. In summer and fall, visitors can watch the U.S. freestyle aerial team train, as plastic mats on the jumps sub for snow and a 750,000-gallon pool at the bottom makes for quite a splash landing

### Olympic Sports Complex at Mt. Van Hoevenberg  (all ages)

**NY 73, Lake Placid, 7 miles southeast of town; (518) 523-4436; www.whiteface.com. Bobsled open selective dates late May through mid-Oct. Winter season runs mid-Oct through late Apr, Wed through Sun 9 a.m. to 4 p.m. $–$$$.**

Cool running on the bobsled "Summer Storm" is offered year-round, with luge rides available in winter at this Olympic event site. and the nearby Cross-Country Center has 31 miles of groomed trails to explore.

### Adirondack Craft Center  (all ages)

**2114 Saranac Ave., Lake Placid; (518) 523-2062; www.adirondackcraftcenter.com. Open daily year-round 10 a.m. to 5 p.m., to 6 p.m. in summer. Closed Thanksgiving and Christmas.**

Folk art from more than 300 artisans of the North Country—from the twig-like Adirondack furniture and intricately woven baskets to the lifelike hand-carved decoys—is gracefully rustic, and there is always a chance to watch an artist at work.

# Take Me to **the Water**

**Adirondack Rent-A-Boat.** 3 George and Bliss Lane, Lake Placid; (518) 523-2378.

**Captain Marney's Boat Rentals.** 3 Victor Herbert Dr., Lake Placid; (518) 523-9746

**Mirror Lake Boat Rental.** 2403 Main St., Lake Placid; (518) 524-7890; www.mlboatrental.com.

**Adirondack Rafting Company.** 7 Patch Lane, Lake Placid; (518) 523-1635 or (800) 510-RAFT; www.adirondackwhitewaterrafting.com.

**Middle Earth Expeditions.** 4529 Cascade Rd., NY 73, Lake Placid; (518) 523-7172; www.adirondackrafting.com.

**Hudson River Rafting Company.** 2609 Main St., Lake Placid; (800) 888-RAFT; www.hudsonriverrafting.com.

**Lake Placid Marina.** Lake Placid; (518) 523-9704; www.lakeplacid.com.

### John Brown Farm State Historic Site (ages 5 and up)

115 John Brown Rd., off NY 73, Lake Placid; (518) 523-3900; www.nysparks.state.ny.us.
Open May through Oct, Mon and Wed through Sun 10 a.m. to 5 p.m. $ guided tour. Call
ahead to confirm changes to hours, activities available, and possible closures due to pending state budget cuts.

This is the home and final resting place of John Brown, the famous abolitionist. Brown and
his followers attempted to seize the U.S. Arsenal at Harpers Ferry on the night of October
16, 1859. He had planned to use the arms and munitions to liberate slaves in the South,
but was captured and executed for treason in Virginia on December 2, 1859.

### Santa's Workshop (all ages)

324 Whiteface Memorial Highway, NY 431, North Pole; (518) 946-2211; www.northpoleny
.com. Open June to Labor Day, Tues through Sat 10 a.m. to 4 p.m.; Labor Day to Columbus
Day, Sat and Sun 9:30 a.m. to 3:30 p.m., plus Fri after Thanksgiving Day to 3 p.m.; in Dec, Vil-
lage of Lights on Sun, Mon, and Tues 4:30 to 7:30 p.m. $$$.

Santa's summer home since 1949, this charming holiday theme park has a talking Christ-
mas tree, a live nativity pageant, a 24-inch gauge Candy Cane Express train, a carousel
of rocking reindeer, a yuletide bounce house, plus live shows by the Mother Goose Guild
and North Pole pals, puppet shows, and parades. Visit the Toymaker's Shop for a chance
to operate a toy assembly line, or the Blacksmith's Shop to watch magical reindeer shoes
forged. Glass glistens to life at the Glassblower's Shop, and delicious fudge is freshly
made daily at the Candy Maker's Shop. Of course, no visit would be complete without

## Lake Placid **Olympic Sites Passport**

A good place to begin your Olympic adventure is the ORDA Store, located at 2426 Main St. in Lake Placid. Information about what's going on at the various venues is offered by the friendly staff, and it's a good place to purchase the popular Olympic Sites Passport, a money-saving ticket to all the sites operated by the Olympic Regional Development Authority. Included in the $29 pass is entry to the Olympic Jumping Complex, where families can ride an elevator to the top of the 120-meter jump tower, then tour the Olympic Sports Complex, habitat of the bobsled and luge, glide aboard a gondola to the top of Little Whiteface, visit the 1932 and 1980 Lake Placid Winter Olympic Museum, skate on the Olympic Speed Skating Oval in winter, and drive along the scenic Whiteface Mountain Veterans Memorial Highway in summer. In addition to admissions, the passport has discount coupons for photo novelties, ice shows, skating sessions, and the bobsled ride. Separate admissions are required for the Bobsled and the Be A Biathlete Experience. Another option in summer is the Gold Medal Adventure ($45), an up-close and personal program designed for families who want to experience their own Olympic miracle, with bobsled and luge clinics, lunch, and a tour of some of the ORDA sites. For more information contact them at (518) 523-1655 or (518) 523-3330; www.orda.org. Children under ten must bring an adult with them.

stopping by Santa's House, so bring your wish list and camera for a quick meet, greet, and photo op. On your way out, mail a friend a letter from the Post Office Gift Shop, postmarked "North Pole, NY." Five family weekends in winter offer opportunities to trim a tree with your own handmade ornaments, join carolers in song, help out at the toy workshop, and attend magic shows and storytelling events.

### Whiteface Mountain Visitor Center (all ages)

Box 277, NY 86, Wilmington 12997; (518) 946-2255 or (888) 944-8332; www.whitefaceregion.com. Open daily 9 a.m. to 1 p.m. in winter, to 4 p.m. in summer. Free.

Stop here for friendly information about area events, then step outside and fish for famously titanic trout along a 5-mile catch-and-release section of the west branch of the Ausable River.

### Whiteface Mountain Ski Center and Gondola (all ages)

5021 NY 86, Wilmington; (518) 946-2223; www.whiteface.com or www.orda.com. Ski season runs late Nov to early Apr. Gondola rides mid-June through mid-Oct and Thanksgiving weekend through mid-Apr. Memorial Highway open mid-May through mid-Oct. Skiing $$$$, gondola $$$, highway $$.

## Mini-golf in the **Lake Placid Area**

**Pirate's Cove Adventure Golf.** 1980 Saranac Ave., Lake Placid; (518) 523-5478; www.piratescove.net.

**Avalanche Adventures.** 1991 Saranac Ave., Lake Placid; (518) 523-1195; www.avalancheadventures.com.

This is the largest ski resort in New York and the only one of the High Peaks reachable by car. With the highest vertical drop in the East (3,216 feet), this was the site of the 1980 Winter Olympics downhill competitions. The eighty trails provide fun for all skill levels, and families will appreciate the Whiteface Kids Kampus, designed for children of all ages and abilities. For nonskiers ages one to six, the Bear's Den Nursery provides a play space with arts and crafts, games, sing-alongs, and movies with surround sound. For potential pint-size skiers ages four to six, there's a Play-n-Ski program with basic snow fun lessons, and for snow beasts seven to twelve, the Junior Adventure program offers instruction in skiing and snowboarding. Teenagers can join the Cloudsplitter Club, with emphasis on safety and mileage. All rental packages come with helmets, and they must be worn. Nearby Lookout Mountain is now open to advanced skiers for the first time, with three challenging trails and a triple chairlift. In summer or fall, ride the new eight-passenger Cloudsplitter Gondola to the summit of Little Whiteface, then hike back to base lodge along the scenic Stag Brook Falls nature trail. For a spectacular 360-degree view from the 4,867-foot summit of Whiteface, take a drive up the Whiteface Mountain Veterans Memorial Highway, an 8-mile ascent to a breathtaking alpine wilderness.

# **Mount** Marcy

The highest peak of the High Peaks region and all of New York is Mount Marcy, towering over the Adirondacks at 5,343 feet. It's also the origin of the Hudson River, flowing from Lake Tear of the Clouds, a mile from the summit. So remote was this area that the source of the Nile River was discovered long before the source of the Hudson. While the trek to the top is a popular one, the grade is a bit steep for younger children, and it can get very crowded in summer. For more information, contact the Department of Environmental Conservation at (518) 402-8013 and www.dec.ny.gov and the Adirondack Mountain Club at (518) 668-4447 and www.adk.org.

# Also in **the Area**

**Uihlein Sugar Maple Research & Extension Field Station.** 157 Bear Cub Lane, Lake Placid; (518) 523-9337; http://maple.dnr.cornell.edu.

**Adirondack Flying Service.** NY 73 (across from ski jumps), Lake Placid; (518) 523-2473; www.flyanywhere.com.

**Lake Placid North Elba Historical Society Museum.** 242 Station St., Lake Placid; (518) 523-1608; www.lakeplacidhistory.com.

### High Falls Gorge (all ages)

**4761 NY 86, Wilmington; (518) 946-2278; www.highfallsgorge.com. Open daily May through Oct; 9 a.m. to 5 p.m., May, June, Sept, and Oct; 9 a.m. to 5:30 p.m., July and Aug. Call for winter hours. $$.**

Follow a 0.5-mile self-guided nature walk alongside the rushing Ausable River, with three waterfalls that plunge past ancient granite cliffs. A new addition is a sluice mine, where kids can pan for gemstones and fossils.

## Where to Eat

**The Boat House.** 89 Mirror Lake Dr.; (518) 523-4822; www.lakeplacidcp.com. Fresh fish, pasta, steaks, and salads, overlooking spectacular sunsets on Mirror Lake. $$$

**Caffe Rustica.** 1936 Saranac Ave.; (518) 523-7511; www.cafferustica.com. Wood-fired pizza, and Mediterranean seafood, pasta, steak and salad specialties. $–$$$$

## Where to Stay

**Adirondack Holiday Lodge.** 8 Whiteface Memorial Highway, Wilmington; (518) 946-2251; www.adirondackholidaylodge.com. Rooms, suites, and apartments, most with private balconies, some with refrigerators and microwave ovens, plus cable TV, free continental breakfast, and a new Wi-Fi cafe and gift shop. Children with an adult free, and fourth night free. $–$$$

**Adirondak Loj.** Adirondak Loj Road, off NY 73, 5 miles south of Lake Placid; (518) 523-3441; www.adk.org. Located on Heart Lake, this rustic camp offers private rooms, family rooms, a loft, a large cabin, and campsites. As this is the home of the Adirondack Mountain Club, numerous workshops and outings are offered year-round for all ages and abilities, from hiking and biking to paddling and rafting, plus ski trips and nature and local culture explorations. If you're wondering why the name is spelled "loj," it's because at one time it was run by Melville Dewey (creator of the Dewey Decimal system), and he thought the English language spellings were difficult and tried to promote a more simplified spelling system. $–$$$$

**Mirror Lake Inn.** 77 Mirror Lake Dr.; (518) 523-2871; www.mirrorlakeinn.com. Five buildings with a variety of rooms and suites, on eight landscaped acres along the shore of beautiful Mirror Lake, plus three restaurants; a spa, salon, and fitness center; Wi-Fi and cable TV; refrigerators; and a private beach with free use of paddleboats and kayaks. Special programs for kids include animal tracking, arts and crafts activities, movies, and "yoga with elephants." In winter, a private ice and hockey rink is maintained, and dogsled rides across the frozen ice are offered, followed by hot chocolate and freshly-baked cookies. $$$$

# Saranac Lake

Take NY 86 west.

When Dr. Edward Livingston Trudeau was diagnosed with tuberculosis in 1876, he decided to come to the Adirondacks to die. Instead, the fresh mountain air and friendly people restored his health and inspired him in 1884 to open the first successful tuberculosis clinic in the country at Saranac Lake.

### Robert Louis Stevenson Memorial Cottage (ages 7 and up)

**11 Stevenson Lane (off junction of NY 3 and NY 86); (518) 891-1462 or (800) 347-1992; www .adirondacks.com/robertlstevenson.html. Open July through Columbus Day, Tues through Sun 9:30 a.m. to noon, and 1 to 4:30 p.m.; closed Mon. $.**

Calling Saranac Lake his "Switzerland in the Adirondacks," the author of Treasure Island and other memorable children's classics used this as his mountain retreat. The cottage is full of Stevenson's personal items, including his ice skates for gliding around nearby Moody Pond, his penny whistle, and his writing desk filled with editions of his works.

## Natural **Attractions**

The Adirondack Nature Conservancy preserves six sanctuaries within the North Country. Each is unique and is home to unusual or rare plants or animals. For more information about these gems of nature, contact the ANC at P.O. Box 65, NY 73, Keene Valley 12943; (518) 576-2082; www.nature.org.

**Silver Lake Bog Preserve.** Old Hawkeye Road, Black Brook

**Clintonville Pine Barrens.** Buck Hill Road, Clintonville

**Spring Pond Bog.** Floodwood Road, Kildare

**Everton Falls Preserve.** Red Tavern Road, St. Regis Falls

**Gadway Sandstone Pavement Barrens.** Cannon Corners Road, Mooers

**Coon Mountain Preserve.** Halds Road, Westport

# Suggested **Reading**

*The Last of the Mohicans*, by James Fenimore Cooper

*Farmer Boy*, by Laura Ingalls Wilder

*The Arrow Over the Door*, by Joseph Bruchac

*The Mystery of the Lake Monster*, by Gertrude Chandler Warner

*Treasure Island*, by Robert Louis Stevenson

*The Great Rope*, by Rosemary Nesbitt

*The Adirondack Kids* series, by Justin and Gary VanRiper

*Adirondack ABC's*, by Joyce Burgess Snavlin and Linda Davis Reed

*Adirondack Gold*, by Persis Granger

*Adirondack Mouse and the Perilous Journey*, by Irene Uttendorfsky

*Adirondack Nightmare: A Spooky Tale in the North Country*, by Rebecca Leonard

## Dewey Mountain (all ages)

NY 3, Harrietstown, Saranac Lake; (518) 891-2697; www.deweyskicenter.com. Season and trails open when snow conditions permit. Open Mon 10 a.m. to 5 p.m., Tues through Fri 10 a.m. to 7 p.m., Sat 9 a.m. to 5 p.m., Sun 10 a.m. to 4 p.m. $.

This family-friendly Nordic-style ski center offers groomed cross-country ski trails for beginners to advanced, plus lighted trails for night ski adventures, lessons, and tours.

## Adirondack Park Visitor Interpretive Center (all ages)

8023 NY 30, Paul Smiths, 1 mile north of Paul Smith's College; (518) 327-3000; www.adkvic .org. Open year-round Tues through Sat 9 a.m. to 5 p.m. Trails open dawn to dusk. Closed Thanksgiving and Christmas. Free.

This 2,885-acre preserve owned by Paul Smith's College features 6 miles of interpretive trails, 8 miles of backcountry trails, and 9.5 miles of cross-country ski trails in winter. There's a sixty-acre marsh, five ponds, several brooks, and a variety of woodlands filled with wildlife, from foxes and beavers to bears and moose. Inside the interpretive center are exhibits about the history of the park, an art gallery, a theater, and a gift shop, and outside are picnic pavilions, a playground, and a native species butterfly house. In summer, naturalists guide visitors on canoe voyages around Barnum Pond and give bird of prey demonstrations, and night hikes are very popular.

### Six Nations Indian Museum (ages 4 and up)

1462 CR 60, Onchiota; (518) 891-2299; www.tuscaroras.com. Open July through Labor Day, Tues through Sun 10 a.m. to 6 p.m. $.

Founded by schoolteacher Ray Fadden, this museum houses more than 3,000 historical and contemporary artifacts of the Haudenosaunee. Of special interest to children are the pictographs used to tell the stories of the Mohawk, Seneca, Oneida, Onondaga, Cayuga, and Tuscarora tribes, and the Fadden family offers interesting lectures and storytelling from the Native American perspective.

### Adirondack Fish Hatchery (all ages)

103 Fish Hatchery Rd., Saranac Lake; (518) 891-3358. Open 9 a.m. to 4 p.m. Apr through Nov. Free.

One of the twelve Department of Environmental Conservation's hatcheries, this one specializes in salmon, producing more than 30,000 pounds of fish a year. Exhibits at the indoor visitor center include a salmon pool, a monitored brood fish pond, and fish facts of life.

### The Wild Center (all ages)

45 Museum Dr., Tupper Lake; (518) 359-7800; www.wildcenter.org. Open daily Memorial Day to Labor Day, 10 a.m. to 6 p.m.; Labor Day to Oct 31, 10 a.m. to 5 p.m.; and Nov 1 to Memorial Day, Fri, Sat, and Sun 10 a.m. to 5 p.m. Adults $$$, children $$, age 3 and under free.

No dusty display cases here—this is a living museum, spread over thirty-one acres, with hundreds of animals in a variety of habitats, along with high-definition multimedia screens that let you choose where to go and what to watch, from tracking a moose to rafting the Hudson Gorge. A film made especially for the center, *A Matter of Degrees,* narrated by Sigourney Weaver, follows the effects of climate change. The Naturalists Cabinet is a large, sunny room filled with drawers and boxes of bones, fur, eggs, and just about everything found in a forest that children can touch. At the Karamazov Theater, performers juggle their way through the Adirondacks, and in the Great Wolf Hall naturalists offer animal encounters with ravens, porcupines, and snakes.

Outside are several easy nature trails and overlooks, and a new exhibit, Mother of Invention, that shows how nature is inspiring a new generation of sustainable inventions.

## Also in the Area

**Mount Pisgah Ski Center.** 92 Mount Pisgah Lane, Saranac Lake; (518) 891-0970; www.saranaclakeny.gov.

**Emerald Springs Ranch.** 651 NY 186, Saranac Lake; (518) 891-3727; www.emerald-springs.com.

The New Path is a behind-the-scenes tour of the Wild Center's green building practices, which have earned it the honor of being the first museum in New York to be certified by Leadership in Energy and Environmental Design (LEED). A very special play place for kids is The Pines, sort of an anti-playground, with logs, sticks, and a fort, designed by and for kids who are tired of artificial playgrounds. When you've worked up an appetite, stop by the Waterside Café, overlooking Blue Pond, for great hot and cold sandwiches, salads, and snacks, and then visit the terrific gift shop for that perfect souvenir.

## Where to Eat

**Blue Moon Cafe.** 46 Main St.; (518) 891-1310. Friendly neighborhood place, serving delicious homemade soups, pastries, great sandwiches, and vegan choices; **free** Wi-Fi. $

**Morgan's 11.** 33 Broadway; (518) 897-1111. Outdoor deck dining, with great wood-fired pizza, pasta, and steak sandwiches, plus kids can sit at the pizza bar and make their own mini-pies. $

**Red Fox Restaurant.** 5034 SR 23; (518) 891-2127. Prime rib, steaks, seafood, and pasta. $$

## Where to Stay

**Hotel Saranac.** 100 Main St.; (518) 891-2200 or (800) 937-0211; www.hotelsaranac .com. The first fireproof hotel built in New York, this landmark lodging has a lobby that's a reproduction of the foyer in the Florentine Davanzati Palace. There are eighty-two rooms and suites, Wi-Fi, cable TV, free cribs, cots and refrigerators, and VCR/DVD players available for extra fee. Dining options include the upscale A.P. Smith's Restaurant and the casual Boathouse Lounge, and in summer, barbecue specials are offered on the terrace overlooking the village. $$$$

**White Pine Camp.** White Pine Road (off intersection of NY 86 and NY 30), Paul Smiths; (518) 327-3030; www.whitepinecamp.com. Built in 1907 and overlooking secluded Osgood Lake, this is a classic Adirondack "Great Camp." The summer White House for President Calvin Coolidge in 1926, the recently restored site encompasses more than twenty buildings, including an indoor bowling alley and a Japanese teahouse on an island. Ten cabins and cottages are available for rent, including the president's cabin, Guest amenities include a concierge grocery shopping service to stock your cabin, an on-site naturalist and guide to customize your Adirondack adventures, in-cabin massages, and complimentary use of canoes, kayaks, and rowboats. A private chef service is available to prepare a variety of gourmet meals, including vegetarian, diabetic, and kids' favorites, or guests can take a walk to the St. Regis Café or the student dining room at the nearby Paul Smith's College campus. $–$$$$

# Malone

Head north on NY 30.

Every August for 150 years, the Franklin County Fair has materialized in Malone. From livestock shows and cooking contests to the magic of the midway, this is a wonderful slice of North Country good-time fun.

# Franklin County **Fishing Fun**

For young fisherfolk who prefer angling with an advantage, several stocked pond preserves almost guarantee you'll catch a good-size trout or salmon quickly. Because these are privately owned ponds, you don't need a license, you pay between $3 and $5 per pound of live weight, and cleaning the catch is often included.

**Hinchinbrooke Fish Hatchery.** Chateaugay; (518) 497-6505.

**Fisherman's Paradise.** Chateaugay; (518) 497-6711.

**Spring Brook Farm.** Chateaugay (518) 425-6879.

**Smooth Flow Ponds.** Malone; (518) 483-7561.

**Cold Brook Farm.** Vermontville; (518) 891-3585.

**Restful Ponds.** Brainardsville; (518) 425-3361.

## Malone Memorial Recreation Area (all ages)

Duane Street; summer (518) 483-3550, winter (518) 483-0680; www.adirondacklakes.com. Open daily Memorial Day to Labor Day, 9 a.m. to 8 p.m. **Free.**

A major migration stop for thousands of Canada geese in their trek southward each fall, this eighty-seven-acre park has a large playground, **free** paddleboats, supervised swimming, tennis courts, ball fields, picnic pavilions, and special children's programs.

## Titus Mountain (all ages)

215 Johnson Rd.; (518) 483-3740; (800) 848-8766 for ski conditions; www.titusmountain .com. Season depends on snow conditions but usually runs Thanksgiving to just before Easter. Open seven days a week, weather permitting; Mon through Wed 9:30 a.m. to 4 p.m., Thurs and Fri 9:30 a.m. to 10 p.m., Sat 9 a.m. to 10 p.m., and Sun 9 a.m. to 4:30 p.m.; holidays, Sun through Wed 9 a.m. to 4:30 a.m., and Thurs through Sat 9 a.m. to 10 p.m. $$$$.

This family ski resort offers twenty-seven trails, ten lifts, night skiing, a terrain park, snow tubing, snowshoeing, a ski school, two lodges, a cafeteria, Wi-Fi, and special children's races and programs on weekends and holidays.

## Almanzo Wilder Homestead (all ages)

Stacy Road, off US 11, Burke; (518) 483-1207 or (866) 483-3276; www.almanzowilderfarm .com. Open late May through Sept, Mon through Sat 11 a.m. to 4 p.m., Sun 1 to 4 p.m. Adults $$, children $.

For fans of the *Little House on the Prairie* TV series, this restored farmhouse was the boyhood home of author Laura Ingalls Wilder's husband, Almanzo. Recollections of his

## Also in **the Area**

**Franklin County Fair.** 606 E. Main St., Malone; (518) 483-0720; www.frcofair
.com.

**Franklin County House of History.** 51 Milwaukee St., Malone; (518) 483-2750;
www.franklinhistory.org.

childhood here were the inspiration for her book *Farmer Boy*. Plans to build a replica of
a one room 1860s schoolhouse mentioned in that book are in the works, and there's a
museum with farm artifacts and a gift shop with Wilder's books on-site.

## Where to Eat

**Hosler's Family Restaurant.** 609 E. Main
St.; (518) 483-0144; www.hoslersrestaurant
.com. Breakfast, lunch, and dinner, with pancakes, omelets, sandwiches, burgers, steaks,
seafood, pasta, kid's meals, and blueberry
pie. $–$$$

**Sansone's Restaurant.** 598 E. Main St.;
(518) 483-9817. Serving great Italian food
since 1939, with lots of fish tanks around the
room, and historical memorabilia under the
glass tabletops. $$

## Where to Stay

**High Falls Park Campground.** 34 Cemetery Rd., Chateaugay; (518) 497-3156; www

.highfallspark.com. With over 200 sites for
tents and RVs, plus a snack bar, playground,
mini-golf, laundry facilities, a swimming pool,
picnic areas, trout fishing, a ball field and
courts, hot showers, a rec room, and nature
trails. And then there is the beautiful 120-foot
private waterfall, formed more than 12,000
years ago by retreating glaciers. $

**Kilburn Manor.** 59 Milwaukee St.; (518)
483-4891; www.kilburnmanor.com. Housed in
an elegant Greek Revival mansion, this lovely
bed-and-breakfast inn offers a 2,000-volume
library, Internet, a seasonal in-ground pool,
landscaped lawns and gardens hemmed by
the Salmon River, fabulous breakfasts, and
special family rates, $–$$

# Blue Mountain Lake

Head south on NY 30.

This azure jewel sparkles in the center of the Adirondacks, surrounded by thick forests of
birch, oak, and pine.

**Adirondack Museum**  (all ages)
NY 28N and NY 30; (518) 352-7311; www.adkmuseum.org. Open daily mid-May through
mid-Oct, 10 a.m. to 5 p.m. Adults $$$, children 6 to 12 $$, 5 and under free.

Called the "Smithsonian of the Adirondacks" by *National Geographic,* this is a must-see museum Twenty-two terrific exhibit areas explore the land and lives of the Adirondackers, along with daily demonstrations, workshops, and nature hikes, The largest public collection of rustic furniture is here, as well as the second largest fleet of inland wooden watercraft in the country, plus over 2,500 paintings of Adirondack art and more than 70,000 historic photographs. Many of the displays have discovery stations and scavenger hunts designed for families, and activities may include churning butter, washing clothes the old-fashioned way, or playing nineteenth-century games in the gazebo. Stop by the Reising one-room schoolhouse to create classroom crafts, play with antique dolls and toys, and romp around outside in the schoolyard on rustic bridges and wooden rockers. Learn about lumberjacks at the Work in the Woods exhibit, where you can make your mark—a logging mark, that is—on a wood-chip keepsake you can take home. For more souvenirs, there's a terrific gift shop, and a lovely cafe has a spectacular view.

### Adirondack Lakes Center for the Arts (all ages)

**NY 28 and NY 30 (next to the post office); (518) 352-7715 and (877) 752-7715; www.adirondack arts.org. Open year-round Mon through Fri 10 a.m. to 4 p.m.; in July and Aug, also Sat 10 a.m. to 4 p.m. and Sun noon to 4 p.m. Free, but $$–$$$ for evening events.**

Known as the Arts Center by the locals, this was the first community center in the Adirondack Park and offers a year-round schedule of art exhibitions, cultural events, and theater, dance, and music performances by classical and cutting-edge artists. Workshops for all ages and abilities are offered, from print and collage creation to drum and mask making, and many of the events occur in a variety of locations throughout the park.

### Adirondack Park Visitor Interpretive Center (all ages)

**5922 NY 28N, Newcomb; (518) 582-2000; www.adkvic.org/newcomb. Open Tues through Sat 9 a.m. to 5 p.m. Closed Thanksgiving and Christmas. Trails open year-round dawn to dusk. Free.**

## Guide to **Adirondack Guides**

**Blue Mountain Outfitters.** 144 Main St., Blue Mountain Lake; (518) 352-7306.

**Living Waters Southern Adirondack Outfitters.** NY 30, Indian Lake; (518) 648-5302.

**G.P.S. Adventures.** NY 28, Indian Lake; (518) 648-5260.

**Fort Noble Adirondack Adventures.** NY 8, Hoffmeister; (315) 826-3771.

**Piseco Guide Service.** Arrowhead Road, Piseco; (518) 548-4442.

**Sabael Guide Co.** 249 Sabael Rd., Indian Lake; (518) 648-5391.

Nestled in the Huntington Wildlife Forest, this is a good place to learn about the natural history of the six-million-acre Adirondack Park. Exhibits explain aspects of life in the wilderness, and outside is a 3.6-mile trail system that winds through old-growth forests and wetlands and past beaver ponds. Mink, moose, white-tailed deer, and red foxes wander through the woods, and many species of birds can be spotted year-round. Bird of prey programs, naturalist-led nature walks, and GPS workshops are some of the activities offered, and in winter there are special snowshoe classes.

## Where to Eat

**Long Lake Diner.** NY 30, Long Lake; (518) 624-3941; Home-cooked diner delights. $–$$.

**Quackenbush's Long View Wilderness Lodge.** 681 Deerland Rd., (NY 28N and NY 30) Long Lake; (518) 624-2862; www.longview lodge.com. Steak, free-range chicken, roasted quail, blackened trout, pasta specials, vegetarian options, and a children's menu. $$–$$$

## Where to Stay

**Hemlock Hall.** Maple Lodge Road; (518) 352-7706 and (518) 359-9065; www.hemlock hall.com. Located on the lake, with fourteen cottages and motel and lodge rooms, a modified American meal plan (breakfast and dinner), packed lunches available, a private beach, free use of canoes, kayaks, and rowboats, a fenced playground, a rec room, and a library. $$–$$$ (no credit cards)

**Prospect Point Cottages.** NY 28; (518) 352-7378; www.prospectpt.com. Fully equipped cottages with big picture windows and screened porches overlooking the lake, plus a hillside lawn sloping to the sandy beach, a playground, free use of canoes, paddleboats, and rowboats, free cable TV, **free** local calls, free Wi-Fi, a vintage nineteenth-century Steinway piano to play, wheelchair friendly, and free gourmet breakfasts from Oct to mid-June. $–$$$$

# North Creek

Take NY 28 east.

Some of the best white water in the East flows through this area's dramatic Hudson River Gorge, and while the high water of spring is best left to the pros, summer is family friendly.

### Gore Mountain (all ages)

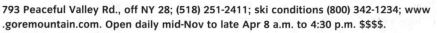

**793 Peaceful Valley Rd., off NY 28; (518) 251-2411; ski conditions (800) 342-1234; www .goremountain.com. Open daily mid-Nov to late Apr 8 a.m. to 4:30 p.m. $$$$.**

This is the second-largest ski resort in New York, with a 2,300-foot vertical drop, ninety trails (eighty-two alpine, fifteen glade, eight cross-country), and twelve lifts. Private and group lessons for children are available at the Kids Klub, for skiers ages four to twelve and snowboarders ages five to twelve, or in the Mountain Adventure programs if you're

## White **Water!** (ages 8 and up)

**Hudson River Rafting Company.** 3268 NY 28 (Main Street), North Creek; (518) 251-3215 or (800) 888-RAFT; www.hudsonriverrafting.com.

**Whitewater Challenges.** NY 28, North River; (570) 443-9727 or (800) 443-RAFT; www.wc-rafting.com.

**Whitewater World.** 307 Main St.; (800) WHITEWATER; www.whitewaterrafting.com.

**Adirondac Rafting Company.** 108 W. Main St., Indian Lake; (518) 523-1635 or (800) 510-RAFT; www.whitwaterrafting.com.

**St. Regis Canoe Outfitters.** 73 Dorsey St., Saranac Lake; (518) 891-1838; www.canoeoutfitters.com.

**Wild Waters Outdoor Center.** 1123 NY 28, The Glen, Warrensburg; (518) 494-4984 or (800) 867-2335; www.wildwaters.net.

**Adventure Sports Rafting Company.** Main Street, Indian Lake; (518) 648-5812 and (800) 441-RAFT; www.adventuresportsrafting.com.

here for longer. For nonskiing snow bunnies ages six months to six years, there's day care available at the Bear Cub Den in the new Northwoods Lodge. At the base lodge is the Tannery Pub & Restaurant, with booths created from vintage red gondola cabins. The terrain park, tubing runs, and family activities are located in the Ski Bowl, where a new lodge is scheduled to open this year. By 2011 trails will connect Gore to this historic area, increasing the resort's vertical drop to 2,500 feet. If you're here in autumn, take the scenic Northwoods Gondola ride to the summit of Bear Mountain, for a picnic-perfect view.

## Barton Garnet Mines  (ages 5 and up)

Barton Mines Road (5 miles from NY 28); (518) 251-2706; www.garnetminetours.com. **Open daily late June through Labor Day, Mon through Sat 9:30 a.m. to 5 p.m., Sun 11 a.m. to 5 p.m., weekends only Labor Day through late Oct. Adults $$$, children $$, ages six and under and over 90 free, plus fee for rocks collected ($1 a pound).**

The garnet has garnered the honor of being New York's state stone. This is one of the largest garnet mines in the world and produces much of the world's industrial garnet. Touring the mine is interesting, but for families the fun is in the finding of these "Adirondack rubies," and this place should please your pebble pups with a plethora of semi-precious gems.

## Also in **the Area**

**Dr. Jacques Grunblatt Memorial Beach.** Ski Bowl Road, North Creek; (518) 251-2421.

**Dynamite Hill Recreation Center & Nature Trail.** NY 8, Chestertown; (518) 494-5160; www.northwarren.com.

## Where to Eat

**Andie's Restaurant.** 296 Main St.; (518) 251-2363. New place serving home-style comfort food, featuring fresh roasted turkey, roast beef, baked ham, hot sandwiches, steaks, seafood, homemade desserts, and a $3.99 children's menu. $

**Durant's.** 3195 State NY 28; (518) 251-2500. Renovated in Adirondack Great Camp style, very family friendly, and serving eclectic American cuisine. $–$$

## Where to Stay

**The Copperfield Inn.** 307 Main St.; (518) 251-2200; www.copperfieldinn.com. Thirty-one newly renovated rooms and suites, outdoor pool, spa, sauna, fitness room, tennis courts, TVs, DVD players, a casual tavern and a gourmet Italian restaurant, plus family-friendly lodging and attraction packages, such as "Go Wild and Find Your Inner Monkey" and the ever-popular "Adirondack Boot Camp."

**Garnet Hill Lodge.** 39 Garnet Hill Rd.; (518) 251-2444 or (800) 497-4207; www.garnet-hill .com. Wonderful rustic lodge with sixteen rooms, plus cottages, with a private beach, stocked lake, nature trails, cross-country ski trails, free canoe use, tennis courts, mountain bikes and horseback rides available, a restaurant, and May family train trip packages aboard Thomas the Tank Engine. $–$$

## Agritainment **of the Area**

**Gore Mountain Farm Alpacas.** 2642 NY 28, North Creek; (518) 251-3040; www.goremountainfarm.com.

**Nettle Meadow Goat Farm and Cheese Company.** 484 S. Johnsburg Rd., Warrensburg; (518) 623-3372; www.nettlemeadow.com.

**Valley Road Maple Farm.** 190 Valley Rd., Thurman, Warrensburg; (518) 623-9783.

**Adirondack Gold Maple Farm.** 90 Bear Pond Rd., Athol; (518) 623-9718; www.thurman-ny.com.

# Old Forge and Raquette Lake

West on NY 28.

The Fulton Chain, a necklace of eight lakes strung along NY 28, links Old Forge to Raquette Lake. Many of the Great Camps were built here, and today the area's beauty attracts hikers, canoeists, mountain bikers, white-water rafters, and snowmobilers.

### Adirondack Scenic Railroad  (all ages)

**Thendara Station, NY 28, Old Forge; (315) 369-6290 or (800) 819-2291; www.adirondackrr .com. Canoe & Rail (315) 369-6286; www.ticknerscanoe.com. Bike & Rail bike rentals (315) 357-3281 or (315) 369-2300. Operating May through Oct, five departures daily in season. $$–$$$$.**

Ride the rails aboard vintage coaches for an hour-long excursion past lush forests and the lovely Moose River. Special events include train robberies by that persistent Loomis Gang every Wed in summer and fall foliage and Halloween spook trains in autumn. A canoe and rail combo allows folks to canoe the Moose, then return by train, or try the two-hour trip aboard air-conditioned coaches to historic Union Station in Utica. For mountain bikers, take the train north to Carter Station, then pedal back to Thendara along 10 miles of trails.

### Old Forge Arts Center  (all ages)

**3260 NY 28, Old Forge; (315) 369-6411; www.artscenteroldforge.org. Open year-round Mon through Sat 10 a.m. to 4 p.m., Sun noon to 4 p.m. Closed major holidays. Free; events $–$$.**

This is the oldest multi-arts center in the Adirondacks, with a gallery of permanent and changing exhibits, special workshops and programs for families, seasonal concerts and art competitions, and guided nature hikes. Nearing completion is the new 28,000-square-foot building that will be the Arts Center's new home. Using recycled and natural materials and alternative energy, from photovoltaic panels to geothermal pipes, this will be the only completely ecologically friendly "green-built" and "green-operating" arts center in the country. A new Wetlands Nature Trail is being planned, as is an Eco Gallery for environmental studies, a theater, a teaching kitchen, and a preschool suite.

## Also in **the Area**

**McCauley Mountain Ski Area.** 300 McAuley Rd., Old Forge; (315) 369-3225; www.oldforgeny.com.

# Cross-country Skiing **in the Adirondacks**

For the quintessential Adirondack experience, it's hard to beat cross-country skiing. There are ski centers throughout the region, but the area around Speculator and Lake Pleasant, known as Big Country, is laced with hundreds of miles of groomed trails surrounded by the West Canada Lake, Silver Lake, and Siamese Ponds Wilderness Areas. The following are some popular cross-country ski centers in the Adirondacks:

**Lapland Lake Cross-Country Ski Center.** 139 Lapland Lake Rd., Benson; (518) 863-4974 or (800) 453-SNOW; www.laplandlake.com.

**Garnet Hill Cross-Country Ski Center.** Thirteenth Lake Road, North River; (518) 251-2444; www.garnet-hill.com.

**Cunningham's Ski Barn.** 1 Main St., North Creek; (518) 251-3215; www.cunninghamsskibarn.com.

**Friends Lake Inn Nordic Ski Center.** 963 Friends Lake Rd., Chestertown; (518) 494-4751; www.friendslake.com.

**Adirondack Woodcraft Ski Touring Center.** Rondaxe Road, Old Forge; (315) 369-6031.

**Ausable Chasm Cross-Country Ski Center.** NY 373, Ausable Chasm; (518) 834-9990; www.ausablechasm.com.

**Cascade Cross-Country Ski Center.** Cascade Road, Lake Placid; (518) 523-9605; www.cascadeski.com.

**The Nordic Ski & Snowshoe Center.** At Whiteface Club & Resort, Whiteface Inn Road, Lake Placid; (518) 523-2551 or (800) 422-6757; www.whitefaceclubresort.com.

**Bark Eater.** Alstead Hill Road, Keene; (518) 576-2221.

### Forest Industries Exhibit Hall (ages 5 and up)

3311 NY 28, Old Forge; (315) 369-3078 or (800) 318-7561; www.northernlogger.com. Open Memorial Day through Labor Day, Mon and Wed through Sat 10 a.m. to 5 p.m., Sun noon to 5 p.m.; Sept and Oct weekends only. **Free.**

More than 5,000 products derived from wood are on display here, along with dioramas and exhibits explaining the history of logging and the importance of sustainable forest management. Five miles from the Hall is the newly acquired Flatrock Mountain

# Old Forge **Family Fun Centers**

When the kids have maxed out on nature's scenic sights, head for:

**Enchanted Forest/Water Safari.** 3183 NY 28, Old Forge; (315) 369-6145; www .watersafari.com.

**Calypso Cove.** 3183 NY 28, next to Enchanted Forest, Old Forge; (315) 369-6145; www.calypsocove.com.

**Nutty Putty Miniature Golf.** Old Forge; (315) 369-6636; www.nuttyputtygolf .com.

**Over the Rainbow Miniature Golf.** Old Forge; (315) 369-6565.

Demonstration Forest. Future plans for that property include a Visitor Interpretive Center, a trail winding through examples of various forest management techniques, including wildlife habitat enhancement, and classrooms for school groups and forest industry training activities.

### Great Camp Sagamore  (all ages)

**Sagamore Road, 4 miles south of NY 28, Raquette Lake; (315) 354-5311; www.greatcamp sagamore.org. Guided two-hour tours Memorial Day to the third week in June, Sat and Sun at 1:30; from the third weekend in June through Labor Day, daily at 10 a.m. and 1:30 p.m.; the Mon after Labor Day through Columbus Day, daily at 1:30 p.m. Adults $$$, children $, preschoolers free.**

Built in 1897 by W. W. Durant, this was Alfred Vanderbilt Sr.'s wilderness retreat and hunting lodge. The classic Great Camp, Sagamore hospitality was extended to movie stars, moguls, and the elite of the gaming crowd. Take a tour of the twenty-seven-building complex, now designated a National Historic Landmark, and you'll see the grown-ups' Playhouse, Mrs. Vanderbilt's bowling alley, and local folk artisans creating wagon-wheel rugs and Adirondack pack baskets.

# Equine **Excursions**

**Flatrock Mountain Ranch.** 1874 NY 28, Old Forge; (315) 369-2657; www.flat rockmountainranch.com.

**Adirondack Saddle Tours.** 4 Uncas Rd., Eagle Bay; (315) 357-4499 and (877) 795-7488; www.adkhorse.com.

**T & M Horseback Riding.** 452 North NY 28, Inlet; (315) 357-3594.

# Excellent **Excursions**

Cool off with a cruise, canoe, seaplane, or even help deliver the mail through the center of the Adirondacks.

**Adirondacks W.W. Durant Cruise & Dine.** Mick Road, Raquette Lake; (315) 354-5532; www.raquettelakenavigation.com.

**Old Forge Lake Cruises.** NY 28, Old Forge; (315) 369-6473; www.oldforgelake cruises.com.

**Mail Boat Tours.** NY 28, Raquette Lake; (315) 354-4441.

**Long Lake Boat Tours.** Lake Street, NY 30, Long Lake; (518) 624-LAKE.

**Tickner's Moose River Canoe Trips.** 3140 NY 28, Old Forge; (315) 369-6286; www.ticknerscanoe.com.

**Frisky Otter Tours.** 148 NY 28, Inlet; (315) 357-3444; www.friskyottertours.com.

**Bird's Marina.** NY 28, Raquette Lake; (315) 354-4441; www.birdsboats.com.

**Rivett's Marina.** 601 S. Shore Rd., Old Forge; (315) 369-3123; www.rivetts marine.com.

**Clark's Marina.** NY 28, Fourth Lake, Inlet; (315) 357-3231; www.clarksmarina .com.

**Burke's Marina.** NY 28, Raquette Lake; (315) 354-4623; www.burkesmarinainc .com.

**Inlet Marina.** 4 S. Shore Rd., Inlet; (315) 357-4896.

**Payne's Boat Livery.** 46 Seventh Lake Rd., Inlet; (315) 357-2628.

**Iggy's Place Boat Rentals.** Moffitt Beach Road, Speculator; (518) 548-8119.

**Adirondack Exposure.** 1872 NY 28, Old Forge; (315) 335-1681; www.adiron dackexposure.com.

**The Stillwater Shop.** 2590 Stillwater Rd., Lowville; (315) 376-2110; www.still waterreservoir.com.

**Dunn's Boat Service.** 1500 Big Moose Rd., Eagle Bay; (315) 357-3532; www .dunnsboats.com.

**Payne's Air Service.** 431 NY 28, Seventh Lake, Inlet; (315) 357-3971.

**Bird's Seaplane Service.** 275 NY 28, Inlet; (315) 357-3631.

**Helms Aero Service.** NY 30, Long Lake; (518) 624-3931.

## Where to Eat

**The Knotty Pine.** 2776 NY 28, Old Forge; (315) 369-6859; www.knottypine.com. Steaks, seafood, pasta, vegetarian specials, and homemade desserts including Turtle Cheesecake and red raspberry pie. $$$

**The Old Mill.** 2888 NY 28, Old Forge; (315) 369-3662; www.oldmilloldforge.com. Terrific homemade soups, prime rib, steak, shepherd's pie, vegetarian lasagna, seafood, and a children's menu. $$$

## Where to Stay

**Brynilsen's Viking Village.** 2387 South Shore Rd., Old Forge; (315) 357-3150 or (925) 827-9179; www.oldforge-ny.com. Weekly or monthly rentals of cottages with a Viking motif, 400 feet of sandy beach on the lake, campfires, vintage movies, fishing, and old-fashioned fun. $$$–$$$$

**North Woods Inn & Resort.** 4920 NY 28, Fourth Lake, Old Forge; (315) 369-6777; www.northwoodsinnresort.com. Hotel/motel rooms and cabins, outdoor heated pool, sandy lakefront beach, boat rentals, cable TV, housekeeping service, a tavern and restaurant, with a partial or full American meal plan, and special stay-and-play package deals with local attractions. $$–$$$

# Oswego

Go south on NY 28 to NY 12 to connect with I-90 toward Syracuse, then head north on NY 481.

The first freshwater port in the country, Oswego today is an angler's paradise and a good place to embark upon the Seaway Trail.

### H. Lee White Marine Museum (all ages)

**West 1st Street. Pier; (315) 342-0480; www.hleewhitemarinemuseum.com. Museum open daily year-round 1 to 5 p.m., except July and Aug, when it opens at 10 a.m. Closed Easter, Thanksgiving and Christmas Eve through New Year's Day; vessels closed Oct through mid-May and subject to weather. Adults $$, children $, 5 and under free.**

Founded by Rosemary S. Nesbitt, a children's theater teacher, this charming museum has exhibits on shipwrecks, archeological artifacts, and the legendary lake monsters believed to inhabit this region. Outside is a rare U.S. Army LT-5 tugboat, the last of its kind, and a veteran of the World War II Normandy invasion, plus a 1925 Derrick Barge, both open for exploration. Special programs for families are offered year-round, including "Kids Pirate Day," "Tales of the Haunted Harbor," and a "Christmas at Sea" Open House. Birthday and non-birthday parties may be booked aboard the LT-5 through the summer, and family boatbuilding workshops are offered so folks can float their own boat.

# Roadster Rooters, **Rejoice!**

**New Oswego Speedway.** 300 E. Albany St., Oswego; (315) 342-0646; www .oswegospeedway.com.

**Brewerton Speedway.** 60 US 11, Brewerton; (315) 668-6906; www.brewerton speedway.com.

**Fulton Speedway.** 1603 NY 57, Fulton; (315) 593-6531; www.fultonspeedway .com.

**MotoMasters Park.** 3098 US 11, Maple View; (315) 963-4999; www.motomaster .com.

**Oswego County Quarter Midget Club.** Silk and Howards Road, Fulton; (315) 592-2555; www.ocqmc.com.

**Thornwood MX.** 1108 Stone Hill Rd., Williamstown; (315) 420-9613; www .thornwoodmx.com.

### Fort Ontario (all ages)

1 E. Fourth St.; (315) 343-4711; www.nysparks.state.ny.us. **Open May through Aug, Tues through Sun, 10 a.m. to 4:30 p.m. Closed Mon, except Monday holidays. $. Call ahead to confirm changes to hours, activities available, and possible closures due to pending state budget cuts.**

Several forts have occupied this site, the original one built by the British in 1755 during the French and Indian War. Destroyed by the French in 1756, it was rebuilt by the British in 1759. During the Revolutionary War, the Americans destroyed the fort; then the British rebuilt it in 1782. Britain finally turned it over to the United States in 1796, then destroyed it during the War of 1812. The Americans rebuilt it again. After the Civil War, no one seemed to care about rebuilding or destroying the place, and it was abandoned in 1901. The U.S. Army decided to expand the post, and by 1941 over 125 buildings had been added. During

# Oswego County **Skating**

**James P. Cullinan Skating Rink.** West 3rd and Niagara Streets, Oswego; (315) 343-6594.

**Anthony J. Crisafulli Skating Rink.** East 9th and Schuyler Streets, Oswego; (315) 343-4054.

**Bilou Roller Skating Rink.** 1804 NY 3, Fulton; (315) 598-9823.

World War II, it became the site of the only refugee camp for Holocaust survivors. Today, Fort Ontario has been restored to its 1868–1872 appearance, with costumed interpreters taking visitors on a time-travel tour of life lived behind the logs. Seasonal events include a Scottish Highlander Encampment, Kite Festivals, and Candlelight Ghost Tours.

### Safe Haven Museum (ages 7 and up)

2 E. 7th St.; (315) 342-3003; www.oswegohaven.org. Open Memorial Day through Labor Day, Tues through Sun 10 a.m. to 4 p.m., and Labor Day to Memorial Day, Wed through Sun 11 a.m. to 4 p.m.; all other Mondays closed. Donation.

With the tide of the war turning in the Allies' favor by 1944, President Franklin D. Roosevelt made the symbolic gesture of bringing nearly a thousand refugees to America. Government officials were sent to Italy on a rescue mission. Priority was given to people who had escaped from Nazi concentration camps, as well as those with skills to run the refugee camp at Fort Ontario. Transported by train to Oswego, they were housed in a barbed-wire fenced-in compound for eighteen months and told to sign papers agreeing to leave the country when the war was over. It wasn't freedom, but it was better than the alternative. The refugees published their own newspaper and put on theatrical productions for entertainment. Children could leave the compound to attend school, and sympathetic Oswego residents passed food through holes in the gate, and a bicycle over it. Eventually, those refugees who wished to remain in America were granted permission. This new museum tells their story and highlights the importance of tolerance and diversity.

# More Oswego County Museums

**Oswego Railroad Museum.** 56 W. 1st St., Oswego; (315) 343-2347; www .oswegocounty.com.

**John D. Murray Firefighters Museum.** East Side Fire Station, East Cayuga St., Oswego; (315) 343-0999.

**Richardson-Bates House Museum.** 135 E. 3rd St., Oswego; (315) 343-1342; www.rbhousemuseum.org.

**Rail City Historical Museum.** NY 3, Sandy Creek; (315) 387-2932; www.rail citymuseum.com.

**Bridge House Museum.** Henley Park, State and Lock Streets, Phoenix; (315) 695-2484.

**Fort Brewerton & Block House Museum.** 9 US 11, Brewerton; (315) 668-8801.

# Oswego **County Bounty**

**Behling Orchards U-Pick.** 114 Potter Rd., Mexico; (315) 963-7068; www.behling orchards.com.

**Greco Family Farm & Orchard.** 297 W. 5th Street Rd., Oswego; (315) 216) 4180; www.grecofamilyorchards.com.

**Ontario Orchards.** 7735 NY 104, Southwest Oswego; (315) 343-6328; www .ontarioorchards.com.

**Sage Creek Orchards.** 139 Minckler Rd., Mexico; (315) 963-3486; www.sage creekorchards.com.

## Selkirk Shores State Park  (all ages)

7101 NY 3, Pulaski; (315) 298-5737 or (800) 456-2267; www.nysparks.state.ny.us. Park open daily year-round; campgrounds open May through Oct. $. Call ahead to confirm changes to hours, activities available, and possible closures due to pending state budget cuts.

Overlooking Lake Ontario, and sandwiched between the Salmon River and Grindstone Creek, this 980-acre park is a major migratory flyway for over 200 species of birds that prefer following the shoreline instead of crossing the big lake. Salmon and steelhead trout spawn in the river every autumn, nature trails wind through the woodlands and marsh, and the sandy beach is beautiful. There's also a playground, picnic pavilions, recreation programs, and cabins and campsites are available.

## Where to Eat

**Raging River BBQ.** 7B Bridie Sq.; (315) 216-6655; www.ragingriverbbq.com. Smoked drunken shrimp, poppers, chili parfait, eleven kinds of burgers, great barbecue, and a kids menu. $–$$

**Vona's.** West 10th and Utica Streets; (315) 343-8710; www.vonasofoswego.com. Homemade pasta, mini-pizzas, fried ravioli, deli sandwiches, shrimp scampi, stuffed peppers, chicken Parmesan, homemade coconut-cream pie and carrot cake, a kids' menu, and family combo take-out dinner special they deliver! $$

## Where to Stay

**Best Western Captain's Quarters.** 26 E. 1st St.; (315) 342-4040 or (800) 528-1234; www.bestwestern.com. On the riverfront, with views of the harbor, ninety-three rooms and suites, cable TV, in-room movies available, free Wi-Fi, indoor swimming pool, hot tub, sauna and steam rooms, fitness center, and deluxe complimentary continental breakfast.

**K & G Lodge.** 1881 CR 1; (315) 343-2475 or (315) 343-8171; www.kglodge.com. Friendly fishing resort, with lodge rooms, cabins, and suites available daily or weekly, in-ground heated pool, golf privileges, charter sport-fishing aboard *Top Gun,* and the rustically elegant Kristi's Restaurant. $$–$$$

# Sackets Harbor

Follow the Seaway Trail along NY 3 north.

In 1804 Augustus Sacket acquired at auction enough land on the shores of Lake Ontario to build a village. His primary interest was to trade with Canada, less than 30 miles away. Unfortunately, the U.S. Embargo Act of 1808 shut down operations, and Sackets Harbor became the major military stronghold of America's northern frontier in the War of 1812. Today the charming town offers families a strong historical and architectural heritage, as well as waterfront concerts, festivals, and fireworks on the Fourth of July.

## Sackets Harbor Visitors Center (all ages)

301 W. Main St.; (315) 646-2321; www.sacketsharborny.com. Open Memorial Day through Columbus Day, daily 10 a.m. to 5 p.m. and by appointment Columbus Day through Memorial Day. Free.

Housed in the mansion of Augustus Sacket, this is one of New York State's Heritage Areas and a good place to get information about historic sites and upcoming events, including waterfront concerts, festivals, and the Official War of 1812 Day.

## The Thousand Islands

This is the longest navigable inland passage in the world, stretching for 2,300 miles and dotted with 1,793 islands. Iroquois legend tells the tale of the Great Spirit's gift of a magical garden, called Manitonna, given to the tribes on the condition they play nice. When the tribes broke their word and started quarreling among themselves, the Great Spirit picked up the paradise and headed home. Somehow, however, the garden slipped from the Spirit's hands, and the Eden of the Iroquois fell into the Saint Lawrence River, shattering into the islands we see today. To qualify as an official island, the land has to be bigger than a square foot, above water year-round, and be the home of at least one tree. Follow the 454-mile Seaway Trail, a National Historic Motor and Water Byway, where the best scenery and most attractions are located. There are forty-five New York and Canadian parks in this region, so bring the camping gear. For maps and information, call (315) 646-1000 or (800) SEAWAY-T, log on to www.seawaytrail.com, or visit the Seaway Trail Discovery Center at Ray and West Main Streets in Sackets Harbor. Open from 10 a.m. to 5 p.m. year-round, daily May through Oct; Mon through Sat, Nov through Apr. For general information check out the official site for the region at www.visit1000islands.com or call (800) 847-5263. $.

## Horseback Riding **in the Area**

**Spencer Valley Farm.** 28925 Rogers Rd., Redwood; (315) 783-4339; www .spencervalleyfarm.com.

### Sackets Harbor Battlefield State Historic Site  (all ages)

504 W. Main St.; (315) 646-3634; cell phone audio tour (585) 672-1011; www.nysparks.state .ny.us and www.sacketsharborbattlefield.org. Open Memorial Day through Labor Day, Tues through Sat 10 a.m. to 5 p.m., Sun 1 to 5 p.m. Grounds open year-round 8 a.m. to sunset. $. Call ahead to confirm changes to hours, activities available, and possible closures due to pending state budget cuts.

In June of 1812, Sackets Harbor became the front line of America's war with Britain. With its deep harbor, large shipyard, and plenty of trees for timber, it was an ideal place for Americans to begin building a fleet of ships in preparation for the invasion and conquest of Canada. A year later, while most of the Americans were away attacking Fort George, the British attacked the Sackets Harbor shipyard, losing the battle but destroying the American military supplies. Guided by costumed soldiers, or self-guided by your cell phone, explore the battlefield, Navy Yard and the Commandant's House, and stay for the spectacular sunsets over Lake Ontario. In August, nineteenth-century garbed interpreters re-create the Battle of Sackets Harbor, with musket and cannon firing, bateaux rowing, craft and cooking demonstrations, children's games, and naval and land battles. The 200th anniversary of the war is in 2012, and special events will be scheduled.

### Seaway Trail Discovery Center  (all ages)

Corner of Ray and West Main Streets; (315) 646-1000 or (800) 732-9298; www.seawaytrail .com. Open daily July through Oct 10 a.m. to 5 p.m. $, under 4 free.

Located in the 1817 Union Hotel, this eclectic museum showcases the Seaway Trail, a signed scenic byway, also known as an awesome road trip. Following the waterways of the St. Lawrence River, Lake Ontario, Lake Erie, and the Niagara River, the 504-mile

## Talking **Farms**

New Yorkers like to talk, and so do their farms. Throughout the Thousand Islands, families can learn about an array of agritainment options by dialing into the new AG Tour audio system, an information source for over a dozen farms, mills, and wineries. Most sites accept visitors on a seasonal basis, but not all may be open at the time of your visit. Still, it's a great way to learn about the agriculture of the area. Call (315) 221-5104 or go online to www .agvisit.com for a list of participating places.

# Parks Near **Sackets Harbor**

**Westcott Beach State Park.** 12421 NY 3, Adams; ; (315) 646-2239; www.nys parks.state.ny.us.

**Southwick Beach State Park.** 8119 Southwicks Place, Henderson; (315) 846-5338; www.nysparks.state.ny.us.

**Long Point State Park.** 7495 State Park Rd., Three Mile Bay; (315) 649-5258; www.nysparks.state.ny.us.

journey winds past farms, forts, museums, parks, and twenty-eight lighthouses. State-of-the-art interactive exhibits on maritime and natural history, the War of 1812, regional agriculture, and architecture offer a virtual preview of this historic path, and an animatronic Ulysses S. Grant and an electronic cow have their stories to tell, too.

### Old McDonald's Farm  (all ages)

North Harbor Road,14471 CR 145; (315) 583-5737; www.oldmcdonaldhasafarm.com. Open daily May through Oct; May through mid-June, Mon through Fri 10 a.m. to 4 p.m., Sat and Sun 10 a.m. to 5 p.m.; in summer open 10 a.m. to 6 p.m. daily; Labor Day through Oct, Mon through Fri 10 a.m. to 4 p.m., and Sat and Sun 10 a.m. to 6 p.m. $.

This 1200-acre working dairy, with over 1000 head of cattle in residence, is a fun place to learn about life on a farm. Corn, soybeans, wheat, alfalfa, and pumpkins are grown on 4,000 acres of fertile land, and dairy tours are given aboard the Moo Town Trolley. Visit Sheepville, Cowville, Goatville, Poultry University, Pork Avenue, the Bunny Trail, the Flying Reindeer Ranch, and the Robbins Rocking Ranch, home to donkeys and miniature horses. Pony rides, an inflatable Adventure Playground, mini-golf, and the Wizard of Oz Hayride provide more agritainment, and the Lazy Cow Café offers pizza, burgers, peanut butter and jelly sandwiches, plus sixteen flavors of ice cream.

## Where to Eat

**Kathy's Barracks Inn.** Madison Barracks; (315) 646-2376; www.colemanrestaurants .com. Located in the historic Madison Barracks, an army post built in 1816 to protect the northern frontier from British invaders, this casual, friendly restaurant on the harbor offers build-your-own pizzas, steaks, seafood, Italian specialties, and homemade desserts, with outdoor deck dining in season and live entertainment on Sat. $$–$$$

**Tin Pan Galley.** 110 Main St.; (315) 646-3812; www.tinpangalley.com. Breakfast chimichanga, build-your-own omelets, fried green tomatoes Benedict, blackberry-crunch pancakes, wraps, sandwiches, jerk salmon, French Quarter chicken, lobster truffle penne, homemade garlic potato chips, and mocha macadamia mousse torte with raspberry sauce, plus live entertainment and a seasonal outdoor patio. $$–$$$

## Where to Stay

**Bedford Creek Marina and Campground.**
16750 Allen Dr., Sackets Harbor; www.bed
fordcreek.com. Located on the shores of Lake
Ontario, with 190 campsites, cabins, park
model homes, and RVs, a 900-foot sandy
beach, boat rentals, a full-service marina, great

fishing, a camp store with groceries, coin laundry, a rustic playground, ball courts, a nine-hole
golf course across the street, a pizza shack on-
site, and special events scheduled throughout
the summer, including fishing tournaments,
barbecues, a kids' carnival, and a Halloween
celebration in Aug. $

**Ontario Place Hotel.** 103 General Smith
Dr.; (315) 646-8000; www.ontarioplacehotel
.com. Thirty-eight rooms and suites, some
with whirlpools and fireplaces, a luxury
penthouse, Wi-Fi, microwave, refrigerator,
coin laundry, and complimentary continental
breakfast. The 40-foot catamaran *Free Astray*,
with four private staterooms, is also available
for overnight stays, with a complimentary
cruise of the Black River Bay, weather permit-
ting. Children under sixteen stay free. $–$$$

# Watertown

Continue north along the Seaway Trail.

Settled by colonists from New Hampshire and named for the numerous waterfalls along
the Black River, this was a major manufacturing hub in the nineteenth century. It was also
the birthplace of the safety pin, and of the "five and dime" store conceived by F. W. Wool-
worth. Factoring in inflation, and the proliferation today of "dollar stores" worldwide, it's a
retail concept that's never gone out of style.

## The New York State Zoo at Thompson Park  (all ages)

1 Thompson Park, off State Street, Watertown; (315) 782-6180; www.nyszoo.org. Open
daily Mar through Oct, 10 a.m. to 5 p.m.; Nov, 10 a.m. to 4 p.m.; Dec through Feb, Sat
and Sun 10 a.m. to 4 p.m. Closed Mon through Fri and Thanksgiving, Christmas, and New
Year's day. Adults $$, children $, children 3 and under free.

Founded in 1920 with two white-tailed deer to exhibit, the Park Zoo Club, under the leadership of a twelve-year-old boy, raised money to feed the animals and create habitats for
small animals such as porcupines and raccoons. Today, this is the only zoo in the world
dedicated to New York's wildlife, and naturalistic habitats feature black bears, bobcats,
cougars, wolves, wolverines, and elk, Summer Zoofaris offer kids half-day programs of
animal activities, crafts, and games, and the Junior Animal Keepers program teaches folks
seven to twelve how to care for the residents. For wild nighttime fun, sign up for a Zoo
Snooze, and camp out with the creatures under the stars.

## Also in **the Area**

**Burrville Cider Mill.** 18176 NY 156, Watertown; (315) 788–7292; www.burrville cidermill.com.

### Sci-Tech Center  (all ages)

154 Stone St., Watertown; (315) 788-1340; www.scitechcenter.org. Open Tues through Thurs 10 a.m. to 2 p.m., Fri and Sat 10 a.m. to 4 p.m. Closed major holidays. $.

This wonderful interactive museum of science and technology offers more than forty hands-on science exhibits.

### Alex T. Duffy Fairgrounds  (all ages)

970 Coffeen St., Watertown; (315) 785-7775. Park free, events $–$$.

Home of the Jefferson County Fair, the oldest continuously operating fair in the United States, this is also home to a variety of local baseball, softball, and football teams, In addition, there's a skate park, an outdoor swimming pool, basketball courts, an indoor athletic center, a picnic and playground area, and walking trails with scenic river views.

## Where to Eat

**Art's Jug.** 820 Huntington St.; (315) 788-8077; www.artsjug.com. Serving Italian cuisine since 1933, featuring steaks, seafood, prime rib, and pizza, with takeout and delivery available. $–$$

**Willie Mae's Soul Food & Hispanic Restaurant.** 30092 NY 3, Black River; (315) 286-2146. American southern and Puerto Rican cuisine, serving barbecued ribs, chicken, collard greens, and arroz con pollo. $

## Where to Stay

**Best Western Carriage House Inn.** 300 Washington St.; (315) 782-8000; www.best western.com. Rooms and suites, microwave, refrigerator, indoor pool, steam and sauna, exercise room, Wi-Fi, free coffee delivered to your room, on-site restaurant, and children twelve and under free with parent. $$

**Candlewood Suites Watertown.** 26513 Herrick Dr., Evans Mills; (315) 629-6990; www .candlewoodsuites.com/watertownny. About 15 miles outside town, but great for extended stays, this all-suite hotel has full kitchens, free Wi-Fi, cable TV, DVD players and library, twenty-four-hour fitness room, barbecue grills, free use of washer/dryers, dry-cleaning pickup/laundry, and on-site convenience store. $$

# Clayton and Cape Vincent

Travel north on NY 180 to NY 12E north.

Where the Saint Lawrence River meets Lake Ontario, Cape Vincent is the village Napoleon wanted to retire to after Waterloo, had he been able to escape the arms of St. Helena. Today it remains a picturesque place full of charming old houses on tree-lined streets. It's also the only place you can ride a car ferry across the Saint Lawrence to Canada. Farther north along the Seaway Trail is the town of Clayton, settled in 1822, famous for its fine shipbuilding. Much later, the town was a popular port for smugglers and rumrunners during Prohibition. Today area anglers are lured by the giant muskellunge, and the arts and crafts community is flourishing.

### Antique Boat Museum (all ages)

750 Mary St.; (315) 686-4104; www.abm.org. Open daily 9 a.m. to 5 p.m. mid-May through mid-Oct. Museum closed for the winter. Haxall Building exhibits free Mon through Sat 9 a.m. to 5 p.m. Boat rides every hour 10 a.m. to 4 p.m. $$, children $, 6 and under free; ask about special family rates.

An impressive armada of more than 250 antique freshwater recreational boats is amassed here, the largest collection of its kind in the country. Housed in ten buildings on a newly designed and landscaped campus, and docked outside along the St Lawrence River, these boats are classically beautiful. Several hundred engines and motors, plus at least 3,000 nautical artifacts, are here as well, and a recent acquisition is the 106-foot houseboat *La Duchesse,* built for the romantic George Boldt. Head outside for a whirl around the waterways aboard a Triple Cockpit Runabout, or row, row, row your skiff through the tranquil waters of French Creek Bay. On Tuesday evenings in July and August, people of all skill levels are invited to paddle or sail with an instructor, or on their own, aboard the museum's fleet, from keelboats to catboats. In Aug 2010 the biennial Antique Racing Boat Regatta arrives, with more than 150 vintage antique racing boats running demonstration laps in front of the museum. This will be the center of the universe for vintage boat buffs.

# Tug Hill **Plateau**

The snowiest place east of the Rockies, yet similar to a Scottish moor, Tug Hill Plateau is a unique landscape of limestone and shale, thick forests, misty swamps, and spectacular river gorges. Technically a cuesta, Tug Hill Plateau covers more than 2,000 square miles. Black bears, bobcats, moose, and migratory songbirds populate the place, and the cross-country skiing and canoeing are excellent. The Tug Hill hamlet of Montague holds the state snowfall record of 77 inches in a single day, due to lake-effect snow. In 2002 New York State and the Nature Conservancy crafted a deal to protect 45,000 acres from development, making it the largest land preservation pact outside Adirondack Park. For more information contact the Nature Conservancy at (585) 546-8030 and www.nature.org; the New York State Department of Environment Conservation at www.dec.ny.gov; and www.visittughill.com.

### Thousand Islands Museum of Clayton (ages 6 and up)

312 James St.; (315) 686-5794; www.timuseum.org. Open May through Columbus Day, Mon through Sun 10 a.m. to 4 p.m.; Oct through Apr, Mon through Fri 10 to 4 p.m. Donation.

Browse through artifacts and photos from the golden years of the Thousand Islands region, including its notorious smuggling history. A replica of the largest muskellunge ever caught (sixty-nine pounds, fifteen ounces), landed by Clayton local Art Lawton in 1957, is mounted at the Muskie Hall of Fame. Duck fans will be delighted by the Decoy Hall of Fame and the annual Decoy and Annual Wildlife Art Show.

### The Handweaving Museum & Arts Center (ages 7 and up)

314 John St.; (315) 686-4123; www.hm-ac.org. Open year-round, Mon through Fri 9 a.m. to 5 p.m., Sat and Sun 10 a.m. to 5 p.m. Donation.

More than 1,400 textiles from around the world, from ancient to modern times, are exhibited here, and the museum also contains an extensive reference library on the hand-weaving arts. Classes are offered year-round, from rug making, pottery, and beading to woodworking, weaving, and writing. Special workshops for kids include tile, mug, and puppet making, sleuthing in the style of *Indiana Jones* and *CSI*, treasure hunts, and theatrical make-believe.

### Cape Vincent Fisheries Station and Aquarium (all ages)

541 E. Broadway, Cape Vincent; (315) 654-2147. Fishery open daily 9 a.m. to 5 p.m. mid-May to Oct. Aquarium open May through Sept, 9 a.m. to 5 p.m. Free.

Five large aquariums stocked with Lake Ontario and Saint Lawrence River fish can be seen here, as well as other aquatic displays and exhibits. Fishing is allowed off the dock, and there's a nice picnic area overlooking the harbor.

### Horne's Ferry (all ages)

At the foot of Saint James Street, Cape Vincent; (315) 783-0638 (New York) or (613) 385-2402 (Ontario); www.hornesferry.com. Operates daily May through mid-Oct, 8 a.m. to 7:30 p.m. Crossing time: ten minutes. Car and driver $$.

New York State's only international auto/passenger ferry crosses the Saint Lawrence River by way of Wolfe Island to Kingston, Ontario.

## Where to Eat

**Koffee Kove Restaurant.** 220 James St.; (315) 686-2472; Local favorite, serving great breakfasts, homemade hash browns, fresh baked cinnamon rolls, fresh fish sandwiches, burgers, and homemade pies. $

**Riverside Cafe.** 506 Riverside Dr.; (315) 686-2940. Greek and American specialties, with outdoor deck dining and river views. $$

## Where to Stay

**Thousand Islands Inn.** 335 Riverside Dr.; (315) 686-3030 and (800) 544-4241; www .1000-islands.com. Open mid-May through mid-Sept. Built in 1897 and on the National and New York Registers of Historic Places, the inn features large renovated rooms and suites, free Wi-Fi, cable TV, complimentary and continental breakfast. The inn's award-winning gourmet restaurant, where Thousand

## Parks & Preserves **in the Area**

**Burnham Point State Park.** 340765 NY 12E, Cape Vincent; (315) 654-2522; www.nysparks.state.ny.us.

**Creative Playground and Village Square Park.** Mary Street; (315) 686-5552.

**Frink Park.** 510 Riverside Dr.; (315) 686-3771.

**Clayton Recreation Park & Arena.** 615 E. Line Rd.; (315) 686-4310.

**Zenda Farm Historic Preserve.** NY 12, west of Clayton; (315) 686-5345; www.tilandtrust.org.

Island salad dressing originated, serves great steaks, chops, local freshwater fish and ocean fish, chicken, duckling, Italian specialties, homemade bread pudding, cheesecake, and a children's menu. Numerous special vacation packages are offered, the most popular with families being the 1000 Island Discovery. $–$$

**West Winds Motel & Cottages.** 38267 NY 12E; (315) 686-3352 or (888) WESTWND; www.westwindsmotel.com. Located on five acres overlooking the St. Lawrence River, with motel rooms and cottages, a heated outdoor pool, picnic facilities, free premium cable TV, free Wi-Fi, free coffee and ice, screened gazebo, golf putting, video games, and a 150-foot fishing pier, plus badminton, beach volleyball, horseshoe and bocci courts, all lighted for nighttime use. $

# Alexandria Bay

Head north on NY 12.

The stomping grounds of millionaires around the turn of the twentieth century, the area now has a variety of mainstream attractions for families. Stroll down Sisson Street to Scenic View Park for a picnic, a concert, or swimming at the sand beach. Or meander down Market Street to Cornwall Brother's Store for a piece of penny candy and a flashback to Alex Bay's golden days.

### Boldt Castle  (all ages)

Heart Island; (315) 482-2501 or (800) 847-5263; www.boldtcastle.com. **Open daily early May through early Oct, 10 a.m. to 6:30 p.m.; during July and Aug, until 7:30 p.m. Accessible only by private boat or tour boat: Uncle Sam Boat Tours (315) 482-2611; www.unclesamboat tours.com; Clayton Island Tours (315) 686-4217; www.claytonislandtours.com. $.**

George Boldt rose from humble beginnings to become, among other things, the owner of New York's Waldorf-Astoria Hotel. Wealthy and passionately in love with his wife,

Louise, he ordered a 120-room, six-story Rhineland-style castle to be built as a summer home. The finest craftspeople in the world were called in, hearts were carved and painted everywhere, and the island itself was even shaped into a heart. Then one day in 1904 a telegram arrived, telling the workers to stop construction. Louise had died suddenly, and George was so heartbroken he never returned to his fairy-tale island again. Restoration was begun in 1977 by the Thousand Islands Bridge Authority, and continues today, at a cost of more than $20 million. The Boldt Yacht House, with three antique boats, has been completely restored and is accessible by a **free** shuttle service.

### Singer Castle on Dark Island  (ages 6 and up)

**Dark Island (315) 324-3275 or (877) 327-5475; www.singercastle.com. Open mid-May through mid-Oct, 10 a.m. to 5 p.m. daily. Accessible only by private boat, shuttle, or tour boat: Schermerhorn Harbor Shuttle (315) 324-5966; www.schermerhornharbor.com; Uncle Sam Boat Tour (877) 253-9229; www.usboattours.com. Adults $$$, children $$, under 4 free, but no strollers allowed, so young children may have to be carried.**

Born in 1851, Frederick Gilbert Bourne got a job while in his teens working for George Clark's sewing thread company. One evening Clark heard Bourne sing and asked him to

# Alex Bay **Area Fun**

**Bonnie Castle Greens Miniature Golf Course.** 43681 NY 12, Alex Bay; (315) 482-5128 or (800) 955-4511; Recreation Center (315) 482-5122; www.bonnie castle.com.

**Alex Bay 500 Go-Karts.** 46772 NY 12, Alex Bay; (315) 482-2021; www.alex bay500.com.

**Wilderness Falls Mini-Golf.** 43772 NY 12, Alex Bay; (315) 482-2021; www .alexbay500.com.

**Mazeland.** NY 12, Alex Bay; (315) 482-2186; www.mazeland.us.

**Alex Bay Drive-In Theater.** NY 26 and Bailey Settlement Road, Alex Bay; (315) 482-3874.

**Champagne Balloon Adventures.** 27 James St., Alex Bay; (315) 482-9356; www.balloonadventures.com.

**Home Again Alpaca Farm.** 37098 Schell Rd., Theresa; (315) 628-5302; www .hafalpacas.com.

**Broken Spur Ranch.** 27768 NY 26, Theresa; (315) 628-5415; www.brokenspur ranch.org.

# More State Parks **in the Area**

**Grass Point State Park.** 42247 Grassy Point Rd., Alexandria Bay; (315) 686-4472; www.nysparks.state.ny.us.

**Wellesley Island State Park.** 44927 Cross Island Rd., Fineview; (315) 482-2722; www.nysparks.state.ny.us.

**Waterson Point State Park.** 44927 Cross Island Rd., Fineview; (315) 482-2722; www.nysparks.state.ny.us.

**Dewolf Point State Park.** 45920 NY 191, Fineview; (315) 482-2722; www.nys parks.state.ny.us.

**Kring Point State Park.** 25950 Kring Point Rd., Redwood; (315) 482-2444; www.nysparks.state.ny.us.

perform for his business associates. He met a lot of leaders in the sewing industry this way, and worked his way up the ladder until he was the director and president of the Singer Sewing Machine Company by the time he was 36 years old. He lived in the Dakota Apartments in Manhattan, and he had a 1,000-acre summer estate on Long Island, but he wanted to surprise his wife, Emma, and their children (they eventually had nine) with an island "hunting " retreat. Designed by architect Ernest Flagg, who later designed the Chrysler Building, Italian stonecutters were brought in to construct a four-story, twenty-eight-room castle inspired by Sir Walter Scott's novel about Scotland's Woodstock Castle. Armored knights stand guard beside a massive marble fireplace, and large Gothic windows frame the river. This castle has its surprises: There are secret tunnels, hidden passageways, portraits you can peek from, grates built into the walls to spy on guests—and there's even a dungeon! Tours are given on the hour, and be prepared to climb some stairs. If you'd like to be king or queen of the castle for a knight, the Royal Suite sleeps six royally.

## Aqua Zoo (all ages)
43681 NY 12; (315) 482-5771; www.aquazoo.com. Open daily May through Labor Day weekend, 10 a.m. to 5 p.m. $$.

This is the only family-owned and -operated aquarium in the country, with more than a hundred fish tanks containing up to 1,500 gallons of water each, filled with fresh and saltwater fish, coral, and invertebrates. Feed a piranha, stare at the sharks, and touch (Sponge Bob and Patrick alert) a sponge or starfish in this arena of aquaria. There are dry exhibits, too, including a fossil collection and a nice gift shop.

### Wellesley Island State Park  (all ages)  ⬤ ⬤ ⬤

**44927 Cross Island Rd. (exit 51 off I-81), Wellesley Island; (315) 482-2722; camping reservations (800) 456-2267; nature center (315) 482-2479; www.nysparks.state.ny.us. Open daily year-round; nature center open Mon through Sat 8:30 a.m. to 8 p.m., to 4 p.m. Sun in summer. $$ in summer.**

This 2,636-acre park is laced with hiking trails and offers swimming beaches, a playground, nice river views, a nine-hole golf course, mini-golf, campsites, and cabins. The Minna Anthony Common Nature Center, a 600-acre portion of Wellesley State Park, has nature trails, a museum with live local animals, a working beehive, a seasonal butterfly house, excellent bird-watching, and guided nature hikes. If you'd like to spend more time here, there's a campground, a cabin colony, and rentals of fully outfitted cottages available.

## Where to Eat

**Admiral's Inn.** 20 James St.; (315) 482-2781. Italian-American cuisine, plus prime rib, fresh seafood, sandwiches, salads, a children's menu, and a seasonal sidewalk cafe. $$–$$$

**Cavallario's Steak and Seafood House.** 26 Church St.; (315) 482-2160. Featuring a Medieval motif, this restaurant serves prime rib, rack of lamb, roast duck, seafood, pasta, and a children's menu. $$$

## Where to Stay

**Captain Thomson's Motel.** 45 James St.; (315) 482-9961; www.captthomsons.com. On the seaway, with sixty-eight rooms overlooking the channel, harbor, or pool; cable TV, free Wi-Fi, outdoor heated pool, kiddie pool, and restaurant. Chartered fishing trips available; motel is next door to Uncle Sam Boat Tours. Children under twelve stay free in parent's room. $–$$$

**Riveredge Resort Hotel.** 17 Holland St.; (315) 482-9917 and (800) 365-6987; www .riveredge.com. Rooms with castle and channel views, as well as loft suites and Jacuzzi suites, Internet access, cable TV, indoor and outdoor pools, hot tubs, fitness room, beauty parlor, two restaurants, plus outdoor seasonal dining dockside or poolside. $$$

# Canton

Head north on NY 37 into Ogdensburg, then turn right onto NY 68 into Canton.

Named in the early nineteenth century after the city in China (now called Guangzhou) because of an interest in the China trade, this was the birthplace of the great western artist Frederic Remington.

### Traditional Arts in New York State (TAUNY) (all ages)

**53 Main St.; (315) 386-4289; www.tauny.org. Open year-round Tues through Fri 10 a.m. to 5:30 p.m., Sat 10 a.m. to 4 p.m., except for major holidays. $.**

TAUNY's mission is to collect, study, and preserve a record of living history of the North Country, from folklore to the crafts and cultures of the region. Holiday celebrations, songs, stories, dances, foods, furniture, and art of the area are all part of this place, with exhibits that change three times a year, demonstrations and workshops ranging from fly tying to fiddling, and a gift shop that is well stocked with one-of-a-kind handmade treasures.

### Frederic Remington Art Museum (ages 4 and up)

**303 Washington St., Ogdensburg; (315) 393-2425; www.fredericremington.org. Open May through Oct, Mon through Sat 10 a.m. to 5 p.m., Sun 1 to 5 p.m.; and Nov through Apr, Wed through Sat 11 a.m. to 5 p.m., Sun 1 to 5 p.m.; closed major holidays. Eva Caten Remington Education Center, 323 Washington St., open July, Sat and Sun 1 to 4 p.m.; and Sept through June, Sat 1 to 4 p.m. $$, children 5 and under free.**

Born on Oct 4, 1861, Frederic Remington headed west when he was twenty years old and sold his first illustration to *Harper's Weekly* a year later. Although the staff at the magazine redrew Remington's drawing, he was not discouraged, but he did move to Kansas and buy a sheep ranch. Two years later, on Oct 1, he married Eva Caten and moved to Brooklyn, but he continued to travel the world, including Cuba, to cover the Spanish-American War for *Harper's*. Prints, paintings, journals, books, and the incredible bronzes created by this multitalented man are displayed in this museum, and next door, at the Eva Caten Remington Education Center, are interactive exhibits and activities for children at the Kid's Place.

## Where to Eat

**Blackbird Cafe.** 107 Main St.; (315) 386-8104; www.theblackbirdcafe.com. Terrific salads, paninis, tapas, Chimichurri Chicken, New England Chop and Chutney, and Cherry Garcia cheesecake, using locally and organically grown bounty of the county, when in season. There's a fun children's menu, or you can order half sizes of any of the pasta entrees, and there's a stack of children's books available to keep kids occupied.

## Where to Stay

**Comfort Suites.** 6000 US 11; (315) 386-1161; www.comfortsuites.com. Sixty-nine rooms and suites, some with microwave and refrigerator, free Wi-Fi, indoor pool, hot tub, sauna, exercise room, game room, guest laundry, free coffee, and free newspaper. $$

## Also in **the Area**

**Jacques Cartier State Park.** 251 Old Mills Rd., off NY 12, Morristown; (315) 375-6371; www.nysparks.state.ny.us.

# Massena

Head north along the Seaway Trail on NY 12 to NY 37 north.

The Seaway International Bridge is the gateway from East Ontario and Quebec, connecting Cornwall, Ontario, with Massena, New York.

### Robert Moses State Park (all ages)

19 Robinson Bay Rd. (4 miles northeast of town off NY 37); (315) 769-8663; www.nysparks
.state.ny.us. Open daily year-round; beach open late June through Labor Day. $–$$.

Located on the Saint Lawrence River, between the Seaway Shipping Channel and the Robert Moses Power Dam, this 2,232-acre park offers hiking and nature trails that start at the nature center, swimming at a sand beach, lake and river fishing, a playground, boat rentals, campsites, and cabins. The nature center offers special programs and events for families year-round, from snowshoe hikes and snow-person sculpting to wood carving, soap making, and lots of bug fun.

### Saint Lawrence–FDR Power Project Visitors Center (all ages)

Hawkins Point Visitors Center. 21 Hawkins Point Rd.; (315) 764-0226 or (800) 262-NYPA;
www.nypa.gov/vc/stlaw.htm. Free.

For an electrifying outing, visit this power plant visitor center on the Saint Lawrence River for hands-on energy-related exhibits, working models, computerized exhibits, a multimedia show on power development, murals painted by Thomas Hart Benton, and views from the 116-foot observation deck overlooking the Moses-Saunders Power Dam and the Canadian border. Power people love to party, and these folks host a lot of fun family events such as holiday pajama and movie nights, Halloween celebrations, and an annual Wildlife Festival.

### Dwight D. Eisenhower Lock (all ages)

NY 131 (2 miles north of NY 37); (315) 769-2049 or (315) 764-3208. Call (315) 769-2422
for ships' origins and expected locking times. Open daily 9 a.m. to 9 p.m. Memorial Day
through Labor Day. $.

More than 3,000 commercial vessels and cruise ships from around the world transit the St Lawrence Seaway every year. Visit the viewing deck to watch these huge ships lifted and lowered 42 feet inside the lock chamber, with an interpretive center and films to explain the process.

### Akwesasne Cultural Center (all ages)

321 NY 37, Hogansburg, about 8 miles east of Massena; (518) 358-2461; www.akwesasne
culturecenter.org. Open year-round Mon through Thurs 8:30 a.m. to 4:30 p.m., Fri 8:30 a.m.
to 3:30 p.m.; call for weekend appointments or scheduled tours. $, children 5 and under
free.

## Other Things to See and Do
## in the North Country

**Coles Creek State Park.** 13003 NY 37, Chippewa Bay; (315) 388-5636 or www
.nysparks.state.ny.us.

**Whetstone Gulf State Park.** RD No. 2, Lowville; (315) 376-6630; www.nys
parks.state.ny.us.

**American Maple Museum.** 9756 Main St., Croghan; (315) 346-1107; www
.americanmaplemuseum.org.

**Fiddlers Hall of Fame & Museum.** 1121 Comins Rd., Osceola; (315) 599-7009;
www.nysotfa.com.

Located on the St. Regis Mohawk Reservation, this small museum and library was started in 1971 in an effort to discourage the dropout rate in the community and encourage an appreciation of the rich heritage of Native American culture. More than 700 ethnographic objects and over 2,000 rare photographic objects have been collected since then, and the library has more than 28,000 books, The Akwesasane are especially gifted at making black ash splint and sweetgrass baskets, and fragments dating back 3,000 years have been found in the area. Other items on display are paintings, pottery, masks, beadwork, and wampum belts.

## Where to Eat

**Trombino's Restaurant.** 181 Center St.; (315) 764-1388; Homemade pizza, calzones, wings, Italian specialties, and takeout available. $

## Where to Stay

**Super 8 Massena.** 84 Grove St.; (315) 764-1065; www.super8.com. Rooms with microwave, refrigerator, free premium cable, free Wi-Fi, and free Super Start Breakfast. $

## For More Information

**Adirondacks.com.** (518) 891-3745; www
.adirondacks.com.

**Adirondack Mountain Club's Information Centers.** (518) 668-4447 or (800)
395-8080, Lake Placid (518) 523-3441; www
.adk.org.

**Adirondack Regional Tourism Council.**
(518) 846-8016 or (800) 487-6867; www.visit
adirondacks.com.

**Adirondack Harvest.** (518) 962-4810; www
.adirondackharvest.com.

**Central Adirondack Association.** (315) 369-6983; www.visitmyadirondacks.com.

**Franklin County Tourism.** (518) 483-9470 or (800) 709-4895; www.adirondacklakes
.com.

**Hamilton County Tourism.** (518) 548-3076 or (800) 648-5239; www.hamiltoncounty.com.

**Indian Lake Chamber of Commerce.**
(518) 648-5112 or (800) 328-5253; www

.indian-lake.com and www.indianlakechamber.org.

**Schroon Lake Chamber of Commerce.** (518) 532-7675 or (888) 724-7666; www.schroonlake.org.

**Lake Placid/Essex County Visitors Bureau.** (518) 523-2445 or (800) 447-5224; www.lakeplacid.com.

**Lewis County Chamber of Commerce.** (315) 376-2213 or (800) 724-0242; www.lewiscountychamber.org. Adirondack Coast Visitors & Convention Bureau. (877) 242-6752; www.goadirondack.com.

**Warren County Tourism.** (800) 95-VISIT, ext. 143; www.visitlakegeorge.com.

**1000 Islands International Tourism Council.** (315) 482-2520 or (800) 847-5263; www.visit1000islands.com.

**Alexandria Bay Chamber of Commerce.** (315) 482-9531 or (800) 541-2110; www.alexbay.org.

**Cape Vincent Chamber of Commerce.** (315) 654-2481; www.capevincent.org.

**Clayton Area Chamber of Commerce.** (315) 686-3771; www.1000islands-clayton.com.

**Greater Watertown-North Country Chamber of Commerce.** (315) 788-4400; www.watertownny.com.

**Oswego County Tourism.** (315) 349-8322; www.visitoswegocounty.com.

**Sackets Harbor Chamber of Commerce.** (315) 646-1700; www.sacketsharborchamberofcommerce.com.

**St. Lawrence County Chamber of Commerce.** (315) 386-4000 or (877) 228-7810; www.northcountryguide.com.

**Seaway Trail Inc.** (315) 646-1000; www.seawaytrail.com.

**Saranac Lake Area Chamber of Commerce.** (518) 891-1990; www.saranaclake.com.

**Lake Luzerne Regional Chamber of Commerce.** (518) 696-3500; www.lakeluzernechamber.org.

**Tupper Lake Chamber of Commerce.** (518) 359-3328; www.tupperlakeinfo.com.

# Western
## New York

Gateway to the Great Lakes, home to the Seneca for centuries, and the last stop on the Underground Railroad, the western frontier of New York is known for its spectacular natural beauty and fertile farmlands, as well as for the unique communities that have flourished within its borders. From the religious idealists of Chautauqua and the freethinkers of Lily Dale to the peaceable Amish in Conewango Valley and the Native Americans in Salamanca, this region is a refuge for a variety of lifestyles.

Water is the theme in the Niagara area, cradled by Lake Erie and Lake Ontario, strung together by the Erie Canal, and crowned by the cascades of Niagara Falls. The forests and lakes in and around the wilderness of Allegany State Park blanket the southern section with thickly wooded hills rimming sparkling sapphire lakes filled with monster-size muskies. From strolling along prehistoric seashores, or cruising the waterways aboard vintage vessels soaking in the beauty of Niagara (literally), to improving your culture quotient at Chautauqua, there is much to see and do here with your family.

### DRIVING TIPS

Paralleling the Erie Canal, NY 31 runs east to west from Rochester to Buffalo. I-90 also runs east and west, heading into Buffalo, then winding south along the scenic Seaway Trail following the shores of Lake Erie. In the Allegany region, east and west travel is easiest on NY 17, passing through Allegany State Park, across to Chautauqua Lake. From Niagara Falls north along Lake Ontario is the continuation of the picturesque Seaway Trail. Dozens of country back roads lace through the region's rolling farmlands and offer interesting detours.

## Buffalo

The French were the first to explore this Iroquois land, calling the Niagara River *beau fleuve,* or beautiful river. Somehow that name morphed into the word Buffalo, or so one

# WESTERN NEW YORK

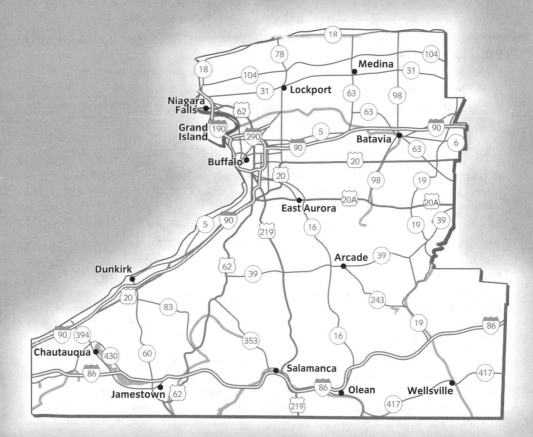

story goes. After the completion of the Erie Canal in 1825, Buffalo boomed, and railroads, factories, and steel mills multiplied. In 1901 the city proudly hosted the Pan-American Exposition, a spectacular world's fair that was unfortunately the place chosen by Leon Czolgosz to assassinate President William McKinley. Today Buffalo is the second-largest city in the state, offering visitors a variety of activities and attractions, from architectural treasures and great theater to spectacular sports and breathtaking scenery.

## Buffalo Niagara Visitor Center (all ages)

Market Arcade, 617 Main St.; (716) 852-BFLO or (800) BUFFALO; www.visitbuffaloniagara .com. Hours vary by season. Please call ahead. **Free.**

Located in the heart of the theater district, this is a good place to pick up maps and brochures and get current information about special events in town.

## Buffalo City Hall (all ages)

65 Niagara Sq.; (716) 851-4200 or (716) 852-3300 (Observation Deck); www.visitbuffalo niagara.com. Open year-round Mon through Fri 8:30 a.m. to 4 p.m., closed holidays and weekends. **Free.**

Take the elevator to the twenty-fifth floor of this Art Deco masterpiece, then walk up three flights to the observation deck overlooking the city, the Niagara River, and Lake Erie.

## Buffalo Zoo (all ages)

300 Parkside Ave.; (716) 837-3900; www.buffalozoo.org. Open daily year-round, except in Jan and Feb, when it is closed Mon and Tues; open July through Aug, 10 a.m. to 5 p.m.; Sept through June, 10 a.m. to 5 p.m. Closed Thanksgiving and Christmas. Adults $$, children $, under 2 **free.**

More than a thousand exotic and endangered animals exist in natural habitats at this twenty-three-acre zoo, from rare white tigers and lowland gorillas to, of course, buffalo. As part of a fifteen-year master plan to create more realistic and immersive animal habitats, a South American rain forest complete with waterfalls has opened recently, soon to be followed by an African Watering Hole and an Arctic Edge exhibit, themed together to highlight the importance of water here and around the world. The Children's Zoo is being transformed into an nineteenth-century farm along the Erie Canal, with rare-breed domestic animals, heritage crops, and local wildlife habitats. Animal demonstrations and interactive stations are offered in season, and a very popular family event is the Zoo Snooze sleepover in summer. Surrounding the zoo is the 350-acre Delaware Park, an emerald oasis designed by Frederick Law Olmstead, where vintage-style rowboats are available for mini-voyages on Hoyt Lake.

## Buffalo Museum of Science (all ages)

1020 Humboldt Parkway; (716) 896-5200 or (866) 291-6660; www.buffalomuseumofscience .org. and www.sciencebuff.org. Winter hours Wed to Sat 10 a.m. to 5 p.m., Sun noon to 5 p.m. Summer hours Mon to Sat 10 a.m. to 5 p.m., closed Sun. Closed holidays. Adults $$, children $, under 3 **free.**

# Water **Explorations**

Cruise the Canadian border along the upper Niagara River or sail on Lake Erie or the Erie Canal for an amazing maritime adventure.

**Buffalo Harbor Cruises.** (716) 856-6696; www.buffalharborcruises.com.

**Moondance Cat.** (716) 854-7245; www.moondancecat.com.

**Spirit of Buffalo.** (716) 796-7210; www.spiritofbuffalo.com.

**Amherst Marine Center.** 1900 Campbell Blvd., Amherst; (716) 691-6707; www.eriecanal.com

**Grand Lady Cruises.** 100 Whitehaven Rd., at Holiday Inn, Grand Island; (716) 774-8594 or (888) 824-5239; www.grandlady.com.

**Classic Cruises.** 5 Austin St., Buffalo; (716) 946-7246; www.wnyclassiccruises.com.

**Buffalo Niagara Riverkeeper Eco Tours.** 1250 Niagara St., Buffalo; (716) 852-7483; www.bnriverkeeper.org.

From anthropology to zoology, this place has a wide variety of permanent and changing exhibits to explore. One of the only Tibetan sand mandalas on permanent exhibition in North America is here, along with dinosaurs, Egyptian mummies, and more than 10,000 gems and minerals. For younger scientists, the Explorations Gallery offers hands-on activities from dino digs to cultural dramatic play areas, and the new (Over) Night at the Museum experience gives kids the chance to solve a museum mystery by collecting clues using flashlights to light the way, followed by a dance party or a movie. A favorite for families is the annual Bubblefest, with bubble performers and activity stations inside the museum and outside in the lovely Rose Garden of Martin Luther King Park.

## Buffalo and Erie County **Botanical Gardens** (all ages)

2655 S. Park Ave. at McKinley Parkway; (716) 827-1584; www.buffalogardens.com. Open daily year-round 10 a.m. to 5 p.m. Open holidays. $, under 6 free.

A dozen glass greenhouses grace the grounds of this eleven-acre garden, filled with an international array of orchids, fruit trees, palms, and cacti. Built in the 1890s, this Victorian conservatory also has spectacular seasonal outdoor displays of roses, tulips, and perennials, plus a special Children's Garden with resident butterflies.

## Buffalo and Erie County **Naval & Military Park** (ages 6 and up)

1 Naval Park Cove; (716) 847-1773 or (716) 847-6405; www.buffalonavalpark.org. Open daily Apr through Oct, 10 a.m. to 5 p.m.; Sat and Sun in Nov, 10 a.m. to 4 p.m. Closed Dec through Mar. Adults $$, children 6 through 16 $, under 5 free.

Located on six acres of Lake Erie waterfront, this is the largest inland naval park in the country. Board the World War II destroyer USS *The Sullivans,* tour the submarine USS *Croaker,* or check out the M-41 tank, an F-101F Voodoo fighter interceptor jet, the guided missile cruiser USS *Little Rock,* or the terrific model-ship collection. Other exhibits focus on women and African Americans in the military and Vietnam veterans, and there are displays of Marine Corps and POW memorabilia.

# Buffalo **Performing Arts**

Buffalo has a lot of places to see and hear great theater and music. Here is a partial list, and you can call or visit the Web sites to get current season and schedule information.

**Theatre of Youth (TOY).** (716) 884-4400; www.theatreofyouth.org.

**UB Center for the Arts.** (716) 645-2787; www.ubcfa.org.

**Shea's Performing Arts Center.** (716) 847-1410; www.sheas.org.

**Studio Arena Theatre.** (716) 856-8025; www.studioarena.org.

**Buffalo State Performing Arts Center.** (716) 878-3005; www.buffalostate .edu/pac.

**Alleyway Theatre.** (716) 852-2600; www.alleyway.com.

**Irish Classical Theatre.** (716) 853-4282; www.irishclassicaltheatre.com.

**Buffalo Philharmonic Orchestra.** (716) 885-5000 or (716) 885-0331; www .bpo.org.

**Paul Robeson Theatre.** (716) 884-2013; www.theatreallianceofbuffalo.com.

**HSBC Arena.** (716) 855-4100; www.hsbcarena.com.

**Buffalo Ensemble Theatre.** (716) 855-2225; www.betbuffalo.org.

**Shakespeare in Delaware Park.** (716) 856-4533; www.shakespeareindelaware park.org.

**Buffalo United Artists.** (716) 886-9239; www.buffalobua.org.

**American Repertory Theater.** (716) 884-4858; www.artofwny.org.

**The New Phoenix Theatre on the Park.** (716) 853-1334; www.newphoenix theatre.com.

**Jewish Repertory Theatre.** (716) 688-4114; www.jewishrepertorytheatre.com.

**Ujima Theatre Company.** (716) 883-4232; www.ujimatheatre.org.

### Ira G. Ross Aerospace Museum  (ages 6 and up)

One Seymour H. Knox III Plaza, HSBC Arena; (716) 858-4340; www.wnyaerospace.org. Open year-round Sat and Sun 11 a.m. to 4 p.m.; closed Mon through Fri and major public holidays. $.

Newly relocated to Buffalo's waterfront in the Canal Side district, this wonderful museum has a variety of historic aircraft, from a barnstorming Curtiss JN-4 Jenny to a lunar launcher, plus the Bell rocket belt James Bond used in *Thunderball.*

### Tifft Nature Preserve  (all ages)

1200 Fuhrmann Blvd.; (716) 896-5200 or (716) 825-6397; www.sciencebuff.org. Trails open daily dawn to dusk, Makowski Visitor Center open Wed through Sat 10 a.m. to 4 p.m., Sun noon to 4 p.m. Closed major holidays. **Free,** donations gratefully accepted.

Fifty years ago, this peaceful 264-acre nature refuge was the city dump. Concerned citizens convinced the city to transform an eyesore into eye candy, and in 1982 the preserve became part of the Buffalo Museum of Science. Five miles of trails and three boardwalks wind through woodlands and wetlands, and a huge seventy-five-acre cattail marsh attracts hundreds of species of birds. Special programs, tours, workshops, and events are offered throughout the year, including nature crafts and Tifft Treks.

### Buffalo and Erie County Historical Society  (ages 5 and up)

25 Nottingham Court; (716) 873-9644; www.bechs.org. Open year-round Tues through Sat 10 a.m. to 5 p.m., Sun noon to 5 p.m. Closed holidays. Resource Center by appointment only; 459 Forest Ave.; (716) 873-9695. $, under 7 **free.**

Housed in the building that was New York's pavilion during the 1901 Pan-American Exposition, this wonderful museum, with more than 10,000 artifacts, has an interesting exhibit on the more than 700 products and inventions that originated in Buffalo, from Cheerios to kazoos. There are also exhibits highlighting the immigrant and Native American heritage of the region, a Pioneer Gallery, and a street of nineteenth-century shops to explore. Nearby is the Resource Center, open by appointment only, which houses the Pan-American Centennial exhibit. Guided tours and chamber theater presentations of American classic plays are offered throughout the year.

### Theodore Roosevelt Inaugural National Historic Site
(ages 4 and up)

641 Delaware Ave.; (716) 884-0095; www.trsite.org and www.nps.gov/thri. Open year-round, museum visit is by guided tour only, scheduled hourly, beginning at 9:30 a.m. weekdays and 12:30 p.m. weekends; last tour at 3:30 p.m. Closed major holidays. Adults $$, children 6 to 18 $, 5 and under **free.**

When President McKinley was assassinated at the Pan-American Exposition in 1901, the library of the Greek Revival Wilcox mansion became the site of Theodore Roosevelt's inauguration. Recently reopened after extensive renovations, this historic house has new exhibits and fresh interpretations of that improvised inaugural event. Seasonal activities and events are scheduled throughout the year, but in summer be sure to make reservations for your favorite kid and bear to attend the popular Teddy Bear Picnic.

## Albright-Knox Art Gallery  (all ages)
1285 Elmwood Ave.; (716) 882-8700; www.albrightknox.org. Open Thurs through Sun 10 a.m. to 5 p.m. Adults $$$, students 13 and up $$, 12 and under **free.**

This small but outstanding museum of modern art has works by Warhol, Picasso, Pollock, van Gogh, Gauguin. Matisse, Mondrian, and others. Special programs for kids include online art games, drawing and painting classes, scavenger hunts, and Sunday Family Fundays.

## The Buffalo Transportation Pierce Arrow Museum  (ages 6 and up)
263 Michigan Ave. at 201 Seneca St.; (716) 853-0084; www.pierce-arrow.com.

This automotive dream destination reopens in spring 2010 after a $15 million renovation. Along with an incredible collection of rare antique cars and trucks, the renewed museum's centerpiece will be a never-before-built 1920s filling station designed by Frank Lloyd Wright. A small movie theater will present historical transportation films, and vintage bicycles and automobile accessories will be displayed for the first time at the museum.

## Woodlawn Beach State Park  (all ages)
S-3580 Lakeshore Rd., Blasdell; (716) 826-1930 or (716) 826-8895; www.nysparks.state.ny .us. Open dawn to dusk year-round; $. Call ahead to confirm changes to hours, activities available, and possible closures due to pending state budget cuts.

Stroll a mile of the easternmost terminus of Lake Erie's beach, where some of its finest freshwater sand dunes are still intact, then wander through wooded wetlands and watch

# The Buffalo **Audubon Society**

For over a century these folks have worked to protect unique areas of biodiversity and connect people to their planet. Along with the Beaver Meadow Preserve, they maintain several other centers and preserves throughout the region, rich with wildlife and rare plants, and offer events designed to entice even reluctant outdoor explorers into budding naturalists. Evening strolls through the Enchanted Forest, where you meet and greet with forest folk, Bird-a-Thons, and a variety of nature hikes and owl prowls are some of the programs they offer. Call or check the Web site for current information and directions; (800) 377-1520 or (585) 457-3228; www.buffaloaudubon.com.

**Allenberg Bog Audubon Nature Preserve**

**North Tonawanda Audubon Nature Preserve**

**Ayer-Stevenson Audubon Nature Preserve**

**Rushing Stream Audubon Nature Preserve**

**Rose Acres Audubon Nature Preserve**

# Buffalo **Sports**

Buffalo boasts some of the best professional sports teams in the country, and there's athletic action available year-round. Call or check the Web for a current season schedule and special family packages.

**Buffalo Bills Football.** Ralph Wilson Stadium. 1 Bills Dr.; (716) 649-0015 or (877) BBTICKS; www.buffalobills.com.

**Buffalo Bisons Baseball.** Coca-Cola Field. 275 Washington St.; (716) 846-2000; www.buffalo.bisons.milb.com.

**Buffalo Sabres Hockey.** HSBC Arena. One Seymour H. Knox III Plaza; (716) 855-4100 or (888) 467-2273; www.sabres.nhl.com.

**Buffalo Bandits Lacrosse.** HSBC Arena. One Seymour H. Knox III Plaza; (716) 855-4100 or (888) 467-2273; www.bandits.com.

**Buffalo Silverbacks Basketball.** 191 Main St., East Aurora; (716) 714-7100; www.buffalosilverbacks.com.

for wildlife atop interpretive boardwalks. Although swimming is sometimes restricted, there is a new nature center and bathhouse complex, plenty of picnic places, a playground, and spectacular sunsets.

### Reinstein Woods Nature Preserve (all ages)
93 Honorine Dr., Depew; (716) 683-5959; www.dec.ny.gov. Trails open sunrise to sunset year-round. Center open Mon through Fri 9 a.m. to 4:30 p.m., Sat 1 to 4:30 p.m. Closed Sun and state holidays. Guided nature walks Sat at 10 a.m. $.

This unique 292-acre preserve is anchored by the new, earth-friendly Environmental Education Center, where interpretive self-guided trails fan out through one of the largest virgin forests in the state and lead past more than a dozen ponds. Wildlife thrives here, from deer and beaver to hawks and herons. Guided ninety-minute walks are offered on Sat, and special programs for families throughout the year include full moon walks and dragonfly talks.

### Niagara Hobby and Craft Mart (all ages)
3366 Union Rd., Cheektowaga; (716) 681-1666; www.niagarahobby.com. Open year-round Mon through Sat 10 a.m. to 9 p.m., Sun 10 a.m. to 5 p.m. Closed Easter, Thanksgiving, and Christmas.

Near the Buffalo Airport and the Walden Galleria Mall is the biggest hobby store in the country, carrying trains of every type and scale, radio-controlled cars, planes, boats, Estes rockets, dollhouses and furnishings, die-cast miniatures, and arts and crafts supplies.

## Where to Eat

**Anchor Bar.** 1047 Main St., (716) 884-4083; www.anchorbar.com. This is home of the original buffalo wings, which were created by Teressa Bellissimo in 1964 as an impromptu snack for her son and his friends. $

**The Broadway Market.** 999 Broadway; (716) 893-0705; www.broadwaymarket.org. Since 1888 this ethnic food emporium has been the main marketplace for the bounty of farms owned and operated by local families. Fruit and vegetable stalls, butcher shops, and bakeries offer a wide variety of exotic delights, and there are delis, restaurants, and specialty stores on-site as well. $

**Ristorante Lombardo.** 1198 Hertel Ave.; (716) 873-4291; www.ristorantelombardo .com. Serving creative Italian specialties, a Caesar salad made table-side, steak, seafood, chops, pastas, with half orders available, and the fabulous Frou-Frou Cake. $$–$$$

## Where to Stay

**Comfort Suites Downtown.** 601 Main St.; (716) 854-5550; www.comfortsuites.com. Rooms and suites, microwave, refrigerator, wet bar, exercise room, free Wi-Fi, free breakfast, and a lounge and restaurant. $$

**Embassy Suites Buffalo.** 200 Delaware Ave.; (716) 842-1000; www.buffalo.embassy suites.com. Suites with two TVs, microwave, mini-fridge, wet bar, pullout sofa, free full breakfast, free nightly manager's reception, free Wi-Fi, indoor pool and whirlpool, fitness center, restaurant, lobby lounge, espresso bar, free valet parking, and free airport shuttle. $$$

# East Aurora

Head south on NY 16.

Elbert Hubbard, the charismatic founder of the Arts and Crafts movement in America, created a community of craftspeople and artisans, known as the Roycrofters, in this pastoral village.

## Vidler's 5 & 10 (all ages)

676–694 Main St.; (716) 652-0481 or (877) VIDLERS; www.vidlers5and10.com. Open Mon through Sat 9 a.m. to 5:30 p.m., Fri 9 a.m. to 9 p.m., Sun noon to 5 p.m. Closed holidays.

Family owned since 1930, this is a time-travel trip to the pre-mall five-and-dime era. Penny candy, old-fashioned housewares, and a toy counter make this a unique shopping experience.

## Also in **the Aurora Area**

**Elbert Hubbard Roycroft Museum.** 363 Oakwood Ave., East Aurora; (716) 652-4735; www.roycrofter.com.

**Millard Fillmore House Museum.** 24 Shearer Ave., East Aurora; (716) 652-8875; www.nps.gov.

**Sinking Pond Wildlife Sanctuary.** Pine Street Extension, East Aurora; (716) 652-8866; www.east-aurora.ny.us.

### Explore and More Children's Museum (ages 1 to 8)
**300 Gleed Ave.; (716) 655-5131; www.exploreandmore.org. Open Wed through Sat 10 a.m. to 5 p.m., Sun noon to 5 p.m.; also open some school holidays. Closed some major holidays. $, under 1 free.**

Solve a puzzle, learn about Mexico and monarch butterflies, harvest faux food from the garden, and design and build a board house at the Frank Lloyd Wright architectural studio inside this small-person–friendly, interactive hands-on museum.

### Hawk Creek Wildlife Center (all ages)
**655 Luther Rd.; (716) 652-8646. Walden Galleria Mall, exit 52 off I-90; (716) 681-7600; www .hawkcreek.org. Open Sat noon to 6 p.m., and sometimes Sun noon to 5 p.m. Donation, $–$$$, depending on event.**

One of the largest raptor rehabilitation centers in the state, this wonderful wildlife sanctuary offers over 2500 educational programs a year and is home to nearly a hundred birds, mammals, and reptiles that can't be released back into the wild. The center is open for several seasonal special events, such as the Wildlife and Renaissance Festival, but is generally closed to the public. They do, however, exhibit several of their star birds and mammals almost every weekend year-round at the Walden Galleria Mall's lower level.

### Knox Farm State Park (all ages)
**437 Buffalo Rd.; (716) 655-7200; www.nysparks.state.ny.us/parks. Open year-round daily dawn to dusk. $. Call ahead to confirm changes to hours, activities available, and possible closures due to pending state budget cuts.**

## New York **Trivia**

George Washington once remarked to Gen. George Clinton, the state's first governor, that New York was "at present the seat of the Empire," giving it the nickname "Empire State."

This 633-acre former farm features a variety of habitats, from grasslands to wood-lands, with scenic nature trails for hiking, biking, and cross-country skiing in season. A phenomenal fiber-arts program and fall festival, as well as interpretive farm animal exhibits, are offered as well, and the visitor center has interesting historic and natural displays.

### Penn Dixie Paleontological and Outdoor Education Center
(all ages)

4050 North St., Hamburg; (716) 627-4560; www.penndixie.org. Open May through Oct, Sat 9 a.m. to 4 p.m., Sun 11 to 4 p.m.; and mid-June to early Sept, Mon through Sat 9 a.m. to 4 p.m. Closed July 4 and Labor Day. $.

During the 1960s, when this site was a quarry for the Penn Dixie Cement Company, a layer of shale was removed, exposing 380-million-year-old Devonian fossils of trilobites, brachiopods, and crustacea that lived in what once was a warm shallow sea. For a small fee your family can collect these little marine critters, the remains of creatures older than the dinosaurs. Owned and managed by the Hamburg Natural History Society, there are also many astronomy programs offered throughout the year, as well as bird-ing expeditions, and the annual Scare-assic Park Pirate Adventure in autumn is very popular.

### The Kazoo Factory and Museum  (all ages)

8703 S. Main St., Eden; (716) 992-3960; www.edenkazoo.com. Open year-round Tues through Sat 10 a.m. to 5 p.m., Sun noon to 5 p.m. Closed Mon. Free.

Established in 1916, this is the only metal kazoo factory in North America. Operated the same way now as then, with twenty machines run by one ten-horsepower motor, this is a real working factory. Watch the creation of a kazoo Wed through Fri, or make your own cool kazoo at the kazoo kiosk, then tour the museum for a look at the many variations of world's most user-friendly instrument.

# Also in **the Area**

**Burchfield Penney Art Center.** 1300 Elmwood Ave., Buffalo; (716) 878-6011; www.yournewburchfieldpenney.com.

**Lasertron.** 5101 N. Bailey Ave., Amherst; (716) 833-8766; www.lasertron.us.

**Dunn Tire Raceway Park.** 57 Gunnville Rd., Lancaster; (716) 759-6818; www.dunntireracewaypark.com.

**Xtreme Wheels Indoor Skate Park.** 356 Hertel Ave., Buffalo; (716) 871-9361; www.xtreme-wheelz.com.

## Where to Eat

**Iron Kettle Restaurant.** 1009 Olean Rd.; (716) 652-5310. Casual, friendly place serving great breakfasts, salads, sandwiches, pasta, and terrific strawberry shortcake, plus a screened outdoor porch for seasonal deck dining. $

**The Old Orchard Inn.** 2095 Blakeley Corners Rd.; (716) 652-4664; www.oldorchardny.com. Formerly a farmhouse, this restaurant is set on twenty-five pastoral acres, with a duck pond to ponder. The Old Orchard Inn serves Italian specialties, chicken fricassee, steak, seafood, rack of lamb, and homemade desserts. $$$

## Where to Stay

**Hampton Inn East Aurora.** 49 Olean St.; (716) 655-3300; www.hamptoninn.hilton.com. Eighty rooms and suites, microwave and refrigerator, indoor pool, whirlpool, exercise room, library, convenience store, coin laundry, laundry service, complimentary breakfast and beverage area, playpens and high chairs available, in-room movies, and free high-speed Internet. $$$$

**The Roycroft Inn.** 40 S. Grove St.; (716) 652-5552; www.roycroftinn.com. A National Historic Landmark, this charming B&B has twenty-eight suites, some with up to five rooms, decorated with original and reproduced Roycroft furnishings. The inn has a gourmet restaurant with a children's menu. $$–$$$

# Grand Island

Take NY 16 north to I-190 north.

Nestled between New York and Ontario and caressed by the Niagara River, this is the biggest island in the stream.

### Beaver Island State Park  (all ages)

**2136 W. Oakfield Rd., Grand Island; (716) 773-3271; www.nysparks.state.ny.us. Open daily year-round dawn to dusk.**

Located on the southern end of Grand Island, this 950-acre park has a half-mile of sandy beach along the Niagara River, a marina, a nature center, nature trails, playgrounds, picnic areas, ball fields, a disc course, an eighteen-hole golf course, and great fishing spots. Also in the park is the River Lea house and museum, home to the Grand Island Historical Society. $.

### Buckhorn Island State Park  (all ages)

**c/o Beaver Island State Park, 2136 W. Oakfield Rd., Grand Island; (716) 773-3271; www.nys parks.state.ny.us. Open daily year-round, dawn to dusk.**

More wild than its sister park on the southern part of the island, this 895-acre wetlands is the last vestige of the vast marshes and meadows that once lined the Niagara River. Ongoing plans include restoration of the habitats for native plants and animals, along with better bird blinds and more nonintrusive trails. **Free.**

### Martin's Fantasy Island (all ages)

2400 Grand Island Blvd.; (716) 773-7591; www.martinsfantasyisland.com. Open mid-May to mid-June, weekends only, 11:30 a.m. to 7:30 p.m.; mid-June through Labor Day, Tues through Sat 11:30 a.m. to 8:30 p.m.; July and Aug, Sat to 9 p.m. Pay one price $$–$$$$; discount coupons available at Wegmans, Wendy's, and the Web site.

Covering eighty acres, this theme park features more than a hundred wet and dry rides; live stage shows, from Wild West shootouts to fairy-tale theater; puppet shows; a petting zoo; and miniature golf.

### Herschell Carrousel Factory Museum (all ages)

180 Thompson St., North Tonawanda; (716) 693-1885; www.carouselmuseum.org. Open Apr to mid-June, Wed through Sun noon to 4 p.m.; mid-June through Labor Day, Mon through Sat 10 a.m. to 4 p.m., Sun noon to 4 p.m.; and after Labor Day through Dec, Wed through Sun noon to 4 p.m. Closed Thanksgiving and Christmas Day. $.

This is the only museum on earth housed in a real carousel factory, and it's filled with a menagerie of magical merry-go-round creatures. Two working whirling rides are offered, one astride steeds crafted in 1916 and one created for children under 43 inches tall. Outside is a short rail trail, and seasonal events range from carousel chats and crafts to holiday themed festivals.

### Adventure Landing (all ages)

2400 Sheridan Dr., Tonawanda; (716) 832-6248 or (716) 692-3122; www.adventurelanding .com. Open year-round Mon through Thurs 3 to 8 p.m., Fri 3 to 11 p.m., Sat 9 a.m. to 11 p.m., Sun noon to 8 p.m. Individual rides $.

Guide your go-kart around a 0.25-mile track of twists and turns, bump your boat and splash your siblings in the new bumper boat pond, or try your luck at the more than forty interactive ticket redemption games in the arcade.

## Where to Eat

**The Beach House.** 5584 E. River Rd.; (716) 773-7119. Kid-friendly, serving homemade soups, great fish and chips, grilled chicken sandwiches, and milk shakes, with indoor and outdoor dining. $

**Mississippi Mudds.** 313 Niagara St., Tonawanda; (716) 694-0787. Burgers, chicken, sandwiches, and homemade waffle cones filled with ice cream, served on a double deck overlooking the Niagara River. $

## Where to Stay

**Holiday Inn Grand Island.** 100 Whitehaven Rd.; (716) 773-1111; www.holidayinn .com. Two hundred and sixty-three rooms and suites, indoor and outdoor pools, kiddie pools, spa, recreation and sports court, game room, Internet, dry cleaning and laundry service, restaurant, room service, and kids under twelve eat free with adult. $$$–$$$$

**Porches of Pendleton.** 5176 Tonawanda Creek Rd., North Tonawanda; (716) 308) 3961; www.porchesofpendleton.com. Charming B&B overlooking the Erie Canal, with Wi-Fi, library, a dock, kayaks, and chocolate-chip pancakes for breakfast. $–$$$

# Niagara Falls

Take I-190 to the Robert Moses Parkway north.

More than ten million people a year come from all over the world to see one of the great-est natural wonders on Earth. Niagara Falls is spectacular. The sheer size of the falls is breathtaking, with more than 0.5 mile of cascades draining four Great Lakes into Lake Erie. As tourist Mark Twain once said, "Niagara Falls is one of the finest structures in the known world."

### Niagara Falls State Park (all ages)
**333 Prospect St., off exit 21 of Robert Moses Parkway; (716) 278-1796; Maid of the Mist (716) 284-8897; Niagara Gorge Discovery Center (716) 278-1070; Cave of the Winds (716) 278-1730; www.niagarafallsstatepark.com and www.nysparks.state.ny.us. Free, but indi-vidual attractions are extra. Ask about the Niagara USA Discovery Pass for one-price pack-age discounts within the park. $–$$$$.**

This is the first and oldest of New York's state parks and the oldest state park in the country. Begin your exploration at the Visitor Center at Prospect Point, where interesting exhibits, displays, and a short film offer a good introduction to this awesome area. It's also a great spot to view the 1,000-foot drop of the American Falls. Outside, vintage trol-leys travel thirty-minute 3-mile loops through the park, stopping at six sites, with hop-on, hop-off options.

Head to the nearby Observation Tower for a ride up the glass-enclosed elevator to the 200-foot platform overlooking the gorge. then descend to the base of the falls and board the famous *Maid of the Mist* boat ride, a legendary tourist attraction since 1846. Another perspective is offered on the Cave of the Winds tour, where families take a 175-foot eleva-tor ride into the Niagara Gorge, then follow a wooden walkway to stand within 20 feet of thundering Bridal Falls. Despite the souvenir ponchos, you will get very wet.

For a drier experience, stop by the Niagara Gorge Discovery Center, where interactive displays, virtual tours, a multiscreen theater, and a fossil-filled rock climbing wall explore the 12,000-year history and geology of the Niagara River. Four short guided trail hikes originate from the Discovery Center, and the nearby Robert Moses Parkway Trail offers year-round hiking and biking opportunities.

## Niagara Falls
# Fun Facts

The edge of the falls was originally 7 miles downstream, but erosion continues to cut away the cliff at a rate of about an inch a year, forming the Niagara Gorge.

When darkness falls, Niagara Falls is illuminated with misty candy-colored lights, and fireworks fill the summer skies. Corny, perhaps, but way cool.

### Daredevil Museum  (all ages)

303 Rainbow Blvd.; (716) 282-4046; www.niagarafallslive.com. Open daily in summer 9 a.m. to 10 p.m. Free.

Immortalizing the late and great challengers of Niagara Falls, this museum has a collection of steel-banded, giant rubber balls, barrels, and other containers used by daring adventurers to plunge headlong over the precipice.

### Aquarium of Niagara  (all ages)

701 Whirlpool St.; (716) 285-3575 or (800) 500-4609; www.aquariumofniagara.org. Open daily year-round 9 a.m. to 5 p.m. Adults $$, children 4 to 12 $, 3 and under free.

Discover denizens of the deep at this terrific aquarium. More than 1,500 aquatic animals live here, from sea lions and sharks to piranhas and Peruvian penguins. Five-dollar cups of fish are available to feed the seals in the large outdoor pool, and with advance reservations longer encounters with penguins and sea lions can be scheduled through the Aqua-Venture program.

### Whirlpool State Park  (all ages)

Niagara Rapids Boulevard, off Robert Moses Parkway, Niagara Falls, 2 miles north of the falls; (716) 284-4691; www.nysparks.state.ny.us. Open year-round dawn to dusk. Free.

This double-decker park, with scenic overlooks of rushing rapids and a swirling whirlpool, has a playground and picnic areas on the upper level, and nature trails skirting the river's edge 300 feet below.

# More Niagara Area **State Parks**

For more information call the parks directly or visit the state park Web site, www.nysparks.state.ny.us.

**Four Mile Creek State Park.** 1055 Lake Rd., Youngstown; (716) 745-3802.

**Golden Hill State Park.** 9691 Lower Lake Rd., Barker; (716) 795-3885 or (716) 795-3117.

**Gallagher Beach State Park.** Fuhrmann Boulevard, Buffalo; (716) 852-2356.

# Niagara Falls
# Fun Facts

Sam Patch was the first daredevil to jump over the falls, in 1829. The first woman to take the plunge was Mrs. Annie Edson Taylor, a 63-year-old schoolteacher, in 1901.

### Devil's Hole State Park (all ages)

Robert Moses Parkway, Niagara Falls, 4 miles north of the falls; (716) 284-5778; www.nys parks.state.ny.us. Open year-round dawn to dusk. **Free.**

Overlooking the raging river, this two-tiered park has picnic places, plus a boardwalk running along the banks of the gorgeous gorge. At the bottom is a large cave, once believed by the local folk to be the home of an evil spirit, and above the cave was the scene of a massacre of a British supply convoy ambushed by the Seneca Indians in 1763.

### Niagara Power Project Power Vista (all ages)

5777 Lewiston Rd., Lewiston; (716) 286-6661 or (866) 697-2386; www.nypa.gov. Reservoir State Park. NY 31, Niagara; (716) 284-4691. Open daily year-round 9 a.m. to 5 p.m. Closed major holidays. **Free.**

The history of hydroelectricity and other sources of energy is explored through more than fifty excellent hands-on displays, exhibits, and interactive computer games. A new Electric Lab displays a working hydropower turbine, the large terrain map has been updated with fiber optics, and families can send an electronic postcard via e-mail, with a variety of virtual views. Take a moment to admire the recently restored 20-foot mural by Thomas Hart Benton, then step outside onto the Observation Deck for a breathtaking panorama of the gorge.

### Old Fort Niagara (all ages)

Fort Niagara State Park, Robert Moses Parkway, Youngstown; (716) 745-7611; www.old fortniagara.org. Open daily year-round 9 a.m. to 5 p.m., and until 7 p.m. July and Aug. Closed Thanksgiving, Christmas, and New Year's Day. Fort Niagara State Park (716) 745-7273; www.nysparks.state.ny.us. Adults $$, children $, under 6 **free.**

Built by the French in 1726 and later occupied by British and American forces, this strategically important stone fortress controlled access to the Great Lakes for nearly three centuries. That turbulent history is brought to life with costumed interpreters, military reenactments, fife and drum drills, and other special events throughout the year. Surrounding the fort is the state park, offering recreation programs, easy hiking trails, fishing, swimming pools, playgrounds, 500 picnic tables, and eighteen soccer fields, with cross-country skiing, snowshoeing, and sledding opportunities in winter.

## Niagara Falls
# Fun Facts

The average flow of water over the Bridal Veil and American Falls is about 75,000 gallons per second.

The Niagara River flows north and is 36 miles long.

The falls were formed 12,000 years ago by melting glaciers.

The Niagara River isn't really a river. Because it connects Lake Ontario and Lake Erie, technically it is a strait.

## Castellani Art Museum  (all ages)

Niagara University campus, NY 104, Lewiston; (716) 286-8200; www.purple.niagara.edu. Open year-round Tues through Sat 11 a.m. to 5 p.m., Sun 1 to 5 p.m. Closed Mon and most university holidays; **Free.**

Contemporary and folk art are the focus of this wonderfully eclectic museum, with more than 3,700 objects and art created by Warhol, Rauschenberg, Dali, Picasso, Matisse, Modigliani, and Grandma Moses.

## Artpark  (all ages)

450 S. 4th St., Lewiston; (716) 754-9000, (716) 754-4375, or (800) 659-7275; www.artpark .net. Open daily 8 a.m. to dusk. Some events **free,** some $–$$, and parking $$.

The only state park in the country dedicated to the visual and performing arts, this 200-acre muse menage has been hosting world-class Broadway and children's theater, dance, and concert events for thirty-five years. Also on the grounds is an ancient Hopewell Indian burial mound, as well as hiking and nature trails and a picnic area. Special seasonal events for children include Family Saturdays, a series of weekly workshops in painting, crafts, and sculpture, and a Tot Spot activity center. Artpark also offers Family Movie Nights, with outdoor screenings of PG classics under the stars.

## Niagara Falls
# Fun Facts

Seven-year-old Roger Woodward survived an accidental fall in 1960 when his boat overturned upriver. He was picked up by a *Maid of the Mist* tour boat at the base of the Falls.

Most fish survive the drop over the falls.

The river rapids speed by at 30 mph.

### Whirlpool Jet Boat Tours (ages 6 and up)

115 S. Water St., Lewiston; (905) 468-4800 or (888) 438-4444; www.whirlpooljet.com. Operating daily mid-June through Labor Day, then on limited days and weekends only, Apr through Sept; times depend on trip type. $$$$+.

Ride the world's most famous rapids aboard jet boats roaring down the river at 65 miles per hour—wow! You will get very, very wet, so bring a change of clothes and your sense of humor.

## Where to Eat

**Michael's Restaurant.** 3011 Pine Ave.; (716 282-4043; www.michaelsniagarafalls .com. Italian and American specialties, homemade soups, sauces, pasta, pizza, chicken wings and fingers, and crispy fried dough sprinkled with sugar. $

**Top of the Falls Restaurant.** Terrapin Point, Goat Island; (716) 278-0340; www.top ofthefallsrestaurant.com. Classic American cuisine, with indoor and outdoor seating overlooking Horseshoe Falls and live music in summer. $–$$

## Where to Stay

**Hampton Inn Niagara Falls.** 501 Rainbow Blvd.; (716) 285-6666; www.hamptoninn.com. Ninety-nine rooms and suites, free premium cable, microwave, refrigerator, free Internet, whirlpool bath, and free hot breakfast or breakfast bags to go. $$–$$$

**The Red Coach Inn.** 2 Buffalo Ave.; (716) 282-1459 and (866) 719-2070; www.redcoach .com. Overlooking the upper rapids, this charming boutique hotel offers rooms and suites with Wi-Fi, premium cable, Jacuzzi tubs, some suites with microwave and refrigerator, and a terrific restaurant on-site. $$–$$$$

# Lockport

Take NY 31 east.

Located along the Erie Canal, Lockport is the home of the fire hydrant and the birthplace of volleyball.

### Niagara County Historical Society (ages 6 and up)

215 Niagara St.; (716) 434-7433; www.niagara-county.org. Open Sept through June, Wed through Sat 1 to 5 p.m.; July and Aug, Mon through Sat 10 a.m. to 5 p.m., Sun 1 to 5 p.m. $.

An incredible eclectic collection of Native American and nineteenth-century pioneer artifacts is housed in this complex of several historical buildings, from farm tools to antique toys, and reenactors guide guests in summer through city and cemetery walks. A new addition to the complex is the Erie Canal Discovery Center at the Hamilton House, where computer kiosks allow kids to "meet" some of the "canawlers," the folks who worked on the Canal. Take the Lockport Trolley in summer, for a narrated tour of the town by costumed interpreters, with hop-on, hop-off options at nine stops.

### Lockport Lock and Canal Tours (all ages)

210 Market St.; (716) 433-6155 or (800) 378-0352; www.lockportlocks.com. Open daily May through mid-Oct. Call for cruise schedule. Adults $$$, children $$, under 4 free.

Take a two-hour narrated cruise of the Erie Canal, where you'll see Lockport's famous "flight of five" original 1825 locks. Dockside is a casual pub serving homemade desserts, and a gift shop with collectible canal curios.

### Lockport Cave and Underground Boat Ride (all ages)

2 Pine St., Lockport; (716) 438-0174; www.lockportcave.com. Open May, Sat and Sun only, noon to 4 p.m.; late May through late June, daily noon to 4 p.m.; and open until 5 p.m. through mid-Oct. Adults $$, children $, under 4 free.

Cruise the historic caves of Lockport, actually a large water-power tunnel that was blasted out of solid rock during the mid-nineteenth century. This is the longest underwater boat ride in the country, and special seasonal events include a spooky Haunted Cave ride in Oct and puzzling Mystery Tours, helmed by time-traveler captains.

### Amherst Museum (all ages)

3755 Tonawanda Creek Rd., Amherst; (716) 689-1440; www.amherstmuseum.org. Open year-round, Apr through mid-Oct, Tues through Fri 9:30 a.m. to 4:30 p.m.; mid-Oct through Mar, Tues through Fri 9:30 a.m. to 4:30 p.m., and Sat and Sun 2:30 to 4:30 p.m. $.

More than a dozen nineteenth-century buildings are scattered around this thirty-five-acre historic park, with authentically outfitted artists demonstrating colonial crafts common on the Niagara frontier. Over 50,000 artifacts, from furniture to photographs, have been collected and protected, and they are displayed on a rotating basis. Special events throughout the year range from Victorian tea parties to Halloween trick-or-treating.

## Where to Eat

**Becker Farms.** 3760 Quaker Rd., Gasport; (716) 772-2211 or (716) 221-7815.; www .beckerfarms.com. Fresh fruits and vegetables, bakery, and ice cream, plus a petting zoo and special family events. Picking tour by reservation. $

**One-Eyed Jack's BBQ Restaurant.** 5983 S. Transit Rd.; (716) 438-5414; www .oneeyedjacksbbq.com. Great barbecue, chili, Brunswick stew, brisket, burgers, catfish, and a little joker's menu. $–$

## Where to Stay

**Holiday Inn Lockport.** 515 S. Transit Rd. (NY 78); (716) 434-6151 or (800) 528-1234. Ninety-five rooms and suites, Internet,

## New York **Trivia**

New York became the eleventh state in the Union on July 26, 1788, and New York City became the first capital of the United States.

restaurant, room service, indoor pool, coin laundry, fitness center, and kids eat free. $–$$.

**Lockport Inn & Suites.** 315 S. Transit Rd.; (716) 434-5595; www.lockportinnandsuites .com. Ninety rooms and suites, some with Jacuzzis and fireplaces, plus microwave, refrigerator, outdoor pool, Wi-Fi, free movies, and valet dry cleaning. $–$$

# Medina

Head east on NY 31, then veer left onto NY 31A.

The fine red sandstone deposits of Medina were prized by architects all over the world, including the builders of Buckingham Palace.

## The Erie Canal Culvert  (all ages)

3699 Culvert Rd., Medina; (585) 798-4287, (585) 589-3230, or (800) 724-0314. Open daily year-round. **Free.**

Worthy of Ripley's Believe It or Not!, this 7-foot tunnel, built in 1823, is the only place where motorists can drive under the Erie Canal.

## Medina Railroad Museum  (all ages)

530 West Ave.; (585) 798-6106; www.railroadmuseum.net. Open daily year-round Tues through Sun 11 a.m. to 5 p.m. $$$, under 2 **free.**

Housed in one of the last surviving freight depots in the country, this is the largest collection of railroad relics and memorabilia anywhere, plus the longest HO scale layout ever built. Two-hour train trips aboard vintage coaches depart the depot for a scenic themed excursions, from foliage and winery tours to a Santa Express.

## Iroquois National Wildlife Refuge  (all ages)

1101 Casey Rd., Basom; (585) 948-5445; www.fws.gov/northeast/iroquois. Open year-round dawn to dusk. $.

This is New York's largest wildlife refuge, encompassing 10,828 acres of wetlands that are home to 268 species of birds, 42 species of mammals, numerous reptiles, amphibians, insects, and unique plants. Three nature trails and four overlooks offer viewing opportunities, and special events include owl prowls, canoe trips, scope watches, and fishing derbies.

## Also in **the Area**

**Cobblestone Society Museum.** NY 98 and NY 104 (Ridge Road West), Childs; (585) 589-9013; www.ahrproductions.com.

**Lakeside Beach State Park.** NY 18, Waterport; (585) 682-4888; www.nysparks .state.ny.us.

**Ridge Road Station.** 16131 Ridge Rd. West, Holley; (585) 638-6000; www .rrstation.com.

**Brown's Berry Patch.** 14264 Roosevelt Hwy., Waterport; (585) 682-5569; www .brownsberrypatch.com.

## Where to Eat

**Zambistro.** 408 Main St., Medina; (585) 798-CHEF; www.zambistro.com. Gourmet American, with great sandwiches, wraps, burgers, steaks, crab cakes, salmon, tuna, homemade meat loaf, terrific mac 'n' cheese, and a fun kids' menu. $–$$

**Rudy's.** 118 W. Center St., Medina; (585) 798-5166. Burgers, fries, hot dogs, and ice-cream sundaes. $

## Where to Stay

**Medina Stone Farm.** 255 North Gravel Rd.; (585) 798-9238; www.medinastonefarm.com. Rural B&B on ninety acres, with hearty breakfasts, free Wi-Fi, barn dances, a corn maze, live entertainment, and a towpath to walk along the Erie Canal. $–$$

**Tillman's Historic Village Inn.** 14369 Ridge Rd., Ibion; (585) 589-9151; www.tillmansvillage inn.com. Eight rooms with private baths, Wi-Fi, telephone, TV, restaurant, and special lunch and dinner packages available. $–$$

# Batavia

Take NY 31A east to NY 98 south.

Built at the crossroad of two Iroquois trails, Batavia is an area of fertile farms, lush orchards, and prosperous dairies.

### Holland Land Office and Museum  (ages 4 and up)
**131 W. Main St.; (585) 343-4727; www.hollandlandoffice.com. Open Tues through Sat 10 a.m. to 4 p.m., also open Mon in summer and Sun from Thanksgiving to New Year's. Closed holidays and Sat in Jan and Feb. Free.**

Exhibits housed in the 1815 stone office include Native American and pioneer artifacts, mastodon bones, Civil War memorabilia, and a gallows.

## Genesee County Park and Forest Interpretive Center

(all ages)

11095 Bethany Center Rd., East Bethany; (585) 344-1122; www.co.genesee.ny.us. Open year-round dawn to dusk. Interpretive Center open Mon through Fri by appointment, Sat through Sun noon to 4 p.m. **Free.**

The first and oldest county forest in the state, this 430-acre popular park contains five small ponds and the headwaters of Black Creek. The interpretive center has interesting exhibits and maps of the trails winding through the woods, and there are picnic places, ball fields, and a playground.

## LeRoy House Museum and Jell-O Gallery (ages 3 and up)

23 E. Main St., LeRoy; (585) 768-7433; www.jellomuseum.com. Open May through Oct, Mon through Sat 10 a.m. to 4 p.m., Sun 1 to 4 p.m., and weekdays in winter. Closed major holidays. $, 5 and under **free.**

Jell-O jiggled into life in this town, and its history is documented in a gallery with cookbooks, molds, and ad campaigns. Another interesting exhibit inside the mansion focuses on Ingham University, the first women's college in America, and a new addition is a twentieth-century transportation exhibit, with historic vintage automobiles.

## Bergen Swamp (all ages)

6646 Hessenthaler Rd., Byron; (585) 548-7304; www.bergenswamp.org. Donation.

This unusual 1,900-acre marl bog has remained unchanged for more than 125,000 years and is home to a wide variety of rare and endangered plants and animals. In 1964 it was

# Genesee County **Family Fun**

**The Gravel Pit Family Entertainment Center.** 5158 E. Main Rd. (NY 5), Batavia; (585) 343-4445; www.geneseeny.com.

**Batavia Muckdogs Baseball. Dwyer Stadium.** 299 Bank St., Batavia; (585) 343-5454; www.muckdogs.com.

**Conquest Golf.** 10188 Alleghany Road, Darien Center Road, Darien; (585) 547-9894.

**Darien Lake Theme Park.** 9993 Allegheny Rd., Darien Center; (585) 599-4641; www.godarienlake.com.

**Polar Wave Snowtubing.** 3500 Harloff Rd., Batavia; (585) 345-1630 or (888) 727-2794; www.polarwavebatavia.com.

**Darien Lakes State Park.** 10289 Harlow Rd., Darien Center; (585) 547-9242; www.nysparks.state.ny.us.

designated as the first National Natural Landmark in the country, and more than 2,500 species of wetland plants grow here, along with the endangered (and poisonous) Massasauga rattlesnake.

### Holiday Hollow  (all ages)

**1410 Main Rd., Corfu; (585) 762-8160; www.holidayhollow.com. Open Oct weekends and Columbus Day, 11 a.m. to 5 p.m. Adults $$, children $, under 2 free.**

Every Oct weekend this place is haunted by talking pumpkins, Captain Hook and Mr. Smee, Dr. Jekyll and Mr. Hyde, and a band of fortune-telling gypsies, silly spooks and goofy ghosts. There's also a Wacky Witch Magical Cooking Show, a fractured fairy tale presentation, a new pirate adventure, a haunted parlor, games of skill, and lots of pumpkins looking for a good home. After providing this Halloween hangout for twenty years, the Walker Family has added "Christmas Enchantment" for 2010, with a holiday show, a festive village to visit, and a chance to meet Santa and his frosty friends.

## Where to Eat

**Center Street Smokehouse.** 20 Center St.; (585) 343-7470; www.centerstreetsmokehouse.com. Authentic southern barbecue, with sides of hush puppies and baked beans, plus live music most nights. $–$$

**D&R Depot.** 63 Lake St., LeRoy; (585) 768-6270; www.dandrdepot.com. Home-cooked Italian specials served in an old depot with an upside-down model train running around. $$–$$$

## Where to Stay

**Edson House.** 7863 Griswold Circle, LeRoy; (585) 768-8579 or (800) 337-8579; www.edsonhousebb.com. Rural B&B featuring four spacious rooms with private baths, cable, phone, refrigerator, and complimentary continental breakfast; children welcome. $–$$

**Lei-Ti Campground.** 9979 Francis Rd.; (585) 343-8600 or (800) 445-3484; www.leiti.com. Located on a five-acre lake, this campground has campsites, cabins, and RV rentals, with fishing, a recreation lodge, arcade, petting zoo, mini-golf, hiking and nature trails, tennis courts, a basketball court, ball fields, playgrounds, a swimming pool, fitness room, small boat rentals, camp store, snack bar, hayrides, Wi-Fi zones, a coin laundry, and special activities for families, from arts and crafts and fireworks to tricycle races and pancake breakfasts. $

# Arcade

Take NY 98 south.

Amid rolling pastures dotted with dairy cows lies Arcade, once a very busy cheese and produce shipping center. For a peek at a pastoral paradise, take a drive along nearby NY 39 and NY 78.

## Also in **the Area**

**New York and Lake Erie Railroad.** 50 Commercial St., Gowanda; (716) 532-5242; www.nylerr.com.

**Schoolhouse No. 8 History Center & Museum.** Library Campus, 2101 School St., North Collins; www.schoolhouse8.info.

### Arcade and Attica Railroad  (all ages)

278 Main St.; (585) 492-3100; www.arcadeandatticarr.com. Open Memorial Day weekend through Dec, Sat, Sun, and some Fridays in Oct; no scheduled departures in Nov; call for hours. $$, under 2 free.

Ride the rails for a two-hour trip back in time aboard the only steam excursion train in New York. Trips are also offered on trains powered by two restored diesel-electric locomotives. Operating between Arcade and Attica, the train's twenty-minute layover at the Curriers Depot allows time to tour the station's mini-museum and model railroad display, and get a quick snack. Seasonal specialty trips include children's trains with costumed characters, Civil War reenactment excursions, murder mystery dinners, Halloween and fall foliage runs, and a North Pole Express.

### Beaver Meadow Audubon Center  (all ages)

1610 Welch Rd., North Java; (585) 457-3228; www.buffaloaudubon.com. Grounds open 24/7 year-round; visitor center open Tues through Sat 10 a.m. to 5 p.m., Sun 1 to 5 p.m. Observatory open Apr through Oct, first and third Sat, dusk to 10 p.m. Closed holidays. $.

This 384-acre sanctuary is laced with 8 miles of trails that wind past beaver ponds, marshes, meadows, and forests. Inside the visitor center are animal and nature art exhibits, a library, and a Children's Discovery Room. Special events include Family Sunday Walks, Full Moon Walks, and a variety of harvest and holiday festivals.

## Where to Eat

**Arcade Center Farm.** 7298 NY 98; (585) 492-3821. All-you-can-eat pancakes from Feb through Apr, with homemade maple syrup you can watch being made, plus a locavore's delight with seasonal summer bounty at the farm market, and apples and cider in autumn.

**Nellie's Restaurant.** 572 Main St.; (585) 492-5531. Fast and friendly, serving breakfast, lunch, and dinner, with homemade sausage, soups, and pies made fresh daily. $

## Where to Stay

**Nellie's Arcade Village Motel.** 574 Main St.; (585) 492-3600. Small, clean motel. $–$$

**Yogi Bear's Jellystone Park.** 5204 Youngers Rd., North Java; (585) 457-9644 or (800) 232-4039; www.wnyjellystone.com. Campsites, cabins, and chalets, Wi-Fi, new laundry room, miniature golf, playgrounds, two heated swimming pools, a stocked fishing pond and store, paddleboats, hayrides, face painting, scavenger hunt, sand and spin art, ceramics center, movies, golf cart rentals, a game room, a mini-market and snack bar, candy bingo, and the new Yogi Bear's Water

Zone, a 16,000-square-foot, multilevel, interactive water playground. $–$$$$

# Olean

Take NY 98 south to NY 16 south.

Inspired by the "black gold" bonanzas of the area, Olean's name is derived from the Latin word for oil: *oleum*.

### Rock City Park (all ages)
**505A Rock City Rd., NY 16 south; (585) 372-7790; www.rockcitypark.com. Open daily May to Oct, 9 a.m. to 6 p.m. $, five and under free.**

Once a natural stone fortress for the Seneca, this is the world's largest exposure of quartz conglomerate, also called puddingstone. More than 300 million years ago, these massive monoliths were the bottom of a prehistoric ocean, but today the giant rocks rest atop the Enchanted Mountains. Trails wind through narrow "streets" and up to panoramic overlooks. A new expanded museum offers a fluorescent mineral room and a video tour for folks preferring not to scramble among the stones.

### Bartlett Historical House and Olean Point Museum (ages 4 and up)
**302 Laurens St.; (716) 376-5642. Open Wed through Sat 1 to 5 p.m., extended hours at Christmas season. $.**

This grand nine-room Victorian mansion is lovely to look at any time of year, but it's especially magical during the festive Christmas season. The Carriage House on the property has been converted into a local history museum, with artifacts and children's discovery area.

### Allegheny River Valley Trail (all ages)
**Access at Gargoyle Park or Henley and Nineteenth Streets, or at the west entrance of Saint Bonaventure University; (716) 372-4433; www.oleanny.com. Open year-round, dawn to dusk. Free.**

This 5.6-mile multiuse recreational loop trail was envisioned and realized by local businessman Joseph Higgins in 1992. Paralleling the Allegheny River, it provides easy paths for hiking, biking, running, and in-line skating.

### Pfeiffer Nature Center (all ages)
**1974 Lillibridge Rd., Portville, and 1420 Yubadam Rd., Portville; (716) 373-1742 or (716) 933-6063; www.pfeiffernaturecenter.org. Open year-round. Free.**

## Also in **the Area**

**Oleans Squirrels.** Various locations throughout the city; (716) 372-5979; www
.woodlandinthecity.org.

**Cutco/Ka Bar Visitors Center.** 1040 E. State St., Olean; (716) 700 7000; www
.cutco.com/company/visitorsCenter.jsp.

Nine miles of trails trace through 188-acres of an old-growth forest at this peaceful preserve, and a recent donation of 430 additional acres nearby of fields, woodlands, and
wetlands have created a birder's paradise. Guided nature walks are offered at both locations, as well as owl prowls, wild herb and food foraging, and Sala-Meanders, a scientific
search for slithery species.

## Where to Eat

**Old Library Restaurant.** 116 S. Union St.;
(877) 241-4348; www.oldlibraryrestaurant
.com. Continental cuisine and a children's
menu, served in Andrew Carnegie's former library, a National Historic Landmark.
$$–$$$$

## Where to Stay

**Microtel Inn & Suites.** 3234 NY 417; (716)
373-5333; www.microtelinn. Rooms and
suites, free phone, free Wi-Fi, free continental
breakfast, twenty-four-hour guest laundry
room and fitness center, free crib use, micro-
wave and refrigerator in some rooms, whirl-
pool, and in-room delivery available. $

# Salamanca

Go west on NY 17.

**Allegany State Park** (all ages)

**2373 ASP Route 1, off NY 17; (716) 354-9121; www.nysparks.state.ny.us. Park open year-
round, campgrounds open mid-May through Labor Day. $. Call ahead to confirm changes
to hours, activities available, and possible closures due to pending state budget cuts.**

Covering 65,000 acres of wooded wilderness, this is New York's largest state park. With
424 campsites, 375 cabins, and 8 fully equipped cottages, a family can settle in and spend
some time enjoying the variety of activities available. Hike or bike more than 90 miles of
trails, fish and swim in two blue lakes with sandy beaches, and challenge your family to a
round of miniature golf. The park is divided into two sections, the Red House and Quaker
Run Areas, and both have lifeguards, ball fields, playgrounds, and picnic places. The boat-
house rents watercraft and bicycles, there's a small nature museum, and naturalist-led
walks and seasonal festivals are offered throughout the year.

## Suggested **Reading**

*Mirette and Bellini Cross Niagara Falls*, by Emily Arnold McCully

*Manny's Cows: The Niagara Falls Tale*, by Suzy Becker

*Seneca Chief, Army General: A Story About Ely Parker*, by Elizabeth Van Steenwyk and Karen Ritz

*The Erie Canal*, by Peter Spier

*Amazing Impossible Erie Canal*, by Cheryl Harness

*The Niagara Falls Mystery*, by Gertrude Chandler Warner

*The Rough-face Girl*, by Rafe Martin

*Maggie Among the Seneca*, by Robin Moore

*Brother Wolf: A Seneca Tale*, by Harriet P. Taylor

*Journey to Nowhere*, by Mary Jane Auch

## Seneca-Iroquois National Museum (ages 4 and up)

814 Broad St.; (716) 945-1760; www.senecamuseum.org. Open year-round Thurs through Mon 9 a.m. to 5 p.m. $, under 7 free.

The history and heritage of the Seneca Nation, known as the "Keeper of the Western Door," is highlighted at this interesting museum. There are exhibits of Native American traditions, medicine, art, artifacts, and culture, and there's even a life-size bark longhouse to explore.

## Salamanca Rail Museum (ages 3 and up)

170 Main St.; (716) 945-3133; http://mysite.verizon.net/bizxyrad/salamancarailmuseumasso ciation. Open Mon through Sat 10 a.m. to 5 p.m., Sun noon to 5 p.m. Closed Mon in Apr, Oct, Nov, and Dec, and all of Jan, Feb, and Mar. Free, donations accepted.

Flash back almost a century to a time when Salamanca was a major railroad center. This fully restored 1912 passenger depot houses exhibits of artifacts and photographs, with a video recalling the golden age of rail travel.

## Holiday Valley Resort (all ages)

US 219 and Holiday Valley Road, Ellicottville; (716) 699-2345 or (800) 367-9691; www.holiday valley.com. Open daily year-round. $$$–$$$$, children 5 and under ski free. Check Web site for additional packages for families and special passports for fourth-graders.

This is the largest public ski area in the state, with fifty-six slopes and trails, thirteen lifts, four terrain parks plus a half pipe, several glades great for cross-country skiing, and

Mountain Adventures, a terrific children's ski and snowboard program, with day care available. Free shuttles are provided to the nearby tubing park, with a special Little Tubers area. Inside the Clubhouse Chalet is the McCarty Cafe, serving pastries and sandwiches, while the Founders Restaurant offers heartier fare. The Yodeler Lodge is the original lodge of Holiday Valley and home to the Marketplace Cafe and two lounges, and the new Tannenbaum Lodge houses the family-friendly Seven Headwalls Cafe, plus a snack bar, with **free** Wi-Fi available throughout the resort.

### Nannen Arboretum  (all ages)

**28 Parkside Drive, Ellicottville; (716) 699-2377 or (800) 897-9189; www.nannenarboretum .org. Open daily year-round dawn to dusk. Donation**

More than 200 species of rare and unusual trees flourish in this eight-acre botanical garden. Perennial, herb, and Japanese stone gardens grace the grounds, there's a picturesque lake, and special programs are offered at the outdoor Northrup Nature Hall and the Chapman Nature Sanctuary.

### Griffis Sculpture Park  (all ages)

**6902 Mill Valley Rd., East Otto; (716) 667-2808; www.griffispark.org. Open May through Oct, dawn to dusk. $, children under 12 free.**

Similar to a surreal dreamscape, more than 250 magical metal and stone sculptures dot the fields and woods of this 400-acre park, the first and largest of its kind in the country.

## Where to Eat

**Myers Steak House & Inn.** 460 Wildwood Ave.; (716) 945-3153; www.myerssteakhouse andinn.com. Serving meals for over a century, now specializing in steaks, seafood, and tavern favorites from pizza to burgers, plus homemade desserts. $–$$$

**Red Garter Restaurant.** Parkway Drive, off exit 21 of I-86; (716) 945-2503; www.redgarter restaurant.com. Atop Round Top Mountain and once the site of a frontier theme park, this western-style panoramic place serves steak, ribs, wings, and pasta, and offers a kids' menu.

## Other Ski Spots **in Western New York**

**Kissing Bridge.** 10296 NY 240, Glenwood; (716) 592-4963; www.kbski.com.

**Cockaigne.** 1493 Thornton Rd., Cherry Creek; (716) 287-3223; www.cockaigne .com.

**Peek'n Peak.** 1405 Old Rd., Clymer; (716) 355-4141; www.pknpk.com.

**Buffalo Ski Club.** 7414 NY 240, Colden; (716) 941-5654; www.bscskiarea.com.

**Holimont.** 6921 NY 242, Ellicottville; (716) 699-2320; www.holimont.com.

# Also in **the Area**

**Gentle Thunder Farm.** 7067 Hencoop Rd., Ellicottville; (716) 699-2940; www .gentlethunderfarm.com.

**R & R Dude Ranch.** 8940 Lange Rd., Otto; (716) 257-5663; www.rrduderanch .com.

**The Crosspatch Horse Ranch.** 5281 Baker Rd., Salamanca; (716) 938-6313; www.thecrosspatch.com.

**James A. Zaepfel Nature Sanctuary & Research Center.** Allegany Road, Napoli; (716) 257-3237; www.zaepfel.org.

**Bradley Alpaca Ranch.** 4898 NY 219, Great Valley; (716) 945-5880.

**Mager Mountain Alpacas.** 69 Mountain View Dr., Little Valley; (716) 938-9077; www.magermountainalpacas.com.

**Gooseneck Hill Waterfowl Sanctuary.** 5067 Townline Rd., Delevan; (716) 942-6835.

**Lana's Little House.** (716) 965-2798; www.lanasthelittlehouse.com.

**Mystic Water Resort.** 620 Parkside Dr., Limestone; (716) 925-8553; www .mysticwaterresort.com.

**Delevan Drive-In Theater.** NY 16, Delevan; (716) 496-5660.

## Where to Stay

**Holiday Inn Express Hotel.** 779 Broad St.; (716) 945-7600; www.hiexpress.com. Sixty-eight rooms and suites, indoor pool, whirlpool, fitness center, guest laundry room, free WIFI, and complimentary breakfast bar. $$–$$$

**The Inn at Holiday Valley.** Holiday Valley Road and US 219, about 2 miles south of Ellicottville; (716) 699-2345 or (800) 323-0020; www.holidayvalley.com. This all-season resort has a variety of lodging options, with ninety-five rooms and seven suites at the inn, some with refrigerators and fireplaces, an indoor/outdoor heated pool, sauna, continental breakfast, and golf packages for the newly redesigned eighteen-hole golf course. Children under seventeen stay free with adult. Town houses and homes in the area are also available to rent, and a recent addition is the Tamarack Club, a new condo project with a heated indoor/outdoor pool, two hot tubs, a fitness center, and the John Harvard's Brew House restaurant. $$$$

# Jamestown

Continue west on NY 17.

### The Lucille Ball-Desi Arnaz Center (ages 6 and up)

300 North Main St.; (716) 484-0800; www.lucy-desi.com. Open Mon, Tues, Wed, and Sat 10 a.m. to 4 p.m., Thurs and Fri 10 a.m. to 5:30 p.m., Sun 1 to 5 p.m. Adults $$, children $, under 6 free.

Celebrating the legacy of the First Couple of Comedy, this charming museum displays Lucy's and Desi's costumes, awards, photographs, and memorabilia, as well as audio clips of their radio shows, songs, and friends' reminiscences. Inside the Desilu Playhouse is a complete re-creation of the Ricardo's New York apartment, an interactive Vitameatave-gamin set ("Do you pop out at parties? Don't be tired and listless or unpoopular!"), and a screening room showing continuous episodes of *I Love Lucy*.

### Roger Tory Peterson Institute of Natural History (all ages)

311 Curtis St.; (716) 665-2473 or (800) 758-6841; www.rtpi.org. Open Tues through Sat year-round 10 a.m. to 4 p.m., Sun 1 to 5 p.m. Closed holidays. Grounds open daily dawn to dusk. $.

Another Jamestown native is the famous ornithologist, artist, and author Roger Tory Peterson. The center has a gallery of wildlife art, nature photography and exhibits, a but-terfly garden, and self-guided nature trails winding through twenty-seven wooded acres. Special programs and field trips are offered year-round, and budding bird-watchers will enjoy the four-day annual Birding Festival in June.

### Jamestown Audubon Nature Center (all ages)

1600 Riverside Rd., off US 62; (716) 569-2345; www.jamestownaudubon.wordpress.com. Open Mar through Oct, Mon through Sat 10 a.m. to 4:30 p.m., Sun 1 to 4:30 p.m.; Nov through Feb, Mon and Sat 10 a.m. to 4:30 p.m., Sun 1 to 4:30 p.m. Sanctuary open dawn to dusk. Closed holidays. $.

This 600-acre sanctuary of mixed forests and marsh is a favorite stop for multitudes of migrating birds. Five miles of trails wind through the woods and swamps that are home to more than 400 species of plants. At the Nature Center Building, you can pick up self-guided trail maps and check out the local reptiles and amphibians in the Discovery Room. Kids ages three to eight can sign up for the Little Explorers nature programs offered on the second Sat of every month, and a variety of nature-themed festivals and events, from Secret Garden tours to Thanksgiving with the Birds, occur throughout the year.

### Jamestown Jammers (all ages)

Russell E. Diethrick Jr. Park, 485 Falconer St.; (716) 664-0915; http://indianapolis.indians .milb.com. Call for ticket and schedule information. $–$$.

Called "The Greatest Show on Dirt," this Class A affiliate of the 2003 World Series Champion Florida Marlins battles the ball clubs of the New York–Penn League from June through Sept.

### Panama Rocks Scenic Park (all ages)

11 Rock Hill Rd. (NY 10), Panama; (716) 782-2845; www.panamarocks.com. Open daily early May through mid-Oct, 10 a.m. to 5 p.m. $, under 6 **free.**

Similar to the rock city outside of Olean, this stone citadel of Paleozoic sea islands is surrounded by an old-growth forest. Massive quartz conglomerate towers, boulders, caves, and crevices are the remnants of weathering and glacial erosion and are a lot of fun to explore. It can get muddy, so wear boots if possible, leave the strollers in the car, put the baby in a backpack, and take the lower trail for the best photo ops.

## Where to Eat

**Alfie's Restaurant.** 986 Fairmont Ave.; (716) 488-7410; www.alfiesrestaurant.com. Family-friendly, serving four kinds of eggs Benedict, chocolate-chip pancakes, sandwiches, salads, burgers, pasta, steak, seafood, and homemade meat loaf. $$

**Johnny's Lunch.** 966 Fairmont Ave.; (716) 664-2881; www.johnnyslunch.com. Nine kinds of hot dogs, burgers, baskets of chicken fingers or fried fish and fries, plus great milk shakes, rice pudding, and special kids' meals. $

## Where to Stay

**Best Western.** 200 W. 3rd St., Jamestown; (716) 484-8400; www.bestwesternnewyork .com. Sixty-one rooms and suites, with indoor pool, spa, exercise room, guest laundry, dry cleaning, Internet, free local calls, microwave available, free newspaper, and complimentary breakfast; children under twelve free with adult. $–$$

**Hampton Inn & Suites.** 4 W. Oak Hill Rd., Jamestown; (716) 484-7829; www.hampton inn.com. Seventy-one rooms and suites, indoor and outdoor pool, fitness room, coin laundry, laundry service, convenience store, cribs and high chairs, and complimentary beverage and breakfast area. $$

# Chautauqua

Take NY 17 west to NY 394.

Home to the world-renowned cultural summer camp for families, the Chautauqua Institution, this area is also known for its vineyards and rolling farmlands.

### Chautauqua Institution (all ages)

1 Ames Ave., NY 394; (716) 357-6200. Ticket office (716) 357-6250; www.ciweb.org. Open late June through Aug. Tours daily. Accommodation and admission packages available. Day pass $$$, under 12 **free;** classes, Children's School, Group One, and Boys and Girls Club $$$$.

# Chautauqua Watershed **Conservancy**

Dedicated to preserving the water quality and scenic beauty of the area, this organization maintains several pristine areas that are home to many rare plants and animals. Contact them for trail maps and more information at 413 N. Main St., Jamestown; (716) 664 2166; www.chautauquawatershed.org.

**Chautauqua Lake Outlet Wetland Greenway,** Ellicott

**Cassadaga Creek Preserve,** Sinclairville

**Dobbins Woods,** North Harmony

**Elm Flats Wetland Preserve,** Chautauqua

**Prendergast Creek Wetland Preserve,** Chautauqua

Founded in 1874 as an arts and education summer camp for Sunday-school teachers, Chautauqua weaves a magical spell around all who visit. For generations families have returned year after year to participate in the wide variety of more than 300 programs offered for all ages, from the performing arts classes and performances of dance, music, theater, and opera to lectures and courses in literature, philosophy, religion, history, and science. Children have always been welcome here, and there are special programs just for them. Visitors can stay for a day or sign up for the full nine-week season.

## Long Point State Park on Lake Chautauqua (all ages)

4459 NY 430, Bemus Point; (716) 386-2722; www.nysparks.state.ny.us. **Open daily year-round dawn to dusk. $. Call ahead to confirm changes to hours, activities available, and possible closures due to pending state budget cuts.**

Reaching out into Chautauqua's waters, this day park has more than 5 miles of hiking and nature trails running through it, as well as playgrounds and picnic areas, excellent swimming, boating, and bicycling opportunities. The lake, at 1,308 feet above sea level, is one of the highest navigable bodies of water on the continent, and is reported to be the habitat of the giant muskellunge.

## Midway State Park (all ages)

4859 NY 430, Bemus Point; (716) 386-3165; www.nysparks.state.ny.us. **Open daily Memorial Day through Labor Day; rides and arcade are open weekends only, Memorial Day through mid-June, and then daily mid-June to Labor Day, Wed through Sun. Operating times vary. Admission charge for rides and games. $–$$$.**

For more than a century, families have been coming to this charming amusement park on the shores of Chautauqua Lake. There's no charge for swimming at the sandy beach, and there are eighteen rides to experience, including go-karts, bumper boats, and an antique carousel, plus an outdoor roller rink, miniature golf, a water wars area, and an arcade.

# Chautauqua **County Bounty**

**The Berry Bush.** 2929 NY 39, Forestville; (716) 679-1240.

**Busti Cider Mill and Farm Market.** 1135 Southwestern Dr., Jamestown; (716) 487-0177; www.busticidermill.com.

**Big Tree Maple.** 2040 Holly Lane, Lakewood; (716) 763-5917; www.bigtree maple.com.

**The Blueberry Patch.** 2918 Carpenter Pringle Rd., Asheville; (716) 782-4942.

**Awald Farms.** 2195 Shirley Rd., North Collins; (716) 337-2997; www.awald farms.com.

**Falcone Farms.** 1707 King Rd., Forestville; (716) 965-2503.

**Meadows Family Farm.** 1707 King Rd., Forestville; (716) 965-2923.

**Whittier Farms.** 3731 Moreley Rd., Asheville; (716) 789-5001; www.whittier farm.com.

**Chadokoin Farms.** 10459 Prospect Rd., Forestville; (716) 965-2674.

**Erdle Farm.** 12229 Hanford Rd., Silver Creek; (716) 934-9599.

**Lembke Farm.** 3107 NY 39, Forestville; (716) 672-267.

**Walker's Fruit Farm and Wine Juice.** 2860 NY 39, Forestville; (716) 679-1292.

Privately owned since 1898, Midway Park was acquired by New York in 2006 and is now one of the state's newest parks. Future plans include construction a new seasonal dock, restoration of the historic Hippodrome, the relocation of the arcade to the Hippodrome, and a new boardwalk along the shoreline. The park will continue to operate the rides, as well as adding and maintaining new ones from the same historical era, and a new system of nature trails and picnic areas will be created.

## McClurg Museum (ages 4 and up)
**Moore Park, US 20 and NY 394, Westfield; (716) 326-2977; www.mcclurgmuseum.org. Open year-round Tues through Sat 10 a.m. to 4 p.m. $.**

This restored fourteen-room, 1818 Federal-style mansion houses a collection of Native American, pioneer, and military artifacts, and a wonderful doll collection in the Victorian nursery. Of special interest is an exhibit on Grace Bedell, an 11-year-old Westfield girl who wrote a letter to Abraham Lincoln in 1860 suggesting that "he would look a lot better" if he grew a beard. He took her advice, and the rest is history.

### Double D.A.B. Riding Stables (ages 6 and up)

5811 Welch Rd., Ripley; (716) 736-4418; www.doubledab.net. Open daily year-round 9 a.m. to 5:30 p.m. by reservation. $–$$.

Day and overnight trail rides as well as pony rides and a petting farm are offered at this family-friendly stable.

## Where to Eat

**Guppy's.** 4663 NY 430, Bemus Point; (716) 386-4422; Casual, friendly place serving excellent Italian specialties, great soups, and homemade desserts. $

**The Italian Fisherman.** 61 Lakeside Dr., Bemus Point; (716) 386-7000; www.italianfisherman.com. Deck dining overlooking Chautauqua Lake, serving fresh seafood, steaks, and pasta, with live entertainment on a floating stage, from rock to country to the Bemus Bay Pops concert series. $$–$$$

## Where to Stay

**Athenaeum Hotel.** On western shore of lake at the Chautauqua Institution; (800) 821-1881; www.ciweb.org. Built in 1881, this Victorian hotel was once the largest wooden building in the country. There's an excellent restaurant, meals are included, and package rates with the Chautauqua Institution are available. $$$$

**The Spencer.** 25 Palestine Ave., Chautauqua; (716) 357-3785; www.thespencer.com. Literary-themed rooms (Lewis Carroll, Jules Verne, C. S. Lewis, E. B. White, Beatrix Potter, etc.) with hand-painted murals, whirlpools, Wi-Fi, cable TV, and spa. $$$$

**We Wan Chu Cottages.** 4434 W. Lake Rd., Mayville; (716) 789-3383; www.wewanchu.com. One- to five-room lakefront cottages and chalets, with Wi-Fi, playground, ball courts, boat rentals, recreation room, fishing dock, and nightly lakefront bonfire. $$$$

## Traveling by Water **in Chautauqua**

***Chautauqua Belle* Steamboat Cruises.** 78 Water St., Lakeside Park, Mayville; (716) 269-2355; www.269belle.com.

***Summer Wind* Lake Cruises.** Docked at Lucille Ball Memorial Park, Celeron; (716) 763-7447; www.thesummerwind.com.

**Chautauqua Marina.** 104 W. Lake Rd., NY 394, Mayville; (716) 753-3913; www.chautauquamarina.com.

# Dunkirk

Take NY 394 west to NY 5 north (Seaway Trail).

Situated on the shores of Lake Erie, Dunkirk was named after the French harbor of Dunkerque.

### Dunkirk Historical Lighthouse and Veterans Park Museum (all ages)

1 Lighthouse Point Dr. North, Dunkirk; (716) 366-5050; www.dunkirklighthouse.com. Open Mon, Tues, and Thurs through Sat, May, June, Sept, and Oct, 10 a.m. to 2 p.m., and July and Aug, 10 a.m. to 4 p.m. Closed Wed and Sun. $, under 4 free.

Tour the tower, reportedly haunted by a ghost, and the eleven rooms of the light keeper's house. Historical maritime and military artifacts are on display in the lighthouse and museum.

### Lake Erie State Park (all ages)

5905 Lake Rd. (NY 5), Brockton; (716) 792-9214; www.nysparks.state.ny.us. Open year-round. free

With breathtaking views from almost a mile of sandy bluffs bordering shallow Lake Erie, this park offers ninety-seven campsites and ten cabins, a playground, picnic places, beach hiking trails, and excellent bird-watching of rare migratory species skirting the lake edge.

## Nature Preserves

The Nature Conservancy maintains several sites of special significance in this area, each one a unique ecosystem. For more information contact the conservancy at 1048 University Ave., Rochester; (585) 546-8030; www.nature.org.

**Chaumont Barrens,** Lyme and Clayton

**El Dorado Beach Preserve,** Ellisburg

**Thousand Acre Swamp,** Penfield

**Moss Lake Nature Sanctuary,** Caneadea

**Deer Lick Sanctuary,** Persia

**French Creek Watershed,** Mina

**Canadaway Creek State Wildlife Management Area, Forestville**

# Other Things to See and Do
## in Western New York

**Ransomville Speedway.** 2315 Braley Rd. off Ransomville Road, Ransomville; (716) 791-3602; www.ransomvillespeedway.com.

**Dart Airport Aviation Museum.** 6167 Plank Rd., NY 430, Mayville; (716) 753-2160.

**Akron Falls Park.** Parkview Drive, Akron; (716) 858-8355; www.erie.gov/parks.

**Kabob Bear Country.** 6347 S. Stockton–Cassadaga Rd., Sinclairville; (716) 962-8270 ; www.kabobbear.com.

**Chestnut Ridge Park.** 6121 Chestnut Ridge Rd., Orchard Park; (716) 662-3290; www.erie.gov/parks.

**Motherland Connextions.** 476 Hyde Park Blvd., Niagara Falls; (716) 282-1028; www.motherlandconnextions.com.

**Amherst Pepsi Center.** 1615 Amherst Manor Dr., Williamsville; (716) 631-7555; www.amherstpepsicenter.com.

## Evangola State Park (all ages)

10191 Old Lake Shore Rd., Irving; (716) 549-1802; www.nysparks.state.ny.us. Open year-round. **free**

Comfort camping is now being offered at this lakeshore park, at sites 56, 62, and 74, complete with furnishings, along with regular campsites. In addition to the beautiful crescent sand beach, there are hiking and biking trails, picnic places and playgrounds, ball fields and courts, recreation programs, and the annual festivals for Pirates and Tomatoes . . . but not at the same time.

## The 1891 Fredonia Opera House (all ages)

9 Church St., Fredonia; (716) 679-0891; www.fredopera.org. Open year-round; call or check Web site for event schedule. $–$$.

This lovely music hall was saved from demolition in 1981 by the Fredonia Preservation Society and restored to its former glory as the arts heart of the area. Offering more than opera these days, this terrific theater provides a variety of family entertainment from movies and magic acts to storytelling festivals and folk music concerts.

**Lily Dale Museum** (all ages)
16-18 Library St., Lily Dale; **(716) 595-8721; www.lilydaleassembly.com. Open late June to Labor Day, Tues through Sun 11 a.m. to 4 p.m. Gate fee $$, 18 and under free with paying adult.**

The childhood home of the Fox sisters and the birthplace of the American Spiritualist Movement, this interesting community on Cassadaga Lake is peopled with mediums, clairvoyants, and tarot card and palm readers. You can schedule a variety of consultations and readings, take a workshop, or attend a lecture on topics ranging from numerology and astrology to mandala making and healing. Classes for children include yoga, meditation, and how to decorate a room using feng shui. The gate fee allows you to tour the town and visit the museum, the Lily Dale Auditorium, the Healing Temple, the Forest Temple, Inspiration Stump, the beach, the Pet Cemetery, and the new work in progress, the Fairy Trails hiking path.

## Where to Eat

**Upper Crust Bake House.** 27 E. Main St., Fredonia; (716) 627-2253. Freshly baked goods, homemade soups from scratch, tasty sandwiches, and incredible desserts. $

**The White Inn.** 52 E. Main St., Fredonia; (716) 672-2103; www.whiteinn.com. Create your own omelet, Belgian waffles, chicken potpie, salads, burgers, sandwiches, filet mignon, barbecue chicken and shrimp, and homemade desserts. $$–$$$

## Where to Stay

**Clarion Hotel & Marina.** 30 Lakeshore Dr. East, Dunkirk; (716) 366-8350 and (800) 526-8350. One hundred and twenty-seven rooms and suites, free premium cable, free local calls, free Wi-Fi, indoor and outdoor pool, fitness center, sauna, hot tub, refrigerators, cribs and roll-away beds on request, pay-per-view movies and games, restaurant, and a dockside cafe. $$

**Days Inn.** 10455 Bennett Rd. (NY 60), Fredonia; (716) 673-1351; www.daysinn.com. Rooms and suites, with free Wi Fi, microwave, refrigerator, free newspaper, coin laundry, indoor pool, spa, Jacuzzi, sundeck, complimentary breakfast, and restaurant. $–$$

## For More Information

**Niagara USA.** (716) 282-8992 and (877) 325-5787; www.niagara-usa.com.

**Buffalo Niagara Convention & Visitors Bureau.** (716) 852-2356; www.visitbuffalo niagara.com.

**Genesee County Tourism.** (585) 343-7440 or (800) 622-2686; www.visitgeneseeny.com.

**Orleans County Tourism.** (800) 724-0314; www.orleanscountytourism.com.

**Wyoming County Tourist Promotion Agency.** (800) 839-3919; www.wyoming countyny.com.

**Chautauqua County Visitors Bureau.** (716) 357-1569 and (800) 242-1459; www .tourchautauqua.com

**Allegany County Office of Tourism and Culture.** (800) 836-1869; www.discoveralleg anycounty.com.

**Cattaraugus County Tourism.** (800) 331-0543; www.enchantedmountains.info.

# Index